Accession no.
36175008

KV-638-485

Secretary of the Invisible

Cross
Cultures

Readings in the Post / Colonial

Literatures in English

114

Series Editors

Gordon Collier	†Hena Maes–Jelinek	Geoffrey Davis
(Giessen)	(Liège)	(Aachen)

Secretary of the Invisible

The Idea of Hospitality in the Fiction of J.M. Coetzee

Mike Marais

LIS LIBRARY

Date	Fund
02/04/13	l-che

Order No

2382994

University of Chester

Rodopi

Amsterdam - New York, NY 2009

Cover painting:
Johann Louw, "Karel se Uur van die Engel"
(2005, oil on plywood, 1600 x 1200 mm.)
Sanlam Collection. Courtesy of the artist.

Cover design: Pier Post

The paper on which this book is printed meets the requirements of
"ISO 9706:1994, Information and documentation - Paper for
documents - Requirements for permanence".

ISBN: 978-90-420-2712-1
E-Book ISBN: 978-90-420-2713-8
© Editions Rodopi B.V., Amsterdam – New York, NY 2009
Printed in The Netherlands

For Sue and Kyle

Contents

———— ৯

Acknowledgements

——————————————— ॐ

I would like to thank the following friends who have in various ways contributed to this book: Luke Alfred, Coleen Angove, Carita and Lasse Backström, Haidar Eid, Johan Geertsema, Stefan Helgesson, Luc Hosten, Dirk Klopper, Craig MacKenzie, John McDermott, Sikhumbuzo Mngadi, David and Carmen Watson, Mary West.

I must also acknowledge the enriching conversations that I have had with many of the students I have taught in the course of my career.

My thanks, too, to Baldrick for warming my lap during the cold Grahamstown winter of 2008 during which much of this monograph was written.

I am especially grateful to Johann Louw for his kindness and generosity.

Some chapters in this book are based on previously published essays. I thank the following journals for permission to use copyright material:
Journal of Commonwealth Literature for allowing me to reprint extracts from an article, entitled "Literature and the Labour of Negation: J.M. Coetzee's *Life & Times of Michael K*," that appeared in 36.1 (2001);
Journal of Literary Studies for letting me use excerpts from "The Novel as Ethical Command: J.M. Coetzee's *Foe*," an article that appeared in 16.2 (2000);
Journal of Modern Literature for allowing me to reprint sections of an article entitled "J.M. Coetzee's *Disgrace* and the Task of the Imagination," which appeared in 29.2 (2006); and
Contemporary Literature for permitting me to include lengthy portions of an article, entitled "Coming into Being: J.M. Coetzee's *Slow Man* and the Aesthetic of Hospitality," from 50.2 (2009).

I also thank Gordon Collier at Rodopi for all his help, patience, and pro-
fessionalism.

Finally, I am grateful to the National Research Foundation of South
Africa for providing me with the financial assistance that has made this
book possible.

Introduction

——————— ২

I
N THE EIGHTH LESSON of J.M. Coetzee's *Elizabeth Costello*,
Elizabeth Costello finds herself "a petitioner before the gate."[1] To
pass through, she must make a statement pertaining to her beliefs.
After the rejection of her first statement, she prepares a second, part of
which reads as follows:

> I am a writer, and what I write is what I hear. I am a secretary of the
> invisible, one of many secretaries over the ages. That is my calling:
> dictation secretary. It is not for me to interrogate, to judge what is
> given me. I merely write down the words and then test them, test their
> soundness, to make sure I have heard right. (199)

Were the judges who hear her statement to ask her who dictates her
writing, Costello's answer would be "*By powers beyond us*" (200).

One of the main purposes of this study is to show that Coetzee stages
the complex processes alluded to in this description in most of his novels.
By implication, I maintain that this novelist conceives of an outside to history, a point of exteriority, of invisibility or otherness, that may inspire the
writer of literature. In short, he assumes not only that the historical enclosure is not total, but also that writing has its origin in what lies beyond
this enclosure. What Costello appears to be saying in the passage, then, is
that the writer creates *ex nihilo*.

I must immediately point out that I, in mounting this argument, diverge
quite markedly from the arguments of Derek Attridge, a critic whose work
has otherwise significantly influenced my reading of Coetzee's fiction.
For Attridge, the other is not transcendent; it does not come from beyond,
from elsewhere, but is, rather, "a product of the identical constituting act

---

[1] J.M. Coetzee, *Elizabeth Costello: Eight Lessons* (London: Secker & Warburg,
2003): 194. Unless otherwise indicated, further page references are in the main text.

that has produced the self/same which perceives it as other."[2] To be sure, he asserts that "There is no 'absolute other' if this means a wholly transcendent other, unrelated to any empirical particularity – or if there is, it is a matter for religious faith alone."[3] At this point, an endnote follows in which Attridge states his departure from Emmanuel Levinas' thinking on the grounds that Levinas' absolute Other is "God."[4] Even if this account of Levinas' understanding of absolute alterity is accurate (and I am by no means convinced that it is: after all, the absolute alterity to which this philosopher refers is not God but the face of the human other), the assumption that informs it: namely, that absolute alterity "is a matter for religious faith alone," is highly questionable. Like Levinas, Maurice Blanchot is a proponent of radical difference. Nevertheless, his understanding of absolute alterity is certainly not grounded in notions of divinity. According to Blanchot, alterity is absolute because it is ultimately irreducible. What is other is not just different to, but always more than what is in history. It is the excess of what I say when I try to represent the other; what is left over after signification has taken place. The other is what remains to be said. It is what exceeds the "constituting act that produced the self/same" to which Attridge refers. Indeed, its transcendence is grounded in exactly this excession.

From what I have stated, it follows that the other can never be accommodated or known, as Attridge suggests is possible. While he may argue that the other's accommodation is only partial, it is fairly clear that, for him, "partial accommodation" does still involve recuperation of the other in the same.[5] Hence, for instance, he contends that the experience of the other "is not the other but the shifts of mental and emotional gear that make it possible for what was other to be apprehended, now ceasing to be, at least momentarily, other."[6] The other is what Attridge's robust subject

---

[2] Derek Attridge, *J.M. Coetzee and the Ethics of Reading: Literature in the Event* (Scottsville: U of KwaZulu–Natal P & Chicago: U of Chicago P, 2005): 99.

[3] Derek Attridge, *The Singularity of Literature* (London: Routledge, 2004): 29. Cf. Attridge, *J.M. Coetzee and the Ethics of Reading*, 99.

[4] Attridge, *The Singularity of Literature*, 151n.22.

[5] *The Singularity of Literature*, 28.

[6] *The Singularity of Literature*, 76.

can "apprehend," "get its teeth into,"[7] and "wrest" into the field of the familiar.[8]

My argument is not that I am right and that Attridge is wrong; that the other is ultimately unknowable rather than produced. Although such a debate would be interesting, it is, in the context of this study, ultimately pointless. What is more to the point is what Coetzee's writing has to say on the matter. And, as I have already intimated, my intention in this book is to establish that this writer's fiction dwells obsessively on an alterity that is figured as being absolute in its irreducibility. In the above passage from *Elizabeth Costello*, the metaphor for such otherness is "the invisible," which is also described as a power that is "*beyond us*." Importantly, the writer is inspired by this power and the process of inspiration is depicted as a form of mastery. The writer is a slave, a secretary who writes under dictation. In his or her writing, s/he, it would seem, has no choice but to follow "the invisible." Implicit here is a contrast between the visible and the invisible, the phenomenal world of history and the domain of the other. Importantly, too, the writer's allegiance, according to Costello, is to the other rather than to history. His or her "responsibility," as Coetzee indicates in *Doubling the Point*, is "toward something that has not yet emerged" and which is therefore invisible.[9]

In this study, I examine Coetzee's preoccupation with this ethic of writing by tracing the metaphors through which he stages it in his fiction. Apart from considering the link between the tropes of inspiration and mastery already evident in the above passage from *Elizabeth Costello*, I also, for instance, trace the metaphor of following. The writer, who is in history, must follow the invisible rather than the visible. Yet s/he can only do so by writing from his or her position within history and in the terms of history. Coetzee's ongoing attempt to negotiate this representational double bind forms the subject-matter of much of this study. Representation, I argue throughout, inscribes an irreducible tension between the domain of history and the order of the other.

In this regard, I focus on what is probably the most prominent metaphor in Coetzee's writing: namely, the lost child. Anyone with even a

---

[7] Attridge, *J.M. Coetzee and the Ethics of Reading*, 41.

[8] Attridge, *The Singularity of Literature*, 79.

[9] J.M. Coetzee, *Doubling the Point: Essays and Interviews*, ed. David Attwell (Cambridge MA: Harvard UP, 1992): 246.

passing acquaintance with Coetzee's fiction will have noticed, and probably puzzled over, the recurring motif of the lost, abandoned, deformed,
dead or unborn child. Part of my purpose in these readings of Coetzee's
novels is to relate the recurrent quest for the lost child to the metaphor of
following the invisible: the child is a deeply self-reflexive metaphor for
the invisible (which, I have pointed out, is itself a trope). The writer writes
in order to render visible what is invisible. As the filial metaphor connotes, s/he bears a parental responsibility for the child. S/he has no
option but to try to find the child. The writer must write. Nevertheless –
and this is an aspect of the double bind to which I have referred – to
render visible the invisible is to destroy the invisible. Hence the salience
of the figure of the damaged child and the theme of betrayal in Coetzee's
writing.

Yet another of my concerns in this study is the effect of Coetzee's
sense of responsibility for what is beyond history on the form taken by his
writing of the apartheid period. My argument here is not just for the
ethical nature of Coetzee's response to apartheid history; it is also that this
writer, in attempting not to follow history by representing the apartheid
state's atrocities, sought to interrupt that history. I argue that this was a
calculated, albeit deeply contradictory and paradoxical, strategy on this
writer's part. Over the course of several chapters, I explicate this dimension of Coetzee's writing of the apartheid years by drawing on Theodor
Adorno's understanding of the ambivalent nature of the aesthetic, its position both in and outside society.

In fact, my eventual argument is that this novelist's continued sense of
responsibility for what has not, and cannot, emerge means that his writing
possesses a certain repetitive quality. If the writer is responsible for what
is other than history, but to which history is refractory, s/he is faced with
an impossible, because always still to be completed, task. If, contra Attridge, the other cannot be accommodated, the writer's task is never done.
The other exceeds and constantly interrupts what has been written, thereby signalling the work's incompletion and inadequacy while at the same
time requiring, indeed demanding, that more be written. Given this restless interplay between representation and its ineliminable excess, there
cannot not be a pronounced similarity between Coetzee's apartheid fiction, his fiction of the transitional period, his post-apartheid fiction, and
his Australian fiction. While there is undeniably considerable difference
on the presentational surface of the texts concerned, the notion of a

responsibility for an otherness that cannot be discharged is most definitely a constant that invests Coetzee's writing across these historical periods and contexts with a certain sameness. Elizabeth Costello's conception of herself as a secretary of the invisible, it will soon become clear, is one already apparent as early as *In the Heart of the Country*, in Magda's relationship with the skygods.

From what I have said, it is perhaps clear that my critical approach to Coetzee's writing takes the form of a close reading of the various works: I trace the intricate, imbricated stock of metaphors in the oeuvre. Nevertheless, my formalism is invested with an abiding sense of the historicity of form and, indeed, is aware of the texts' awareness of their implication in history. Since I conduct a close reading of them, it follows that my discussion of the novels' concern with alterity, responsibility, engagement and so on proceeds incrementally in this study. Although I trace the motifs and metaphors in the oeuvre as a whole, I do so through readings of the individual works. One benefit of this approach is that my study consists of what is rather rare in Coetzee criticism: i.e. critiques of the works that pay some attention to their formal features.

I do not wish to suggest that the practice of close reading is somehow nearer to the literary text than other hermeneutic methods, that it, in being 'true' to the text, avoids the danger of reducing it to a term in an interpretative paradigm. On the contrary, I know that close reading is all too often simply a form of literary fundamentalism: by scrutinizing the word on the page, one invokes the word of the author in support of one's necessarily questionable assertions. One masters the work while purporting to follow it. If anything, such literary fundamentalism is actively resisted by Coetzee's writing. In following the individual text's metaphors, it will become clear in the chapters ahead, I often reach a point at which they become ambiguous and ambivalent, where their meanings slip and multiply and they, in the process, raise questions about my reading, my following of the work's following of the invisible. Even as they invite it, Coetzee's novels resist being followed.

Finally, I must briefly comment on my use of the ethical philosophies of Levinas and Jacques Derrida in developing the arguments that I have here introduced. I have already noted that Coetzee's writing is informed by his sense of responsibility for what is not yet present in history, by the sense that it is the writer's task to make of the text a home for the other. The text must *host* the other and so enable it to interrupt history. Indeed, the notion of hospitality implicit here is directly related to the process of writerly inspiration: to be a secretary of the invisible is precisely to become a home for the other and then to try to make for it a home of language, of the text. Dostoevsky's following sentiment in *The Master of Petersburg* holds for most of Coetzee's writer–protagonists: "He will give a home to any word [...] if there is a chance it is an anagram for Pavel."[10] It is in explicating Coetzee's understanding of hospitality that I have found Levinas' and Derrida's writings on the subject invaluable. Having said that, I must also add that I have been at pains not to lose sight of the fact that Coetzee's project is principally a literary-aesthetic one, and that this focus means that his writing is not reducible to an allegory of either of these thinker's thoughts. I invoke what Levinas and Derrida have said about hospitality to elucidate Coetzee's conception thereof rather than to subsume his understanding under either of theirs. It follows that the conception of hospitality adumbrated in this study is not intended accurately to reflect either Levinas' or Derrida's thought on the matter. What is ultimately important to me, once again, is the arduous task of providing an account of what *Coetzee* says about hospitality in his works.

ℐ ৯

---

[10] J.M. Coetzee, *The Master of Petersburg* (London: Secker & Warburg, 1994): 141.

1 Hospitality in the Early Fiction

———————————————————————— ২

T HE SECOND PART of *Dusklands*, "The Narrative of Jacobus Coetzee," opens with the following three sentences: "The one gulf that divides us from the Hottentots is our Christianity. We are Christians, a folk with a destiny. They become Christians too, but their Christianity is an empty word."[1] The "we" and "us" here invoked: i.e. the community of European settlers at the Cape in the eighteenth century, situates itself in opposition to a "they" and "them": namely, the "Hottentots." In other words, this community defines itself negatively: that which "we" are not constitutes what "we" are. The movement of inclusion through which this community shapes itself is clearly premised on exclusion. Moreover, Jacobus Coetzee, the "I" who invokes this "we," quite self-consciously situates himself in the community that it implies. The "we" in which he is located locates his perceptions, attitudes, and values.[2] In fact, his identity or sense of self is enabled by this "we." Hence, after his sojourn with the Khoi, he "composes" and sings the following "little ditty" in order to reassure himself of who he is: "*Hottentot, Hottentot, / I am not a Hottentot*" (101).

From the first, then, Coetzee's writing announces its preoccupation with community and, by inevitable extension, the idea of hospitality. The basic question posed by this writer's oeuvre may be couched as follows: how does the individual, who is part of a community, respond to the stranger *as* a stranger: i.e. without simply positioning this outsider in

---

[1] J.M. Coetzee, *Dusklands* (Johannesburg: Ravan, 1974): 61. Unless otherwise indicated, further page references are in the main text.

[2] See Teresa Dovey, *The Novels of J.M. Coetzee: Lacanian Allegories* (Craighall: Ad. Donker, 1988): 86, and Sue Kossew, *Pen and Power: A Post-Colonial Reading of J.M. Coetzee and André Brink* (Cross/Cultures 27; Amsterdam & Atlanta GA: Rodopi, 1996): 42.

opposition to the "we" in which s/he is located? In the case of "The Narrative of Jacobus Coetzee," the variant of this question would be: how does Jacobus Coetzee respond to the "Hottentots" other than as "Hottentots"? How does he respond to them without the knowledge of who they are that is always already inscribed in this name?

In Derrida's understanding, "unconditional" hospitality involves saying "yes *to who or what turns up*, before any determination, before any anticipation, before any identification."[3] If this is so, and Emmanuel Levinas would certainly concur, unconditional hospitality is both exacted and disabled by the exclusionary movement through which community establishes itself. To be what it purports to be, hospitality must be unconditional or, to use another of Derrida's terms, "unlimited."[4] No less is demanded by the exclusionary gesture through which community comes into being and which, in fact, calls for a mechanism such as hospitality. (If there were, or could be, something like an 'open' or inclusive community, hospitality would be inconceivable.) Hospitality, then, must exclude community's exclusions. Yet, if it were to do this, it would negate the very gesture through which community constitutes itself and thereby undo community (and, in the process, itself). By its very nature, community cannot exclude exclusion.

Nevertheless, unconditional hospitality does not pose much of a threat to community, because of the fact that the individual, on a reflective level at least, must respond to the otherness of the stranger from within community's forms of knowledge and the expectations of others which these inscribe. Being implicated in community, s/he is simply unable to respond without knowledge to what "turns up." The stranger or other is always expected and so recognized and known from the self's position within culture and its structures of knowledge. By implication, the relationship between host and stranger is predetermined by community's protocols of inclusion and exclusion. On a reflective level, the kind of hospitality exercised from within community can only ever be limited and "conditional."[5] Although s/he invites the guest into his or her home, the

---

[3] Jacques Derrida, *Of Hospitality: Anne Dufourmantelle Invites Jacques Derrida to Respond*, tr. R. Bowlby (*De l'hospitalité: Anne Dufourmantelle invite Jacques Derrida à répondre*, 1997; Stanford CA: Stanford UP, 2000): 77.

[4] Derrida, *Of Hospitality*, 77.

[5] *Of Hospitality*, 25ff.

host thus always does so on his or her own terms. The mere existence of such terms means that the host has in advance exercised the right and power of discrimination. As sovereign of his or her home, the power that invites, s/he screens his or her guests.

Conditional hospitality, it would seem, is premised on the distinction between 'friend' and 'enemy', which assumes the us–them distinction through which community defines itself.[6] In presupposing this distinction, conditional hospitality presupposes the conflict that it *necessarily* inscribes in the history of community. Quite ironically, then, conditional hospitality defends community against the stranger by reducing the threat of his or her otherness through naming and so identifying him or her. As Derrida puts it, the "perversion and pervertibility" of the law of hospitality "is that one can become virtually xenophobic in order to protect or claim to protect one's own hospitality, the own home that makes possible one's own hospitality."[7] Implicitly, at least, conditional hospitality conceives of the stranger as an enemy and is itself therefore a form of hostility, a means through which community negotiates the danger of radical difference, the threat of being invaded and so undone by what it seeks to exclude in constituting itself.

Moreover, in defending community by endorsing its exclusions, conditional hospitality emerges as one of the mechanisms through which community continually affirms itself. It facilitates the oppositional process through which community defines itself against what it is not. That is, it enables community to continue defining itself through conflict. Crucially, in this regard, the power that invites still affirms itself when it chooses *not* to invite someone home. Even if the stranger is named an enemy, this identity reduces his or her alterity and thereby affirms the host. In this respect, the ultimate effect on the host of identifying the stranger as an enemy is not so very different from what it would have been had s/he invited the stranger home. The stranger who is named an enemy is a guest: in being named and identified, s/he is incorporated into community's system of differential relations and, in the process, the primary threat of his or her otherness is reduced.

---

[6] See Tracy B. Strong, "Foreword," in Carl Schmitt, *Political Theology* (Chicago: U of Chicago P, 2005): xv–xvi.

[7] Derrida, *Of Hospitality*, 53.

Only the stranger's strangeness is therefore excluded or, more accurately put, rendered not present. In naming the stranger an enemy, community thus welcomes the enemy as a guest (a paradox which, Derrida points out, is implicit in the Latin *hostis*, which means both 'guest' and 'enemy'[8]), and thereby ensures that it is affirmed by this guest. In *Dusklands*, this paradox is evident in Eugene Dawn's call for the pacification of resistance in Vietnam. Hamilton, playing on Dawn's use of the family metaphor, explains that this is a call "to condition the Vietnamese body by bringing it into the American/Western 'family' of the selfsame: to transform the incomprehensible *Other* into the known value of *Subject* [sic] by means of identification through representation to become 'the sons' of the imperial father."[9]

If hospitality is a means by which community affirms itself, it follows that the host needs a guest. To feel at home, Derrida argues, the host must identify the outsider.[10] Precisely this logic of dependence in the economy of hospitality emerges in Jacobus Coetzee's extermination of the Khoi community in *Dusklands*. In identifying the Khoi as savages, he not only legitimizes his violence but also asserts his existence and that of his community:

> No more than any other man do I enjoy killing; but I have taken it upon myself to be the one to pull the trigger, performing this sacrifice for myself and my countrymen, who exist, and committing upon the dark folk the murders we have all wished. (113)

The doubt implicit in the words "who exist" exposes Jacobus Coetzee's dependence on those he calls "savages."

Since the host can only be a host through inviting a guest, his or her sovereignty is deeply ambivalent. While s/he has the power to name, select, elect, and receive, s/he is always dependent on the arrival of the guest s/he has invited. To all intents and purposes, then, his or her power renders him or her vulnerable. In Coetzee's early fiction, obsessed as it is with waiting and arrival, the instability and ambivalent nature of the host's power is a constant theme. Indeed, this preoccupation accounts for some

---

[8] Derrida, *Of Hospitality*, 21, 45.
[9] Grant Hamilton, "J.M. Coetzee's *Dusklands*: The Meaning of Suffering," *Journal of Literary Studies* 21.3–4 (2005): 299.
[10] Derrida, *Of Hospitality*, 54–55, 61.

of the ambiguity with which acts of violence are so often described in these novels.[11] For example, Eugene Dawn, in the following passage from *Dusklands*, describes the invaders in the American assault on Vietnam as visitors who, in arriving, expect and await an arrival:

> We brought them our pitiable selves, trembling on the edge of in-existence, and asked only that they acknowledge us. We brought with us weapons, the gun and its metaphors, the only copulas we knew of between ourselves and our objects. [...] Our nightmare was that since whatever we reached for slipped through our fingers, we did not exist; that since whatever we embraced wilted, we were all that existed. We landed on the shores of Vietnam clutching our arms and pleading for someone to stand up without flinching to these probes of reality: if you will prove yourself, we shouted, you will prove us too, and we will love you endlessly and shower you with gifts.
>
> But like everything else they withered before us. We bathed them in seas of fire, praying for the miracle. In the heart of the flame their bodies glowed with heavenly light; in our ears their voices rang; but when the fire died they were only ash. (18)

The invaders are depicted as both visitor and aspirant host: they await, and so depend on, the arrival of the guest they have invited: i.e. the enemy.

Understandably, many critics have noted that passages such as these draw on Hegel's account of the master's dependence on the slave.[12] While this is certainly so, I think it untenable to argue, as does Lois Parkinson Zamora, that Coetzee's fiction simply "reiterates" this "basic political

---

[11] See Dominic Head, *J.M. Coetzee* (Cambridge: Cambridge UP, 1997): 34. Head refers to "The presentation of imperial violence as a quest for ontological reassurance" in *Dusklands*.

[12] See Georg Wilhelm Friedrich Hegel, *Phenomenology of Spirit*, tr. Arnold V. Miller (*Phänomenologie des Geistes*, 1807; Oxford: Oxford UP, 1977); see also David Attwell, *J.M. Coetzee: South Africa and the Politics of Writing* (Berkeley: U of California P, 1993), Dovey, *The Novels of J.M. Coetzee*, Rosemary Jolly, *Colonization, Violence, and Narration in White South African Writing: André Brink, Breyten Breytenbach, and J.M. Coetzee* (Athens: Ohio UP, 1996), George Steiner, "Master and Man," review of *Waiting for the Barbarians*, *New Yorker* (12 July 1982): 102–103, Stephen Watson, "Colonialism and the Novels of J.M. Coetzee" (1986), in *Critical Perspectives on J.M. Coetzee*, ed. Graham Huggan & Stephen Watson (Houndmills: Macmillan, 1996): 13–36, and Lois Parkinson Zamora, "Allegories of Power in the Fiction of J.M. Coetzee," *Journal of Literary Studies* 2.1 (1986): 1–15.

allegory."[13] To explain my disagreement, I shall have to rehearse Hegel's analysis of power relations. In discussing the master–slave relationship, this philosopher is, of course, treating the problem of recognition between self-conscious individuals. When an individual who has asserted his or her independence by pitting him-/herself against nature encounters another individual, his or her autonomy is challenged. Such an individual may seek to solve this problem by eliminating the challenger. This "life-and-death struggle," however, turns out to be a false solution, because what the challenger contests is not so much the individual's independence as his or her legitimacy. And, in the absence of the challenger, there is thus no one left to affirm that legitimacy.[14]

As a solution to the problem of independence and recognition, enslavement constitutes an advance on the life-and-death struggle: while the loser remains alive, the victor gains both independence and recognition.[15] However, this relation of dominance and subservience is fundamentally unstable and "self-frustrating,"[16] since the master can never know whether the recognition which "he" receives from "his" slave is a function of "his" subjection of the individual concerned. The slave's recognition is worthless because the slave is a slave rather than an independent being. Toward the end of *In the Heart of the Country*, one of the voices that Magda hears cites Hegel's contention in this regard: "*It is the slave's consciousness that constitutes the master's certainty of his own truth. But the slave's consciousness is a dependent consciousness. So the master is not sure of the truth of his autonomy. His truth lies in an inessential consciousness and its inessential acts*" (129).[17] The relation of dominance and subservience is rendered even more unstable by the possibility that the slave may realize that it is through his or her labour that nature is dominated and, accordingly, that the master is superfluous.[18] Rebellion is thus inherent in the very structure of this relationship.

---

[13] Zamora, "Allegories of Power in the Fiction of J.M. Coetzee," 3.

[14] Hegel, *Phenomenology of Spirit*, 113–15.

[15] *Phenomenology of Spirit*, 115–19.

[16] J.N. Findlay, "Foreword," in Hegel, *Phenomenology of Spirit*, xvii.

[17] J.M. Coetzee, *In the Heart of the Country* (1977; Johannesburg: Ravan, 1978): 129; see Hegel, *Phenomenology of Spirit*, 116–17. Unless otherwise indicated, further page references to Coetzee's novel are in the main text.

[18] Hegel, *Phenomenology of Spirit*, 117–19.

While he clearly invokes Hegel's dialectic of recognition in his novels, it does not follow that Coetzee allegorizes it. To be sure, this writer invokes the master–slave relationship in order to foreground the absence of its dialectical structure from the relationships he depicts in his works.[19] In Hegel's account of the independence and dependence of self-consciousness, only a mutual recognition between self-conscious individuals, an acknowledgement on the part of each of the other's right to exist, can bring about an end to the entire struggle for affirmation.[20] In fact, such mutual recognition is the actual point of the struggle: throughout, each party has sought recognition from the other, but has failed to realize that such recognition must come from an individual whose independence has itself been acknowledged.

It is such mutual recognition that is missing from the relationships depicted in Coetzee's early fiction. Magda, who tries to reconfigure her relationship with the servants Hendrik and Anna in *In the Heart of the Country*, is ultimately forced to concede that "There has been no transfiguration" (113). What is at stake in this novel is the impossibility of achieving the kind of mutual recognition that, according to Hegel, would resolve the conflict between master and slave. In *In the Heart of the Country*, and the other two novels under discussion, the relational modes depicted are not dialectical or, more accurately, not dialectizable. What we have, at best, is relationships in which the dialectical movement towards the synthesis of a mutual recognition is conspicuously absent.

It follows that Coetzee's point in his descriptions of colonial violence in *Dusklands* and *Waiting for the Barbarians* is not simply that community needs its others in order to invest itself with a sense of identity. Instead, it is that such recognition cannot be obtained and therefore that community is tenuous, always only in the process of coming into being, yet to construct for itself a full identity and thereby complete itself. To use Magda's words in *In the Heart of the Country*, it is "a hole crying to be

---

[19] See Watson's following observation: "so much of Coetzee's work can be viewed as a failed dialectic, a world in which there is no synthesis, in which the very possibility of a synthesis would seem to have been permanently excluded" ("Colonialism and the Novels of J.M. Coetzee," 28).

[20] Hegel, *Phenomenology of Spirit*, 104–19, 263–94, 355–63; see also Findlay, "Foreword," xvii, and David Carr, *Time, Narrative and History* (Bloomington: Indiana UP, 1986): 143.

whole" (41; see also 9, 114). Although Magda here describes herself, she is as deeply embedded in her community as Jacobus Coetzee is in his.

In the communities depicted in *Dusklands* and *Waiting for the Barbarians*, the guest who has been invited does not arrive and so cannot affirm the host that issues the invitation. The problem is, of course, that the strategy of affirmation in the communities represented is profoundly aporetic: it consists in naming, and therefore presenting in a recognizable form, the stranger who is, precisely, unknowable. In being named in this way, the stranger is addressed and thus required to reply to the name with which s/he has been addressed. By extension, the name seeks to predetermine the reply; it exacts from the stranger a response that confirms the expectations which it from the first has inscribed. The stranger, in his or her reply, must fit the description provided by the name. Since the name has been posited by the host and is therefore a construct, this is obviously impossible. The act of naming, in relating him or her to and distinguishing him or her from the host's community, *ensures* that the stranger cannot be presented and so confronted or opposed. Ultimately, then, the name that is invoked by the host indicates only the absence of what it purports to signify.

Because they invite and thereby name and determine the other, the host-figures in Coetzee's early fiction never encounter what they address; they encounter only non-presences that cannot affirm their vestigial identities. They are left with a name that corresponds to no phenomenal reality, a sign without a referent that signifies but a failure of presence. This is why the latter part of the above passage describing the American invasion of Vietnam takes the form of an address. The addressee that is apostrophized, is, as is usually the case in apostrophe, absent and thus unable to do what the invaders expect of him: i.e. to respond in a way that affirms their identity. The invited guest fails to arrive.

In the second part of *Dusklands*, the theme of the absent guest is again evident in the depiction of Jacobus Coetzee's encounter with the Khoi:

> Early on the fifth morning we saw small figures advancing toward us across the plain. Ever cautious, I readied my party by distributing the smaller pieces to Klawer and a steady boy named Jan Plaatje, with instructions that they load but show no hostility, biding my sign. Plaatje came up behind the wagon with the oxen to ensure that no sudden clamour from the enemy should drive my second span helter-

skelter away. Klawer sat beside the driver with his gun ready. I rode
out ahead.

Thus we approached each other. [...]

When we came near enough to make out each other's faces I held
up my hand and the wagon stopped. The Hottentots stopped too, the
mounted man in the middle, the others shuffling up in a cluster around
him. [...] I rode out slowly toward them. My men stayed back, obey-
ing orders. The mounted Hottentot rode forward, matching his step to
mine. [...] (68–70)

In this colonial encounter, both Jacobus Coetzee and the Khoi play the
parts of host and guest. While he, logically speaking, is a foreigner who is
received by them in their land, they – and this is apparent from the expectations he brings to the encounter – are also received by him. On the most
obvious level, these expectations are present in his ascription of the names
"Hottentot" and "the enemy" to them. By contrast, they, in welcoming
him, refer to themselves as the "Khoikhoin":

We were welcome in the land of the [Khoikhoin], the people of the
people, who were always glad to receive travellers and eager to hear
what news they brought. (72)[21]

Through this discrepancy in names, *Dusklands* indicates the Khoi's self-
ascription, a point that is stressed when it is later revealed that the name
"Hottentot" is a term of European derivation imposed upon the Khoi:
"'Aten taten, aten taten,' sang the natives of the Cape to the shipwrecked
sailors of the *Haerlem*, 'aten taten, aten taten,' and danced in 2/4 time.[8]
Hence the appellation *Hottentot*" (120). Significantly, the note number in
this quotation directs the reader to an endnote indicating the source of this
information (namely, European travel writing), and thus suggests that the
term which Jacobus Coetzee applies to the Khoi is one that has been constituted in European colonial discourse, a discourse which determines its
signification. It is worth noting here that Coetzee, in an essay entitled
"Idleness in South Africa," describes the constitution of the 'Hottentot' by

---

[21] The parenthetical inclusion of the word "Khoikhoin" in this citation is ostensibly
the work of "J.M. Coetzee," the putative translator and editor of Jacobus Coetzee's
supposed travel report. Since this "editorial" adjustment is followed directly by the
translation "people of the people," it serves to emphasise the Khoi's self-ascription.

colonial discourse. His basic argument is that the early writings on the Khoi by seamen, ships' doctors, and Company officials – what he refers to as the "discourse of the Cape" – constantly recycle the same material in their representation of the 'Hottentots', and that they therefore construct their object of study. Such writing produces rather than represents the Khoi.[22]

If read in the context of this argument, Jacobus Coetzee's use of the name 'Hottentot' clearly exposes his linguistic and discursive separation from the Khoi. That is, it betrays the fact that his knowledge of them is not acquired through perception in the present but from a conceptual system formed *a priori*. When he approaches the Khoi, Jacobus Coetzee does so from a location, place, and position in language and discourse. In other words, he approaches them from the perspective provided by home. Language, as Derrida maintains, is "the home that never leaves us," "the "mobile habitat" that one carries with one and which carries one "from birth to death."[23]

The expectations inscribed by the name 'Hottentot', and indeed the appellations 'savage' and "enemy," are also foregrounded by the narrative scenarios that Jacobus Coetzee constructs as he approaches the Khoi tribe. These scenarios, which punctuate what initially appears to be a relatively realistic description of a colonial encounter, are easily recognizable as standard variations on the formulaic plot that characterizes the colonial adventure novel:[24]

> Tranquilly I traced in my heart the forking paths of the endless inner adventure: the order to follow, the inner debate (resist? submit?), underlings rolling their eyeballs, words of moderation, calm, swift march, the hidden defile, the encampment, the greybeard chieftain, the curious throng, words of greeting, firm tones, Peace! Tobacco!, demonstration of firearms, murmurs of awe, gifts, the vengeful wizard, the feast, glut, nightfall, murder foiled, dawn, farewell, trundling wheels, the order to follow, the inner debate, rolling eyeballs, the ner-

---

[22] Coetzee, "Idleness in South Africa," in Coetzee, *White Writing: On the Culture of Letters in South Africa* (New Haven CT: Radix, 1988): 12–35.

[23] Derrida, *Of Hospitality*, 89.

[24] See Attwell, *J.M. Coetzee*, 49; Susan VanZanten Gallagher, *A Story of South Africa: J.M. Coetzee's Fiction in Context* (Cambridge MA: Harvard UP, 1991): 66; and Allan Gardiner, "J.M. Coetzee's *Dusklands*: Colonial Encounters of the Robinsonian Kind," *World Literature Written in English* 27.2 (1987): 181.

vous finger, the shot, panic, assault, gunfire, hasty departure, the
pursuing horde, the race for the river, the order to follow, the inner
debate, the casual spear in the vitals (Viscount d'Almeida), the fleeing
underlings, pole through the fundament, ritual dismemberment in the
savage encampment, limbs to the dogs, privates to the first wife, the
order to follow, the inner debate, the cowardly blow, amnesia, the dark
hut, bound hands, the drowsing guard, escape, night chase, the dogs
foiled, the dark hut, bound hands, uneasy sleep, dawn, the sacrificial
gathering, the wizard, the contest of magic, the celestial almanac,
darkness at noon, victory, an amusing but tedious reign as tribal demi-
god, return to civilization with numerous entourage of cattle. (70)

The self-consciously textual nature of these plot outlines indicates that
what Jacobus Coetzee meets is not the actual Khoi but the verbal, discursive construct constituted in his mind by colonial discourse. He positions himself in relation to the Khoi according to the foreknowledge of
them that he has gained from this discourse. This is also true of those plots
in which he is killed or forced to flee as, even here, the Khoi's behaviour
still conforms to European expectations regarding native savagery. As
long as this remains the case, these strangers are familiar and knowable
and therefore affirm, rather than threaten, both him and his community.

What these narrative scenarios reveal, then, is that Jacobus Coetzee, in
approaching the Khoi, names and thereby extends an invitation to them.
The guest's failure to arrive is apparent in the way in which the Khoi's
behaviour, quite unintentionally on their part, disrupts his expectations.[25]
To begin with, they do not provide the display of submission that would
affirm not only Jacobus Coetzee's reality, but also that of his community.
When he addresses them "as befitted negotiations with possibly un-
friendly powers" (71), they merely become bored and drift "out of [his]
firm but friendly line of vision" (71); when he anticipates an attack, he
finds that they display "no organized antagonism" (74); when he thinks
that they probably regard him as a god (75) and pictures himself as "an
equestrian statue" (77), he finds that they call him "Long-Nose" (77); and,
rather than the "greybeard chieftain" (70) he expects, he finds that the
Khoi have "only perfunctory reverence for authority" (77), and direct him
to a dying man quite incapable of according him the ceremonious welcome he so desires. Finally, the epic flight which he envisages in one of

---

[25] See Head, *J.M. Coetzee*, 38–39.

his scenarios becomes an abject scramble in which he is debased to a cari-
cature of the glorious, intrepid "tamer of the wild" that he imagines himself to be (82): "Held in position by Klawer I evacuated myself heroically
over the tailgate" (80).

The name 'Hottentot' that Jacobus Coetzee ascribes to the Khoi describes not them but a dissonance between itself and what it seeks to
name. In the process, this word reveals its tropological status. By extension, it points to both language's capacity for tropological substitution and
what Johan Geertsema, in another context, refers to as the human propensity to misrecognize "a linguistic order for a natural one."[26] Indeed,
Jacobus Coetzee himself begins to suspect that this name, and likewise
'savage,' signifies only its inability to signify what it purports to signify:

> They had introduced poison into me. Yet could I be sure I had been
> poisoned? Had I not perhaps been sickening for a long time, or simply
> been unused to Hottentot fare? [...] But how could savages be un-
> familiar with treachery and poison? But were they true savages, these
> Namaqua Hottentots? Why had they nursed me? Why had they let me
> go? Why had they not killed me? Why had their torments been so
> lacking in system and even enthusiasm? (103)

The failure of the Khoi to satisfy the expectations that he brings to his encounter with them cannot fail to call into question Jacobus Coetzee's identity. He complains of having been treated like an "irrelevance" or just
another "accident" by them. Rather than this, we read, he "would gladly
have expired in battle, stabbed to the heart, surrounded by mounds of
fallen foes." He would even have preferred "to die at the sacrificial stake"
(88). Death at the hands of the Khoi would, at least, have confirmed his
reality and that of his community.

Like *Dusklands*, *Waiting for the Barbarians* explores the colonizer's
dependence on naming by exposing the tropological status of the word
'barbarian'. In this novel, it becomes increasingly apparent that the native
inhabitants of the region do not fit Empire's description of them as "barbarians" and "enemies." There is little certainty, in each reported attack or
case of rape or plundering, that the barbarians are actually responsible.
The purpose of Colonel Joll's visit to the frontier – to crush a barbarian

---

[26] Johan Geertsema, "Irony and Otherness: A Study of Some Recent South African
Narrative Fiction" (doctoral dissertation, University of Cape Town, 1999): 88.

rebellion – is questioned by the simple detail that before his arrival "There were no border troubles."[27] As the Magistrate tells one of Joll's men, "We are at peace here [...] we have no enemies" (77). There is no rebellion and there are no barbarians. After Joll's expeditionary force returns and parades its prisoners in public, the Magistrate sceptically reflects on the existence of barbarians: "The circuit is made, everyone has a chance to see the twelve miserable captives, to prove to his children that the barbarians are real" (103).

The outcome of this sustained scepticism concerning the reality of the barbarians, is, as Laura Wright points out, that the word "'barbarian' [...] becomes a floating signifier devoid of specific meaning" in Coetzee's narrative.[28] Because of the dissonance between this word and what it purports to designate, Empire's strategy of self-affirmation must always fail. The barbarians cannot come, because they do not exist and therefore cannot affirm Empire's identity.[29] When the defeated soldiers return from their attempt to confront them, it is with the news that the barbarians have not met Empire's expectations:

> We froze in the mountains! We starved in the desert! Why did no one tell us it would be like that? We were not beaten – they led us out into the desert and then they vanished! [...] They lured us on and on, we could never catch them. [...] they would not stand up to us! (147)

Like the Vietcong and the Khoi in *Dusklands*, then, the barbarians in *Waiting for the Barbarians* refuse to 'stand up' to Empire. They do not allow Empire to define itself by assuming a position in opposition to them. Ashcroft makes this point succinctly: "The failure to find the barbarians has been the failure to constitute self against other, the failure of imperial discourse to constitute the subjectivity of its subjects."[30] Accordingly, Empire is a "duskland," on the threshold of light and darkness,

---

[27] Coetzee, *Waiting for the Barbarians* (Johannesburg: Ravan, 1981): 114. Further page references are in the main text.

[28] Laura Wright, *Writing "Out of All the Camps": J.M. Coetzee's Narratives of Displacement* (New York: Routledge, 2006): 82.

[29] See Attwell, *J.M. Coetzee*, 71.

[30] Bill Ashcroft, "Irony, Allegory and Empire: *Waiting for the Barbarians* and *In the Heart of the Country*," in *Critical Essays on J.M. Coetzee*, ed. Sue Kossew (New York: G.K. Hall, 1998): 107.

being and non-being. In this regard, it is, of course, important that Empire is unnamed in the novel. This, together with what Barbara Eckstein refers to as the novel's "temporally and geographically enjambed setting,"[31] emphasizes Empire's lack of identity and definition. Like the USA, it trembles "on the edge of inexistence."[32] Empire is only ever in the process of coming into being. In not being able to present the barbarians, it is unable to present itself and therefore exists in a perpetual state of waiting. Empire awaits the invited guest, the barbarians, whose arrival would affirm its existence, provide it with an identity. Indeed, through their failure to arrive, the "barbarians" gain a messianic dimension in this novel. Like the USA's invasionary force in Vietnam, Empire, in wishing the barbarians' arrival (and, through Joll's mission, even attempting to orchestrate it), prays "for the miracle."[33] The coming of the barbarians would be a salvation of sorts.

In all three of the works under discussion, a host therefore awaits the arrival of a guest who will enable him or her to feel at home, to feel settled. Waiting is, in fact, the dominant action in these texts. At the end of *In the Heart of the Country*, Magda, in the farmhouse from which her guests, Hendrik and Anna, have absconded, waits, "like a maiden waiting for the holy ghost" (127), for the voices that speak to her from flying machines. As its title announces, *Waiting for the Barbarians* is a novel about waiting. Similarly, the communities in *Dusklands* are "dusklands" because the guests they await do not arrive. In this novel's remarkable description of the American invasion of Vietnam, the stress falls squarely on the invaders' hope that they will encounter what they expect and thereby come into being. With terrible irony, J.M. Coetzee describes the invasion of Vietnam as a prayer for salvation. In the second part of this novel, the emphasis on Jacobus Coetzee's expectations of the Khoi depicts his encounter with them as a form of waiting. Importantly, waiting is here represented as an intentional activity: Jacobus Coetzee waits *for* something of which he has some form of foreknowledge. In encountering the Khoi, he awaits the arrival of the 'Hottentots'. His subsequent extermination of the Khoi tribe is also, of course, a form of waiting, a vain attempt

---

[31] Barbara Eckstein, "The Body, The Word, and the State: J.M. Coetzee's *Waiting for the Barbarians*," *Novel: A Forum on Fiction* 22.2 (1989): 175.

[32] Coetzee, *Dusklands*, 18.

[33] *Dusklands*, 18.

to force them into conformity with his expectations of them, to coerce the guest whom he has invited to arrive. Most of the activities in these texts – from imperial invasion to genocide – are forms of waiting for a guest who does not exist and whose arrival is thus endlessly deferred.

ᚤ ᚦ

While the early novels all treat the problem of identifying the stranger from a position within community, there is a definite development in their negotiation of this issue. For the most part, *Dusklands* is content to stage Eugene Dawn's and Jacobus Coetzee's entrapment in their respective communities' structures of knowledge. Even so, while wandering the desert like a "pallid symbol" (113), the latter, who seems to be familiar with Immanuel Kant's philosophy and William Blake's poetry, does entertain the possibility that he suffered "a failure of imagination" in his encounter with the Khoi (109), that they may have comprised "an immense world of delight" that was, however, "closed off" to his "senses" (113). It is this suggestion that it may be possible to respond to the stranger in terms that have not always already been prescribed by community's epistemological and discursive regimes that is developed in *In the Heart of the Country* and *Waiting for the Barbarians*.

The most striking difference between Magda and, say, Jacobus Coetzee is that her author invests her with some knowledge of her entrapment in her community. She is, from the first, wholly dissatisfied with who she is: "I live inside a skin inside a house. There is no act I know of that will liberate me into the world. There is no act I know of that will bring the world into me" (10). In these sentences, the house-metaphor, which becomes increasingly prominent in the later novels, signifies the protagonist's detachment from the world. The house, it would seem, is a prison of sorts, as emerges quite clearly in Magda's later claim: "I could have burned my way out of this prison" (101). To be sure, the old farmhouse begins to look suspiciously like the prisonhouse of language. After describing herself as dithering "in the empty house, feeling the comfort of the sunlight glancing off the same rows of copperware it glanced off before I was born into this world," Magda goes on to say: "I would not be myself if I did not feel the seductions of the cool stone house, the comfortable old ways, the antique feudal language" (43). This character's dissatisfaction with herself is precisely a dissatisfaction with the way in which she has been constituted in language.[34] As she puts it, "I create myself in the words that create me" (8). Language, again to invoke Derrida's description, is the "mobile habitat" that the self carries with it and which, indeed, bears the self from birth to death. Magda is inscribed in a linguistic and discursive system that pre-exists her entry into the world.

The metaphor of the house thus signifies the subject's linguistic and discursive separation from the world. Magda's wish *not* to be the self that responds to "the seductions of the cool stone house" signals a desire to transcend language, to live "a life unmediated by words" and to experience and know "these stones, these bushes, this sky [...] without question" (135). Earlier in the novel, she, after having referred to "the ache to abdicate the throne of consciousness and enter the mode of being practised by goats and stones," articulates a similar sentiment:

> Seated here I hold the goats and stones, the entire farm and even its environs in this cool, alienating medium of mine, exchanging them item by item for my word-counters. (26)

Crucially, Magda's language alienates her from not only goats and stones, but also other human beings. So, for instance, she comments as follows on her relationship with Hendrik:

> I know nothing of Hendrik. The reason for this is that in all our years together on the farm he has kept his station while I have kept my distance; and the combination of the two, the station and the distance, has ensured that my gaze falling on him, his gaze falling on me, have remained kindly, incurious, remote. [...] We have our places, Hendrik and I, in an old old code. With fluid ease we move through the paces of our dance. (24–25)

In identifying Hendrik as a servant: i.e. in trying to *present* him as a servant, Magda's language, and the code it bears, negates him. This is why she reflects that "Hendrik is not only essence but substance, not only servant but stranger" (14).

Tellingly, the same code, and the distances its identifications inscribe, is again evident in Magda's description, or perhaps construction, of her

---

[34] See Head, *J.M. Coetzee*, 55; and Brian May, "J.M. Coetzee and the Question of the Body," *Modern Fiction Studies* 47.2 (2001): 398.

father's "dialogue" with Hendrik upon his arrival on the farm. The most striking feature of this "dialogue" is its formulaic nature, its aura of repetition. Although a stranger, Hendrik is immediately identified as a servant by the language that *both* he and Magda's "masterful" father use (3):

> 'Baas [...], middag baas, ek soek werk, baas.'
> [...]
> 'Wat se soort werk soek jy?'
> 'Nee, werk, my baas.'
> 'Waar kom jy vandaan?'
> 'Van Armoede, my baas. Maar nou kom ek van baas Kobus, baas, baas Kobus sê baas het werk.'
> [...]
> 'Nouja, luister nou goed. Hoe noem hulle jou?'
> 'Hendrik, my baas.' (20)

> ['Master, afternoon Master, I'm looking for work, Master.'
> 'What kind of work are you looking for?'
> 'No, work, my Master.'
> 'Where do you come from?'
> 'From Armoede, my Master. But I now come from Master Kobus, Master Kobus says Master has work.'
> 'Now yes, listen well now. What do they call you?'
> Hendrik, my Master.'][35]

The point of the dialogue is that there is nothing unique about it and the positions it installs. It is, to use Magda's metaphor, a dance, the steps of which are well-rehearsed and have been executed on countless previous occasions. On the surface, the one dancer leads the other. In Magda's description, the rhythm of the dance even approximates a rudimentary two-step of sorts: "question and answer, word and echo" (20). The two dancers are locked together in a relation of total dependence: the one that leads depends on the one that follows; the one that follows depends on the one that leads. In fact, though, both leader and follower are led by the dance, the steps of which are always already there, waiting only to be oc-

---

[35] In the South African edition of *In the Heart of the Country*, dialogue is rendered in Afrikaans. This is my translation of this particular 'exchange'.

cupied by the dancers. When the dancers follow the steps, they dance to a
tune to which they and numerous others have previously danced.

The dance-metaphor thus foregrounds the dialogue's repetitive, and
therefore generic and entirely impersonal, nature. The words of which it is
formed say nothing that is remotely specific about either Hendrik or
Magda's father. These two simply occupy already-given, fixed, oppositionally defined positions that annul the specifty of whomsoever fills
them. Well before he reveals his name to be 'Hendrik', Hendrik has been
named and known by the discourse of *baasskap* or racial mastery that
informs the dialogue. Importantly, in this regard, it is not just Magda's
father who names Hendrik through this discourse. Having internalized it,
Hendrik identifies *himself* in its terms: he introduces and so presents himself to Magda's father in the code of *baasskap*. At the same time, Magda's
father presents himself to Hendrik by assuming the position that the code
inscribes for him. Ironically, in presenting themselves through this code of
racial mastery, in being mastered by it, these characters, in fact, fail to
present themselves.

So, although Attridge is correct in contending that "Hendrik and Anna
remain enigmatic presences never wholly grasped by the machinery of the
text, never securely 'in their place',"[36] it must be added that exactly the
same should be said of Magda's father. In truth, we know very little about
the character called "Magda's father." One of the only things that we do
know about him is that he "creates absence" (37). "Wherever he goes,"
says Magda, "he leaves absences behind him" (37). While this is clear in
the case of the absence that he leaves for Hendrik in the cited passage, it is
equally apparent that he, in the process of creating this absence, creates
another for himself. Tellingly, Magda, after having described him in terms
of a failure of presence, numbers her father among the absences that he
has created: "The absence of himself above all – a presence so cold, so
dark, so remote as to be itself an absence, a moving shadow casting a
blight on the heart" (37). In *In the Heart of the Country*, master and servant are positions inscribed by a language and a discourse that subject and
fail to present whomever occupies them. Brian Macaskill is, I think, quite

---

[36] Attridge, *J.M. Coetzee and the Ethics of Reading*, 28–29.

right when he maintains that "one of the central subjects of this novel is
the struggle against subjection by language."[37]

Language distances or alienates individuals not just from others but
from themselves or, rather, their potential selves. I have suggested that
Magda's dissatisfaction with her life stems from her sense that she is entrapped in the house of language. The danger of this statement is that it
implies a distinction between an essential self and language. For this
reason, I must emphasize what is, in fact, already implicit in my argument: Magda's dissatisfaction with her home is a dissatisfaction with the
way in which her self has been defined by language. This, indeed, is the
implication of her aforementioned observation that she creates herself in
the words that create her. The "word," she confesses elsewhere, has always "come down" to her and she has "passed it on" (10). Magda is
linguistically and discursively separated from what she *might* be. As she
says to Anna, "I could have been another person" (101). To liberate herself from her house entails, not freeing an essential self, but *becoming*
other than herself. If she is, for instance, to relate to that in Hendrik which
their language excludes, to what makes of him not just a servant but a
stranger, she will become a stranger to herself, to what she presently is.
She will have brought "the world" into herself.

It is when Magda tells Anna she might have been a different person
that she boasts that she "could have burned" her "way out of this prison"
(101). Significantly, though, her attempt at liberating herself does not assume the form of burning or, in an allusion to the fable of the three little
pigs, "blow[ing]" her house down (10). Instead, she attempts to renego-
tiate her relations with Hendrik and Anna by killing her "masterful
father."[38] The death of the father, she hopes, will bring about her rebirth.[39]
After the murder, Magda, in contemplating how to dispose of the corpse,

---

[37] Brian Macaskill, "Charting J.M. Coetzee's Middle Voice: *In the Heart of the
Country*," in *Critical Essays on J.M. Coetzee*, ed. Kossew, 76.

[38] Given the novel's aleatory nature, we, of course, never know whether Magda
does, in fact, kill her father. As Attwell points out, Magda is at the end of the novel still
serving her father tea (*J.M. Coetzee*, 60). It should be added, though, that even this
detail is highly ambiguous: there is a suggestion that it may be the *remains* of her
father that she serves: "I pick him up without difficulty, a mannikin of dry bones held
together by cobwebs" (*In the Heart of the Country*, 135).

[39] See Dovey, *The Novels of J.M. Coetzee*, 163.

reflects that "Until this bloody afterbirth is gone there can be no new life for me" (15).

The Hegelian dimension of this character's strategy is obvious: she wishes to alter the master–slave relationship through achieving some form of mutual recognition. As she later puts it, "The medium, the median – that is what I wanted to be! Neither master nor slave, neither parent nor child, but the bridge between, so that in me the contraries should be reconciled!" (133). To this end, she invites Hendrik and Anna into her house:

> We make up two beds in the guestroom, decently, with sheets and blankets. Then we push the beds together. I see to it that there is a chamberpot. I fill the waterjug. I am failing in no observance, nor are my intentions impure. In the heart of nowhere, in this dead place, I am making a start; or, if not that, making a gesture. (110)

Moreover, she sleeps with Anna and, subsequently, Hendrik. As I have already observed, however, Magda eventually comes to realize that nothing has changed, that that for which she longs, "whatever it is, does not come" (113). In terms of the birth-metaphor, which is hereafter systematically developed in Coetzee's fiction, what she expects, even labours to bear, in killing her father remains unborn. Her earlier words therefore prove proleptic: "Labouring under my father's weight I struggle to give life to a world but seem to engender only death" (10–11). There is no virgin birth, no salvation, and therefore no "new life" for her. In failing to reconfigure the master–slave relationship, she fails to become other than she is.

The killing of the master, it would seem, cannot solve the problem of recognition that, according to Hegel, underlies the conflict between master and slave: the positions inscribed by the language and discourse of mastery remain intact. This much emerges in this account by Magda of her relationship with Anna:

> Anna is oppressed by my watching eyes. She is oppressed by my invitations to relax, to sit by my side on the old bench in the shade of the sering-tree. She is oppressed particularly by my talk. (112)

Ironically, as the following description of her "talk" shows, even the language in which Magda expresses her desire to find "words of true exchange" oppresses Anna: "I crane over her from the stiff kitchen chair and hector: she hears only waves of rage crashing in my voice, and sobs drearily" (101). The language they share locks these two characters in oppositionally defined positions that render Magda's hospitality nothing more than, to use her word, a "gesture."[40]

In fact, though, language makes of her hospitality more than just a gesture; it becomes an act of hostility. Hence Magda wonders to herself "whether Hendrik and Anna are guests or invaders or prisoners" (112), and earlier realizes that Anna may well perceive herself to be "trapped in the dark house with the witchwoman" (101). The persistence of the power relationship, despite Magda's attempt at hospitality, is further apparent in Hendrik's invasion of her body. In Hegelian terms, his rape of her is a rebellion against her tyranny. Irrespective of her reluctance to do so, of her intentions to the contrary, Magda remains a master.[41] Her hospitality is an oppression. Through it, she, like the father she kills, "creates absences," including her own.

Seemingly, then, Magda's hospitality fails because it is rendered conditional by language. If she is to achieve her ambition to reconcile the contraries, to be neither master nor slave but "the bridge between," she must recognize and act on the recognition that it is language which enables relations of power, the economy of dominance and subservience. Such a recognition seems to be implicit in her desire to transcend language. Indeed, as we have seen, Magda does initially consider burning or blowing the house down as a potential solution to her problem. However, we are also told that the house is made of stone (43). No amount of huffing and puffing will bring it down. The possibility of transcending language by eliminating it is further negated by the novel's ending, which finds Magda still in the house on the farm. Clearly, she has not managed to escape the

---

[40] See Kossew, *Pen and Power*, 73.

[41] See Stephen Watson's argument that most of Coetzee's "major protagonists are colonisers who wish to elude at almost any cost their historical role as colonisers. All of them [...] are wrought to a pitch of desperation in their efforts to escape the intolerable burdens of the master–slave relationship. [...] If there is [...] a pessimism in them [i.e. Coetzee's novels], it is because the majority of these characters [...] beat against the shackles of their historical position in vain" ("Colonialism and the Novels of J.M. Coetzee," 22–23). Watson then cites Albert Memmi's argument on the predicament of the colonizer who refuses – the colonizer who, despite his or her reluctance, is implicated in the colonial system. The crucial point here is that colonial relations derive not from individual intention and action but exist before the arrival or birth of the individual.

prisonhouse of language. Moreover, this novel's sequence of concluding paragraphs marks Coetzee's first use of the notion of the castaway as a metaphor for the human subject's linguistic and discursive detachment from the world: "We are the castaways of God as we are the castaways of history. *That* is the origin of our feeling of solitude. [...] I wish only to be at home in the world as the merest beast is at home" (135; see also 123, 125, 131, 132). Magda's entrapment in her home precludes her from being at home in the world.

Nevertheless, even as it suggests this character's failure to transcend her linguistic subjection, the ending of *In the Heart of the Country* foregrounds her attempt to alter language through her stone poems. On the one hand, the medium of these poems equates their words with the "cool stone house," thereby rendering ironic Magda's efforts to contrive a transcendental language of "pure meanings" (125). On the other hand, the analogy between poetic language and stone cannot but extend to the stone desert from which Magda's language separates her and yet to which she so often refers.[42] Given the ambivalence of this analogy, we find, in Magda's poems of stone, *both* a recognition that the attempt at transcending language occurs in language *and* a concerted attempt not so much to "burst through the screen of names into the goatseye view of [...] the stone desert" (18) as to make language *like* the stone desert it excludes. Since it cannot be transcended, language must be altered. It must be made a home for the alterity that it excludes. It will be recalled that Magda, at the beginning of the novel, knows of "no act" that will "liberate" her "into the world," or "bring" it into her (10). Whether or not they can or will do so, her stone poems are an act designed to make language similar to the environment it screens.

This ambition is, of course, sheer madness. From a rational perspective at least, Magda's paradoxical enterprise to make language accommodate what it excludes is driven by her insanity. Still, it is its very madness that is perhaps the point of this enterprise. The metaphor of madness – and this is also the case in some of the later novels – implies this character's unconditional hospitality to an uninvited guest. Paragraph 238 describes a visit paid Magda by a boy, and ends with the following sentence: "That

---

[42] Chiara Briganti, "'A Bored Spinster with a Locked Diary': The Politics of Hysteria in *In the Heart of the Country*," in *Critical Essays on J.M. Coetzee*, ed. Kossew, 93–94.

was the one visit" (125). Paragraph 239 then commences with the words
"I also hear voices" (125). The implication, then, is that these voices *visit*
Magda. At night, when she is asleep and thus no longer has the power, the
self-possession, to invite, name, and therefore select, her guests, she receives these voices. They arrive uninvited "from another world" (127), we
are told. Magda's description of the visitation of the voices emphasizes
the absence of intentionality in her hospitality:

> The words I hear [...] sift down as they grow colder, just as the dew
> does [...] and to reach my ears by night, or more often in the early
> morning just before dawn, and to seep into my understanding, like
> water. (126–27)

She becomes host to invisible and therefore uninvited visitors.

Earlier in this chapter, I suggested that *In the Heart of the Country* concludes with its protagonist waiting for these voices. It is now necessary to
add that the kind of waiting at issue in this novel's ending is qualitatively
different from that in *Dusklands*. When she waits for the voices, Magda
does so, paradoxically, without waiting for anything that may be defined
as an object constituted by an intentional act of consciousness. That is, she
waits without inviting, without awaiting, without expecting anything. As
the following description indicates, her kind of waiting is a non-intentional activity: "I do not dream at all nowadays, but sleep a blissful pas-
siveness waiting for the words to come to me, like a maiden waiting for
the holy ghost" (127).

What is connoted here is Magda's openness to what is *outside* the
house of language she inhabits. Significantly, in this respect, the voices
she hears speak a language of "pure meaning" (125): i.e. no recognizable
language or, more accurately, a "language" beyond language. While she is
entrapped in the house, its interior therefore presupposes an exterior. Its
walls and apertures demarcate not only an inside but also an outside.
Teasing out the implications of the metaphor of the house in the ethic of
hospitality, Derrida notes that "in order to constitute the space of a habi-
table house and home, you also need an opening, a door and windows,
you have to give up a passage to the outside world."[43] The very circum-
scription of this space opens it to intrusion.

---

[43] Derrida, *Of Hospitality*, 61.

Magda becomes not simply a host but also a home for the invisible. In not being able to name and so exclude the stranger, she is taken over by him or her or it. The host, that is to say, loses her sovereignty over and distance from this visitor. She is opened up to and invaded by the visitor's otherness. For both Derrida and Levinas, such an invasion is an inevitable consequence of the unannounced and therefore wholly unexpected arrival of the stranger. Because the visitor does not "knock," as Levinas puts it, s/he "assigns me before I designate him" or her,[44] and this assigning "is entry into me by burglary" (145). In arriving uninvited, then, the visitor unsettles and unhomes the host. The host becomes the other's home. Unconditional hospitality is thus an effect of the host's being taken hostage by the visitor, of the visitor's visiting itself upon the host. In the process, the host becomes a stranger unto him-/herself. Tellingly, Magda is unsettled in precisely this way. "This cannot go on," she complains, "I am losing myself" (127).

It is because she loses possession of her self in being possessed by her invisible visitors that Magda writes. She writes beside or outside herself in an ecstasy of madness. Inspiration, in both this novel and Coetzee's subsequent ones, is figured as a form of unconditional hospitality. Magda writes because she has been mastered – not by an agent in a Hegelian economy of power but by the invisible, which is outside this economy. Her writing is her involuntary response to being visited by what is beyond her prisonhouse of language. Magda writes, and therefore acts, in being acted upon by these invisible visitors.[45] In other words, she is *obliged* to obey the voices that dictate to her. She is Coetzee's first "secretary of the invisible."

ࣾ ࣾ

In the Heart of the Country thus suggests that language and culture are not total, that their apparent totality, in fact, presupposes infinity, a beyond, a point of exteriority. Equally importantly, Magda's accommodation of the voices that visit her implies the possibility of a non-phenomenological

---

[44] Emmanuel Levinas, *Otherwise Than Being or Beyond Essence*, tr. Alphonso Lingis (*Autrement qu'être ou au-delà de l'essence*, 1974; The Hague: Martinus Nijhoff, 1981): 87.

[45] See Attridge's discussions of the nexus between otherness and creation in *The Singularity of Literature*.

response to this exteriority. What this character waits for, I have argued, is not intentionally assumed. It would seem, then, that for Coetzee, as for Levinas, it is necessary to distinguish between the order of the same and of the other. In terms of the phenomenological model of intentionality, the same would consist of both the intentional acts of consciousness and the intentional objects that are constituted by these acts and, in turn, invest them with meaning. Conversely, the other is what is exterior to the same. Since it cannot be reduced to an object before intentional consciousness, it cannot be presented or represented.

Waiting for the Barbarians develops this idea of an alterity that lies beyond the same, language, and history. While the Magistrate is implicated in history, he receives constant intimations, in his dreams, of what is outside history. In this section of my discussion, I examine not only this novel's suggestion of an outside to history, but also the notion of responsibility, of ethical action, attendant on it.

Earlier in the chapter, I argued that *Waiting for the Barbarians* foregrounds the manner in which the word 'barbarians' signifies a failure of presence. Given that my discussion may have created the impression that a failure of presence is simply to be equated with absence, it is now necessary to emphasize that a form which fails to present something nevertheless gestures toward what has not been presented. In Coetzee's novel, the point is precisely that the word 'barbarians', rather than exhausting what it seeks to name, leaves a remainder or surplus. What is staged in the Magistrate's relationship with the barbarian girl is his attempt to relate to this excess, to what the word 'barbarians' has failed not only to present but also to render absent.[46]

Importantly, in this regard, Empire has inscribed itself and its forms on the girl's body. This is what is suggested by Colonel Joll's torture of her. For instance, the Magistrate refers to the girl's scars as "the traces of a history" that "her body bears" (64). In his interactions with her, he tries to

---

[46] See Abdul JanMohamed's argument that even though the colonizer's identifications negate him or her, the indigene's "presence as an absence can never be cancelled" ("The Economy of Manichean Allegory: The Function of Racial Difference in Colonialist Literature," in *"Race," Writing, and Difference*, ed. Henry Louis Gates, Jr. [Chicago: U of Chicago P, 1986]: 86). See also Lance Olsen, "The Presence of Absence: Coetzee's *Waiting for the Barbarians*," *ARIEL: A Review of International English Literature* 16.2 (1985): 47–56.

read what these signs have rendered neither present nor absent.[47] He tries
to read what cannot be read, to relate to what the signs have failed to say.
In fact, he intuits that it is his desire for the "marks on her" to be "erased,"
and thus for her to be "restored to herself" (64), that draws him to the girl.
He wants to *see* her in the absence of Empire's history, without knowledge, from outside his linguistic and cultural enclosure. In terms of the
notion of unconditional hospitality, the Magistrate wishes to receive the
girl without naming and identifying her in advance. At least, this is the
tenor of one of his concluding thoughts in the novel: "I wanted to live
outside the history that Empire imposes on its subjects, even its lost subjects. I never wished it for the barbarians that they should have the history
of Empire laid upon them" (154).

   What we find in the Magistrate's relationship with the barbarian girl is
therefore a form of waiting akin to that staged in the closing pages of *In
the Heart of the Country* in Magda's relationship with the voices. The
Magistrate waits, not for the "barbarians," but for the unexpected visitor,
for that of which he can have no expectation, and which can therefore,
strictly speaking, not be awaited. Herein lies the significance of his recurring dream of the hooded girl. In his sleep, when his intentional consciousness is relaxed, the dream, we are told, "comes back" (37). Like
Magda's voices, it arrives and visits him when he is in a state devoid of
expectation and intentional assumption. The dream is a vision of a child.
In and through it, the child arrives; she arrives when the Magistrate is
unable to welcome her, to respond to her with advance knowledge and so
place her, and himself, in the subject positions installed by his culture.
This is why, in one instance of the dream, his face is covered in ice (52):
he, quite literally, cannot confront the child, adopt a position in opposition
to her. Notably, too, in none of the dream's visits is the Magistrate able to
address the girl in language.

---

[47] See the following discussions of the Magistrate's attempt to read the barbarian
girl's body: Eckstein, "The Body, The Word, and the State"; Head, *J.M. Coetzee*; May,
"J.M. Coetzee and the Question of the Body"; Michael Valdez Moses, "The Mark of
Empire: Writing, History, and Torture in Coetzee's *Waiting for the Barbarians*," *Ken-
yon Review* 15.1 (1993): 115–27; and Jennifer Wenzel, "Keys to the Labyrinth: Writing, Torture, and Coetzee's Barbarian Girl," *Tulsa Studies in Women's Literature* 15.1
(1996): 61–71.

In his sleep, then, the Magistrate responds to the child as a stranger. That is to say, he responds to her without knowledge and is accordingly able to see her immediately, as she is in herself:

> I fear, at this last instant, that she will be a disappointment, that the
> face she will present to me will be obtuse, slick, like an internal
> organ not meant to live in the light. But no, she is herself, herself as I
> have never seen her, a smiling child, the light sparkling on her teeth
> and glancing from her jet-black eyes. "So this is what it is to see!" I
> say to myself. (53)

The child of the Magistrate's dreams is thus other than history, beyond the domain of the same. By extension, the child signifies what history has corrupted, defaced, effaced, rendered invisible. In juxtaposing the dream-child and the barbarian girl,[48] the novel therefore exposes Empire's violation of otherness in its attempt to know it from within its linguistic and conceptual economy. Its attempt to make a face for the other, the child, defaces it. The history of Empire, it follows, is both the violation and the loss of the child. In terms of the logic of the child-metaphor, history is the realm of abandonment, of parental irresponsibility. "Somewhere, always," the Magistrate thinks despairingly, "a child is being beaten" (80). As I have already suggested in my introduction, and will show in subsequent chapters, this understanding of history as a realm characterized by irresponsibility to the other is a feature of Coetzee's fiction. Indeed, it, and the child-metaphor through which it is conveyed, is already apparent in *Dusklands* in Eugene Dawn's stabbing of his son, and in Jacobus Coetzee's brutalization of the Khoi child.

In *Waiting for the Barbarians*, the juxtaposition of the dream-child and the barbarian girl suggests that the Magistrate, in his relationship with the latter, must *see* the former. He must see beyond the visible marks of Empire on the barbarian girl's body. Differently put, he must see what is not phenomenally apparent, what is invisible, and has been rendered such by the forms of history and their logic of manifestation. It is, moreover, the Magistrate's *responsibility* to see the invisible. He has no say in the matter. Having been visited by the vision of the lost child, he acts under inspiration. The fact that the dream commences before the Magistrate's

---

[48] See Attwell, *J.M. Coetzee*, 81.

first encounter with the barbarian girl implies that it inspires his attempt to
see her without the knowledge of her that Empire's codes inscribe. Consequently, the dream affects, even mediates, the Magistrate's relationship
with the barbarian girl.

By implication, the Magistrate is never in control of his actions. Like
Magda in *In the Heart of the Country*, he is unsettled, unhomed, by his
uninvited visitor. For example, he is quite unaware why it should be that
he offers the barbarian girl shelter and succour. In the first of the scenes in
which he washes her feet, the Magistrate's confusion is very apparent. As
Attridge points out, the scene is developed in a way that enables us to
sense this character's "awareness that he is playing out the standard rituals
of seduction – the fire, the drawn curtains, the lamp" and so on.[49] The
Magistrate's words to the girl, "This in not what you think it is" (27), are,
of course, the stock disclaimer of the seducer. At the same time, though,
they reveal to us that *he* thinks that he knows what it is that he has in mind
for the girl. Clearly, he assumes that he desires her sexually. He assumes
that he is acted upon by his desire for her. Thus, for instance, he hears
himself speak in a "new thick voice" that he hardly recognizes. He knows
that he is not himself, that he has been mastered by something he believes
to be sexual desire. It is therefore all the more striking that what he anticipates will be his seduction of the girl should culminate in his washing of
her feet. While he is acted upon, and knows that this is so, it is by nothing
that he can recognize.[50]

Throughout their time together, the Magistrate fails to understand his
attraction to and treatment of the girl. He repeatedly dismisses sexual
desire as an explanation – "I have no desire to enter this stocky little body
glistening by now in the firelight. It is a week since words have passed between us. I feed her, use her body, if that is what I'm doing, in this foreign
way" (30) – and constantly dwells on his inability to account for his actions in *rational* terms:

---

[49] Attridge, *J.M. Coetzee and the Ethics of Reading*, 44.

[50] Josephine Donovan is perhaps the only critic to have commented on this aspect of
the Magistrate's relationship to the barbarian girl. After noting that "nearly all of his
reactions are visceral ones that he is unable to explain," she refers to the Magistrate's
"unmediated and otherwise inexplicable empathy" for the girl; Donovan, "'Miracles
of Creation': Animals in J.M. Coetzee's Work," *Michigan Quarterly Review* 43.1
(2004): 78–93, online http://name.umdl.umich.edu/act2080.0043.112 (8 June 2008).

> What this woman beside me is doing in my life I cannot comprehend.
> (47)

> I am with her not for whatever raptures she may promise or yield but
> for other reasons, which remain as obscure to me as ever. (64)

In fact, the Magistrate is quite obviously surprised, perplexed, and bewildered by his own behaviour. A few pages after the foot-washing scene,
we encounter the following description of his interaction with the girl:

> I lie beside her, speaking softly. This is where my hand, caressing her
> belly, seems as awkward as a lobster. The erotic impulse, if that is
> what it has been, withers; with surprise I see myself clutched to this
> stolid girl, unable to remember what I ever desired in her, angry with
> myself for wanting and not wanting her. (33)

Evidently, the Magistrate no longer knows himself. Since they bear little
relation to his assumptions, intentions, and ostensible desires, he finds his
actions wholly unpredictable.

   In his relationship with the barbarian girl, the Magistrate is therefore
certainly not in control of himself. Although he acts, he does so under inspiration by the invisible. His actions are informed by his desire to see the
invisible. For this reason, he unintentionally, and unbeknownst to both
himself and the girl, assumes responsibility for her. In the process, he
becomes a stranger to himself, notwithstanding his protestations to the
contrary:

> If a change in my moral being were occurring I would feel it [...]. I
> am the same man I always was; but time has broken, something has
> fallen in upon me from the sky, at random, from nowhere: this body
> in my bed, for which I am responsible, or so it seems, otherwise why
> do I keep it? For the time being, perhaps forever, I am simply bewil-
> dered. (43)

The unintentional, involuntary nature of this form of responsibility, the
fact that it is accompanied by a dispossession of self, accounts for the
Magistrate's "fits of resentment" against what he refers to as his "bond-

age" to the foot-oiling ritual.[51] He even feels that he has been mastered by the girl: "I light a candle and bend over the form to which, it seems, I am in a measure enslaved" (42). The Magistrate, it would appear, is a servant not of sexual desire, but of responsibility.

Significantly, this responsibility extends well beyond this character's relationship to the girl. In the scene in which Joll first inscribes the word "ENEMY" on the backs of the prisoners and then has it erased through flogging, we again see the Magistrate acting against his conscious intentions. Upon observing Joll's arrival with the prisoners, the Magistrate consciously decides on a course of action. At least, we infer as much from his actions: he returns to the prison yard, where he collects an empty bucket, which he then fills. Even so, we certainly do not know what he intends doing. When he reflects that "As a gesture it will have no effect, it will not even be noticed" (104), we do not know the nature of the "gesture" he has in mind. Nor do we know the antecedent of the impersonal pronoun "it." All we know is that when he finally does intervene by speaking out against the brutalization of the prisoners, the Magistrate utterly disregards whatever action it is that he had decided on when he quite deliberately and very purposefully collected the bucket. Tellingly, too, he again hears himself when he speaks. In an ecstasy of responsibility – beside himself, outside himself – he hears what he says and sees what he does:

> "*No!*" I hear the first word from my throat, rusty, not loud enough.
> Then again: "*No!*" This time the word rings like a bell from my chest.
> The soldier who blocks my way stumbles aside. I am in the arena
> holding up my hands to still the crowd: "*No! No! No!*" (106)

His actions are involuntary. He acts in being acted upon.[52]

---

[51] See Sam Durrant, *Postcolonial Narrative and the Work of Mourning: J.M. Coetzee, Wilson Harris, and Toni Morrison.* (Albany: State U of New York P, 2004): 44.

[52] Our sense of the disparity between the Magistrate's intentions and actions is, of course, compounded by Coetzee's use of first-person, present-tense narration. Anne Waldron Neumann notes that "Present-tense narration is well suited to narrate the magistrate's childlike confusion," and that this technique "records present uncertainty without always drawing retrospective connections, certainly without drawing them simultaneously with the event." See Neumann, "Escaping the 'Time of History'? Present Tense and the Occasion of Narration in J.M. Coetzee's *Waiting for the Barbarians*," *Journal of Narrative Technique* 20.1 (1990): 67; see also Ene–Reet Soovik, "Prisoners of the Present: Tense and Agency in J.M. Coetzee's *Waiting for the Bar-*

Apart from shouting "*No!*", the Magistrate also shouts "*Men!*" (107), in an attempt to remind the torturers, and their spectators, of the humanity they share with the prisoners. By implication, the Magistrate is responsible not just for the barbarian girl but for all human beings. The form of responsibility that Coetzee thematizes in this novel is even more hyperbolic than this would suggest, though. As the Magistrate shouts "*Men!*" he reflects that "beetles, worms, cockroaches, ants, in their various ways" are also "miracles of creation" (107). Responsibility, if it is to deserve this appellation, must encompass all.

The notion of infinite responsibility emerges earlier in the novel when the Magistrate goes hunting. In many respects, this is a pivotal scene: this character obviously goes hunting with the intention of killing animals. On a conscious and rational level, he subscribes to the anthropocentric notion that human animals have dominion over other animals. To be sure, we learn on the very first page of the novel that hunting is one of his favourite pastimes (one, it should be noted, that he shares with Colonel Joll[53]). It is all the more surprising, therefore, that, once he has a waterbuck ram in his sights, he does not shoot it. "Never before," he later explains to the girl, "have I had the feeling of not living my own life on my own terms" (40). Her response foregrounds the breakdown in intentionality that is here at stake, the fact that the Magistrate is not in control of his actions. "Didn't you want to shoot this buck?" she asks, then adds: "If you want to do something, you do it" (40).

What is adumbrated in *Waiting for the Barbarians*, then, is a form of ethical action that is *not* grounded in the perceptions, experiences, and understanding of a rational, autonomous individual. Very clearly, this novel treats knowledge and reason with the utmost suspicion. Knowledge,

---

barians and M. Atwood's *The Handmaid's Tale*," *Interlitteraria* 8 (2003): 259–75. I would add that this form of narration heightens our sense of the Magistrate's ultimate inability to elucidate his actions. What is at issue is not just "present uncertainty." In James Phelan's words, "teleology is beyond his control" ("Present Tense Narration, Mimesis, the Narrative Norm, and the Positioning of the Reader in *Waiting for the Barbarians*," in *Understanding Narrative*, ed. James Phelan & Peter J. Rabinowitz [Columbus: Ohio UP, 1994]: 234). Even retrospectively, this character is unable to explain his actions. Although we leave him after the events of which we have read have transpired, he has yet to comprehend them: he "feel[s] stupid, like a man who lost his way long ago but presses on along a road that may lead nowhere" (156).

[53] Soovik, "Prisoners of the Present," 363.

that which invests the rational subject with control of both the world and self, enables only conditional hospitality, the comprehension of others within the subject's previously formed conceptual system. By implication, knowledge is one of the mechanisms through which community differentiates itself from its others and, in the process, requires its members to respond to them with indifference. In Coetzee's novel, it is after the barbarians have been identified as barbarians and enemies that it becomes possible to violate them physically. The Magistrate's inability to know either the world or himself must be read in the context of such epistemological violence.[54] For that matter, so must his description of his parting with the barbarian girl, which suggests that he does not know her, that, at some or other pre-reflective level, he has responded to her as a stranger:

> I see only too clearly what I see: a stocky girl with a broad mouth and hair cut in a fringe across her forehead staring over my shoulder into the sky; a stranger; a visitor from strange parts now on her way home after a less than happy visit. (73)

It is worth noting that the barbarian girl, owing to her impaired vision, does not confront the Magistrate in this scene. He cannot define himself in opposition to her. In other words, he cannot know her from within the subject positions inscribed by his culture.

The novel closes shortly after the Magistrate's conscious reflection that "There has been something staring me in the face, and still I do not see it"

---

[54] After arguing that torture has "transformed" the girl's body into "a text to be read," Wenzel seems to ascribe the Magistrate's failure to understand the otherness of the girl's body to some kind of moral flaw. "It is this sense of otherness," she contends, "that allows torturers to ignore the pain of their victims" ("Keys to the Labyrinth," 65). Laura Wright tends toward a similar conclusion when she maintains that the Magistrate's "inability to see what motivates his actions is a kind of blindness that results in a failure of the sympathetic imagination" (*Writing "Out of All the Camps,"* 80). In my argument, it is precisely the Magistrate's sense of her otherness that renders him responsible for the girl. Wenzel, I suspect, conflates radical otherness with the cultural inscription of difference, i.e. 'othering'. The otherness that proceeds from othering is an attempt to domesticate and so understand radical otherness. At the same time, radical otherness is what inevitably exceeds the reductions of othering. In his relationship with the barbarian girl, the Magistrate encounters the excess of Empire's forms of understanding. He encounters a strangeness that asserts commonality and proximity rather than the cultural difference that enables indifference.

(155). What stares him in the face, I have argued, is precisely that which can only be seen without knowledge: i.e. pre-reflectively. This, I have also argued, is the point of the novel's dream sequence. Through his vision of the child, the Magistrate is visited by what is beyond history and the domain of the same. In receiving difference with unconditional hospitality: i.e. "before any determination, before any anticipation, before any *identification*,"[55] he becomes host to that of which history is the loss. No matter how slightly, how ambiguously (and these qualifications are necessary), his actions in history are affected by what is outside history, and history is accordingly altered. Albeit almost imperceptibly, perhaps even inconsequentially, and certainly ambivalently, history is interrupted as a result of the self's visitation by what is beyond it.

✆ ༀ

One can only respond to history's exclusions from within history and in the terms of history. In other words, one cannot not respond to what is other than the same, other than in the very terms through which it has been excluded. It is for this reason that the Magistrate's reaction to the barbarian girl is so ambiguous. The following reflection by him, which again invokes the image of the child, the metaphor for what is other than history, expresses his desire to relate to her paternally: "I gave the girl my protection, offering in my equivocal way to be her father" (80). By implication, he wishes to treat her differently from her torturers. The Magistrate, however, is aware that he is a part of "the time of history" that "Empire has created," and therefore "no less infected with it than the faithful Colonel Joll" (133). To respond to what history excludes in the terms of history may well be to repeat, rather than repair, the original violation. Hence the Magistrate, after describing himself as swooping and circling "around the irreducible figure of the girl," asks himself what it is that she sees: "The protecting wings of a guardian albatross or the black shape of a coward crow afraid to strike while its prey yet breathes?" (81). While he wishes to "assert" his "distance from Colonel Joll" (44), the truth may be that he and the torturer are "Two sides of imperial rule" (135). One must remember, here, that not only Joll but also the Magistrate hosts the girl in her "less than happy visit" to the outpost.

---

[55] Derrida, *Of Hospitality*, 77.

There is clearly a literary corollary to the Magistrate's concern over the equivocal, ambivalent nature of his response to the girl. The novel asks itself whether it is possible to respond responsibly to the stranger in writing. It asks itself whether it is able to recover, protect, shelter, and succour the lost child. Is it able to host *and* parent what has been abandoned by history? If it is to do so, the work, it seems, would somehow have to transcend history. In expressing the Magistrate's desire "to live outside" history, the novel thus speaks of its own desire to contrive a degree of autonomy. Indeed, Coetzee moots exactly this possibility in an essay entitled "The Novel Today." After observing that history proceeds from the oppositional structure of social relations, he distinguishes between a mode of writing which "supplements" history by "depending on the model of history" for "its principal structuration" and another which "rivals" history by "occupy[ing] an autonomous place." The latter "operates in terms of its own procedures and issues" and, in the process, is able to "show up the mythic status of history."[56]

If writing could somehow occupy an "autonomous place," the text would be able to host the other unconditionally. It would be able to recover and protect the lost child. As Coetzee is well aware, though, matters are not nearly so simple as this rather crude distinction between the rivalry and supplementation of history in literary writing would seem to suggest. In this connection, it will be recalled that Magda, in the concluding scenes of *In the Heart of the Country*, writes under the inspiration of voices "from another world" (127). Nevertheless, as I pointed out, she writes in stone, the very material of which the house, symbol of her entrapment in language, has been built. In rendering radically ambivalent her response to the voices, this detail erodes and complicates precisely the opposition between supplementing and rivalling history that Coetzee posits in "The Novel Today."[57] Writing that attempts to respond to what lies beyond it,

---

[56] Coetzee, "The Novel Today," *Upstream* 6.1 (1988): 2–3.

[57] I agree entirely with Rachel Lawlan's argument that Coetzee is *"polemicizing"* when he constructs this rigid opposition in "The Novel Today," and that "what we find in the novels may be quite different and infinitely more complex than a dogmatic either/or" (*"The Master of Petersburg*: Confession and Double Thoughts in Coetzee and Dostoevsky," *ARIEL: A Review of International English Literature* 29.2 (1998): 132). Although he also distinguishes between supplementarity and a rivalry premissed on autonomy in essays like "Into the Dark Chamber: The Writer and the South African State" (in *Doubling the Point*, 361–68) and "Erasmus' *Praise of Folly*: Rivalry and

may well end up supplementing history. To respond to the other in writing may be to reduce it to the same.

In raising these questions, *Waiting for the Barbarians* asks not only whether *it* is able to *see* the invisible but also whether or not its figure for the invisible, the image of the child, is not itself already a corruption and reduction of that of which it is a figure.[58] Is it not, in other words, a prosopopeia? If we agree with Hillis Miller's description of prosopopeia as the ascription of "a name, a face or a voice" to what no longer has one or never had one: i.e. to "the absent, the inanimate, or the dead,"[59] the figure of the child in this novel is an instance of exactly this trope. If it is a metaphor, it is a metaphor for what cannot be metaphorized. Properly speaking, then, it is a catachresis rather than a metaphor. What the image of the child purports to signify is absent; it figures that which corresponds to no phenomenal reality and therefore cannot be figured. The image tries to present as an object an otherness that is beyond the same and therefore not presentable. As such, this figure cannot not reduce the otherness that it figures. Miller points out that such irony is typical of prosopopeia, which, he maintains, "always buries what it invokes"; the making of the "face" is "at the same time an act of effacement or defacement."[60] Ultimately, then, we have to ask whether the figure of the child is so very different from the name "barbarian" which, we have seen, is also a trope.

Notwithstanding their scepticism concerning the possibility of responding responsibly to the other in language, both *In the Heart of the Country* and *Waiting for the Barbarians* make it clear that the writer inspired by

---

Madness" (*Neophilologus* 76.1 [1992]: 1–18), the modes of writing thus opposed are not presented as a choice that is open to the writer.

[58] See Marianne de Jong's related argument: namely, that "Novels may be about the ethical without themselves being ethical actions" ("Is the Writer Ethical?: The Early Novels of J.M. Coetzee up to *Age of Iron*," *Journal of Literary Studies* 20.1–2 [2004]: 75). Later in her essay, she elaborates as follows: "The writer is guilty by the mere fact of his act of writing, it seems, since he cannot avoid positing substantial being and by the same token fail it" (85).

[59] J. Hillis Miller, "Prosopopeia in Hardy and Stevens," in *Tropes, Parables, Performatives: Essays on Twentieth-Century Literature* (Durham NC: Duke UP, 1991): 245.

[60] Miller, "Topography and Tropography in Thomas Hardy's *In Front of the Landscape*," in *Tropes, Parables, Performatives*, 210. For a truly insightful overview of this trope, its relation to catachresis, irony, and alterity, see Johan Geertsema's "Irony and Otherness."

the other has no choice but to attempt to make of the order of the same, history, a home for the other. As I have noted, Magda writes in an ecstasy of madness and the Magistrate, whose attempt to recover the lost child in his dealings with the barbarian girl is self-consciously literary, is not in control of his actions. The complex subject of responding involuntarily to an other whose alterity may be reduced by one's response is something I shall turn to in the succeeding chapters of this study.

What one finds in Coetzee's early fiction is thus an intense awareness of the ethics of writing, a protracted self-reflexive meditation on how to respond responsibly to what is other than history in order to interrupt, and so alter, history. Already in these novels, then, this writer raises, and at the same time questions, the possibility that the literary work, through its relation to what is other than history, may affect relations in history. In the next three chapters of this study, I trace at some length this writer's self-reflexive articulation (and complication) of this possibility in his fiction of the late-apartheid period and show how he, in these works, attempted to develop a form of writing that could engage affectively with apartheid history.

In the process of doing this, I pay special attention to the later fiction's concern with the nature of reading. If the literary text is to affect relations in history, it must affect the reader, who is in history and who therefore approaches the text from within a horizon of expectations. By implication, the reader names and identifies the text in advance. In reading a text, s/he waits for *the* text that has already been invited. The question that is self-reflexively raised by Coetzee's later novels may be phrased as follows: is it possible to read non-intentionally, or is reading necessarily a Hegelian struggle in which a masterful reader and an apparently servile text, both of whom know their places "in an old old code,"[61] move through the paces of their dance, the follower following the leader, the leader following the follower? Although this question of reading hospitably is implicit from the first in Coetzee's oeuvre, it becomes increasingly explicit after *Waiting for the Barbarians*.

ॐ ॐ

---

[61] Coetzee, *In the Heart of the Country*, 25.

2 A Goatseye View of the Stone Desert
∞ *Life & Times of Michael K*

T
HE DESIRE FOR TRANSCENDENCE so evident in the earlier novels gains a structural dimension in *Life & Times of Michael K*, *Foe*, and *Age of Iron*. The principal feature of these three novels is the opposition they inscribe between the realm of history and a setting that putatively transcends this realm. In *Life & Times of Michael K*, this setting is the insular Karoo farm, in *Foe*, the island, and, in *Age of Iron*, Mrs Curren's dilapidated old house. By staging a forfeiture of subject-centred consciousness, these utopian settings suggest the possibility of a relational mode that is wholly different from what has shaped the realm of history that they apparently transcend, and, in the process, provide an image of that whose absence has enabled the colonial history of South Africa.

The occurrence of these utopian settings in Coetzee's fiction of the late-apartheid period cannot but be related to the aforementioned desire of this writer to write fiction that "rivals" rather than "supplements" the conflictual relations out of which South Africa's history has "erected itself."[1] While I do explore this self-reflexive dimension of Coetzee's depiction of Michael K's utopian existence on the farm in my reading of *Life & Times of Michael K*, my ultimate argument is that the purpose of this portrayal is not simply to project a relational mode that is non-existent in history, but to affect the reader in such a way that his or her reading of this novel enacts the very relationship of which s/he reads.

Importantly, in *Life & Times of Michael K*, the farm is *not* initially shown as an "autonomous place";[2] it only becomes so after Michael K undergoes a *Bildung* of sorts. On first visiting the farm, this character

---

[1] Coetzee, "The Novel Today," 2–3.
[2] "The Novel Today," 3.

dominates nature, as is evident in the following description of his hunting of the goats:

> Almost under his feet one slipped and slid, kicking like a fish in the mud to regain its footing. K hurled the whole weight of his body upon it. [...] He could feel the goat's hindquarters heaving beneath him; it bleated again and again in terror; its body jerked in spasms. K straddled it, clenched his hands around its neck, and bore down with all his strength, pressing the head under the surface of the water and into the thick ooze below. The hindquarters thrashed, but his knees were gripping the body like a vice.[3]

The emphasis in this passage falls squarely on K's physical mastery of the goat. Quite clearly, he is here represented as being a part of the nature-dominating rational world rather than of nature itself. So, while Attwell contends that K is a "different kind of creature from the coloniser,"[4] I believe that he, by virtue of cultural location rather than design, is initially a "tamer of the wild" and "Destroyer of the wilderness,"[5] and therefore has something in common with Jacobus Coetzee, a fact already implicit in the seemingly innocuous detail that he was once employed as a gardener in Wynberg Park, Cape Town.[6] Tellingly, too, K's killing of the goats alludes to Defoe's *Robinson Crusoe*, in which the protagonist's possession and settlement of the island on which he has been cast away includes the domestication of the goats that he finds there.

Among Coetzee's many other allusions to Defoe's novel, which include the arrival of Visagie, the grandson of the erstwhile owners of the

---

[3] *Life & Times of Michael K* (Johannesburg: Ravan, 1983): 73–74. Unless otherwise indicated, further page references are in the main text.

[4] Attwell, *J.M. Coetzee*, 96.

[5] Coetzee, *Dusklands*, 82, 84.

[6] While most readers of the novel assert such an opposition between K and colonizer, some do detect a change in K's relation with the earth. Karin van Lierop, for instance, argues for a "reversed process of initiation": i.e. for an "entry into nature rather than culture," and for a regression from adulthood to infancy ("A Mythical Interpretation of J.M. Coetzee's *Life and Times of Michael K*," *Commonwealth: Essays & Studies* 9.1 [1986]: 47). Derek Wright makes a similar point ("Black Earth, White Myth: Coetzee's *Michael K*," *Modern Fiction Studies* 38.2 [1992]: 438–39). See also Stefan Helgesson's contribution to this discussion (*Writing in Crisis: Ethics and History in Gordimer, Ndebele and Coetzee* [Scottsville: U of KwaZulu–Natal P, 2004]: 208–10).

farm, who attempts to make of K a Friday of sorts, is Michael K's reflection that he had deemed the farm to be "one of those islands without an owner" (84).[7] In terms of the concept of ownership, K's occupation of the deserted farmhouse is a deeply symbolic gesture. As becomes clear when Visagie later dispossesses him of it and relocates him to the servants' quarters, the house signifies ownership and mastery. The farm is a *farm*: i.e. terrain that has previously been mastered and possessed by the human subject. In occupying the farmhouse, then, the suggestion is that K subsumes the land under a field of human interest. This character's first act on the farm, like Crusoe's on the island, is therefore to possess the land conceptually.

By contrast, on his second visit to the abandoned farm, K refuses to stay in the farmhouse and, instead, takes up residence in a burrow in the earth. Given the symbolism of the farmhouse, this gesture would seem to suggest a change in his relationship with the land:

> whatever I have returned for, it is not to live as the Visagies lived, sleep where they slept, sit on their stoep looking out over their land. If this house were to be abandoned as a home for all the ghosts of all the generations of the Visagies, it would not matter to me. It is not for the house that I have come. (134)

In the burrow, we now read, K "felt at home [...] as he had never felt in the house" (147). Quite clearly, his relocation from the farmhouse to the burrow, to what Coetzee, in another context, refers to as "an unsettled habitation in the earth,"[8] connotes an overcoming of the separation be-

---

[7] Kossew comments in passing on the allusions to Defoe in this novel (*Pen and Power*, 143–44). See also Patricia Merivale ("Audible Palimpsests: Coetzee's Kafka," in *Critical Perspectives on J.M. Coetzee*, ed. Huggan & Watson, 52–67). Some readers have found evidence of Coetzee's intertextual citation of Defoe in the earlier novels. See, for example, Allan Gardiner's reading of *Dusklands* as a Robinsonade ("J.M. Coetzee's *Dusklands*," 174–84). Interestingly, although Michela Canepari–Labib sees *Robinson Crusoe* as a literary analogue for both *Dusklands* and *In the Heart of the Country* (*Old Myths – Modern Empires: Power, Language and Identity in J.M. Coetzee's Work* [Oxford: Peter Lang, 2005]: 71–73, 81–86), she suggests that, in the later texts, apart from *Foe*, "the points of contact" with this novel are "more erratic" (85). From my reading of *Life & Times of Michael K*, it should be clear that I disagree with this view.

[8] Coetzee, "Reading the South African Landscape," in *White Writing*, 173.

tween human subject and natural object. Without this opposition, the impulse to possess and dominate is structurally impossible.

Significantly, in this regard, Coetzee, in his depiction of K's changed
relationship to the land, emphasizes the absence of the will to possess by
means of a number of allusions to *Robinson Crusoe*. The most notable of
these is K's reluctance to salvage the material that he has found in the
homestead:

> He scratched among the odds and ends in the shed and there was
> nothing for which he could not imagine a use. But he was wary of con-
> veying the Visagies' rubbish to his home in the earth and setting him-
> self on a trail that might lead to the re-enactment of their misfortunes.
> The worst mistake, he told himself, would be to try to found a new
> house, a rival line, on his small beginnings out at the dam. (142–43)

Michael K's attitude to the farmstead and the tools it contains stands in
direct contrast to Robinson Crusoe's fascination in Defoe's novel with the
wreck and his concerted effort to salvage from it all that is "portable and
fit to hand out."[9] It is, of course, by means of these tools that Crusoe
transforms the island into a "little England,"[10] reducing it to his rational
and technological will. Martin Green tellingly argues:

> The ship is a wreck; it is no longer any use; the island is a desert; it has
> never been of any use. But Crusoe, swimming out to the wreck, and
> paddling back with loads of planks, ropes, nails, carpenters' tools,
> sews the two together and creates something new out of the two of
> them; creates a property.[11]

In this intertextual context, then, K's avoidance of the tools and material
that he finds in the homestead connotes his recognition that the land exists
for itself rather than for him, that it is independent of human culture and
systems of interest. To possess it is to transform it; to make of it something other than what it is in itself.

K's eschewal of the will to possess is also foregrounded by the intertextual contrast between the burrow in this novel and its analogue in

---

[9] Defoe, *Robinson Crusoe* (London: Dent, 1975): 43.

[10] Pat Rogers, "Crusoe's Home," *Essays in Criticism* 24 (1974): 390.

[11] Martin Green, *Dreams of Adventure, Deeds of Empire* (London: Routledge &
Kegan Paul, 1979): 76.

Robinson Crusoe – the cave.[12] In Coetzee's novel, the burrow is depicted as being situated between "two low hills" (137), a depiction that recalls the following description of the location of the cave in *Robinson Crusoe*:

> I found a little plain on the side of a rising hill, whose front towards this little plain was steep as a house-side, so that nothing could come down upon me from the top; on the side of this rock there was a hollow place worn a little way in like the entrance or door of a cave, but there was not really any cave or way into the rock at all.[13]

The rest of this passage evinces an obsession with security which, of course, presupposes possession:

> I drew a half circle before the hollow place which took in about ten yards in its semi-diameter, from its beginning and ending.
>
> In this half circle I pitch'd two rows of strong stakes, driving them into the ground till they stood very firm like piles, the biggest end being out of the ground about five foot and a half, and sharpen'd on the top. The two rows did not stand above six inches from one another.
>
> Then I took the pieces of cable which I had cut in the ship, and I laid them in rows one upon another, within the circle, between these two rows of stakes, up to the top, placing other stakes in the in-side, leaning against them, about two foot and a half high, like a spurr to a post, and this fence was so strong that neither man or beast could get into it or over it. This cost me a great deal of time and labour, especially to cut the piles in the woods, bring them to the place, and drive them into the earth.
>
> The entrance into this place I made to be by not a door, but by a short ladder to go over the top, which ladder, when I was in, I lifted over after me, and so I was compleatly fenc'd in, and fortify'd, as I thought, from all the world and consequently slept secure in the night, which otherwise I could not have done [...].[14]

Indeed, as Green argues, Defoe's novel "gives us a very complete and all-round exploration of the emotions of possession"[15] – emotions that arise once it becomes possible for a subject to possess items in a world of ob-

---

[12] See Merivale, "Audible Palimpsests," 161.
[13] Defoe, *Robinson Crusoe*, 44–45.
[14] *Robinson Crusoe*, 45.
[15] Green, *Dreams of Adventure, Deeds of Empire*, 77.

jects. What is most conspicuous in Coetzee's repetition of this scene from *Robinson Crusoe* is the total absence of such "emotions of possession." Through his intertextual foregrounding of their absence, then, this writer makes it quite clear that K, in his relationship to the farm, has overcome the separation between subject and object.

If anything, though, the nature of the change that Michael K undergoes on his second visit to the farm is even more apparent in the depictions of his interactions with the land, which are now increasingly characterized by a state of languor and somnolence.[16] Passages such as the following are frequent in this section of the novel: "Sometimes he would emerge into wakefulness unsure whether he had slept a day or a week or a month. It occurred to him that he might not be fully in possession of himself" (163–64). An absence of self-possession, of subject-centred consciousness, the novel suggests, renders impossible cognitive control over entities. This is further evident in K's apparent inability to relate to things other than as they are in themselves:

> He could lie all afternoon with his eyes open staring at the corruga-
> tions in the roof-iron and the tracings of rust: his mind would not
> wander, he would see nothing but the iron, the lines would not trans-
> form themselves into pattern or fantasy: he was himself, lying in his
> own house, the rust was merely rust. (158–59)

What is absent from the consciousness here described is the constitutive dimension of subject-centred intentionality. What K sees is not always already intentionally assumed in consciousness. His consciousness no longer mediates things; it no longer produces objects for experience.

By extension, the above passage implies a non-intentional mode of consciousness in which the self forgoes control over the world of things. It would seem that Coetzee's depiction of K's second visit to the farm suggests a state that is akin to what Levinas refers to as the *il y a* – the experience of consciousness without a subject, a wholly impersonal, neutral situation in which Being is detached from beings that control it. Levinas describes this anonymous and impersonal state, in which the subject is no longer able cognitively to control objects and which, in fact, is the end of objectivizing consciousness and intentional assumption, as follows:

---

[16] See Michael Valdez Moses, "Solitary Walkers: Rousseau and Coetzee's *Life and Times of Michael K*," *South Atlantic Quarterly* 93.1 (1994): 131–56.

There is is an impersonal form, like in it rains, or it is warm. Its anony-
mity is essential. The mind does not find itself faced with an apprehended exterior. The exterior – if one insists on this term – remains
uncorrelated with an interior. It is no longer given. It is no longer a
world. What we call the I is itself submerged by the night, invaded,
depersonalised, stifled by it. The disappearance of all things and of the
I leaves what cannot disappear, the sheer fact of being in which *one*
participates, whether one wants to or not, without having taken the
initiative, anonymously. Being remains, like a field of forces, like a
heavy atmosphere belonging to no one, universal, returning in the
midst of the negation which put it aside, and in all the powers to which
that negation may be multiplied.[17]

Being an experience in which consciousness is divested of a controlling
subjectivity, the *il y a* is precisely a condition in which the self is not
"fully in possession of himself."

An obvious corollary of Coetzee's depiction of such a state of impersonal consciousness and indeterminate being in K's interaction with the
land would be that the land absolves itself from the appropriative relationship that K at first establishes with it. That is, the description of K's
second visit to the Karoo farm should suggest this character's respect for
the openness of the land, his refusal or inability to foreclose on and thereby control it by viewing it as property, as a 'farm'. By implication, the
description should suggest that what he experiences is not produced: it is
the land in-itself and not a negation thereof. Precisely this point is connoted in the novel by the fence-motif. Following his escape from the
Jakkalsdrif camp, K, on his way back to the farm, passes through an apparently empty landscape, which he eventually notices is traversed by
fences. In what amounts to a rejection of the desire to control and so transform the land, he reflects upon and distances himself from the business of
erecting fences and thus "dividing up the land" (133). His commerce with
the land is therefore no longer characterized by negation and transformation. In fact, the reader is told that "He thought of himself not as something heavy that left tracks behind it, but if anything as a speck upon the
surface of the earth too deeply asleep to notice the scratch of ant-feet, the
rasp of butterfly teeth, the tumbling of dust" (133).

---

[17] Emmanuel Levinas, *Existence and Existents*, tr. Alphonso Lingis (*De l'existence
à l'existant*, 1947; The Hague: Martinus Nijhoff, 1978): 58.

Cumulatively, these descriptions suggest a suspension of intentionality in K's interaction with the land. In his relationship with it, the Karoo farm loses its status as property and domesticated wilderness – both of which are implied by the appellation 'farm' – and becomes open space. Coetzee, in his depiction of K's interaction with it, thus suggests the decommodification and decolonization of the Karoo farm. He quite consciously reverses the pattern of colonization that one finds in *Robinson Crusoe* – the transformation of the island from wilderness to property to colony.

Nevertheless, there is more at stake in this section of the novel than merely a suspension of intentionality. When we read of K's "yielding up of himself" to the land (158), it becomes apparent that *he* is drawn into the environment and, in the process, becomes *like* it. This "yielding attitude to things," the tendency "to lose oneself in the environment instead of playing an active role in it," Adorno and Horkheimer, after Caillois, term mimeticism.[18] Unlike projective intentionality, which "makes the environment like itself," mimesis "imitates the environment"; in mimesis, "the outside world is a model which the inner world must try to conform to."[19] It is precisely such a mimetic move that defines K's interaction with the Karoo farm. As the following passage indicates, the change that the erstwhile gardener undergoes involves the recognition that, as Coetzee states elsewhere, "the true South African landscape is of rock, not of foliage":[20]

> When he thought of Wynberg Park he thought of an earth more vegetal than mineral, composed of last year's rotted leaves and the year before's and so on [...] an earth so soft that one could dig and never come to the end of the softness [...]. I have lost my love for that kind of earth, he thought [...]. It is no longer the green and brown that I want but the yellow and the red; not the wet but the dry; not the dark but the light; not the soft but the hard. I am becoming a different kind of man. (92–93)

In the final stages of this mimetic development, K is described as "A hard little stone, barely aware of its surroundings, enveloped in itself and its

---

[18] Theodor Adorno & Max Horkheimer, *Dialectic of Enlightenment*, tr. John Cumming (*Dialektik der Aufklärung*, 1944; London: Verso, 1997): 227.

[19] Adorno & Horkheimer, *Dialectic of Enlightenment*, 187.

[20] Coetzee, "Reading the South African Landscape," 167.

LIBRARY, UNIVERSITY OF CHESTER

interior life" (185). He has become like the landscape of the Karoo, a place-name derived from a Khoi word for 'dry'.

K's behaviour is mimetic, then, in the sense that he makes himself like the environment. Through perceiving the discrete nature of objects and thereby establishing their uniqueness, he achieves a utopian reconciliation with nature. In other words, in its relationship with him, the farm is not a 'farm'. This is why it is described as a "pocket outside time" (82), in which K is able to "escape the times" and "Cape Town and the war [...] slip[] further and further into forgetfulness" (159). What renders the farm an "autonomous place" is the way in which K relates to it. It is constituted as such by his perception of its radically discrete nature.

Importantly, what enables K's mimetic behaviour is the fact that he relates to the farm in the virtual absence of language. Coetzee's novel repeatedly stresses the tenuous nature of K's grasp of language. Apart from his speech impediment, which is mentioned in the opening sentence of the novel and emphasized thereafter (3), he describes himself as "not clever with words" (190). Moreover, his existence on the farm, following the departure of Visagie, is purely sensory and marked by the absence of language:

> He had become so much a creature of twilight and night that daylight hurt his eyes. He no longer needed to keep to paths in his movements around the dam. A sense less of sight than of touch, the pressure of presences upon his eyeballs and the skin of his face, warned him of any obstacle. His eyes remained unfocussed for hours on end like those of a blind person. He had learned to rely on smell too. He breathed into his lungs the clear sweet smell of water brought up from inside the earth. It intoxicated him, he could not have enough of it. Though he knew no names he could tell one bush from another by the smell of their leaves. He could smell rain-weather in the air. (158)

Somehow or other, Michael K has realized Magda's desire, in *In the Heart of the Country,* to "burst through the screen of names into the goatseye view of [...] the stone desert" (18). From predating on goats, he has become like a goat. Whereas Magda knows of "no act" that will "liberate" her "into the world," or "bring the world into" her (10), he, in overcoming his linguistic separation from the world, becomes like the world, part of it. He hosts it unconditionally by becoming part of it.

This depiction of K's ability to relate to the sensuous particularity of things accords not only with Adorno's understanding of mimesis as a form of preverbal cognition[21] but also with Blanchot's postulation that it is the absence of language that distinguishes the *il y a*, or what he refers to as the "*other* dark." The "*other* dark" is "things" and existents "prior to the day" – prior to their negation by language and human systems of order.[22] In arguing that the subject negates the being or presence of things through language, Blanchot cites Hegel's observation that "Adam's first act, which made him master of the animals, was to give them names, that is, he annihilated them in their existence."[23] Unlike Hegel's Adam, Coetzee's K does not name entities: he relates to them sensuously and immediately through "the pressure of presences."

ᛏ ᕼ

Coetzee's focus on K's mimetic practice on the Karoo farm, rather than simply on the social world it transcends, would seem to gesture toward the possibility of a better world. That is, it appears to hold out the possibility of a utopian reconciliation with nature which would render structurally impossible the conflictual relations that have shaped human history, the "times" that Michael K escapes on the farm. In depicting K's forfeiture of projective intentionality on the farm, this writer therefore ostensibly refuses to "supplement" the contestatory relations out of which history "erects itself" and, in the process, contrives a degree of autonomy in and for his writing. Such a conclusion, though, would be both premature and naive. After all, K's autonomous mode of existence on the farm is not just a model of nothing that is, but also of nothing that can be in the irrevocably linguistic realm of history. Accordingly, Coetzee's portrayal of

---

[21] Theodor Adorno, *Aesthetic Theory*, tr. C. Lenhardt, ed. Gretel Adorno & Rolf Tiedemann (*Ästhetische Theorie*, 1970; London: Routledge & Kegan Paul, 1984): 80, 263; see also Miriam Hansen, "Mass Culture as Hieroglyphic Writing: Adorno, Derrida, Kracauer," *New German Critique* 56.Spring–Summer (1992): 53.

[22] Maurice Blanchot, "Orpheus' Gaze" (1955), in *The Siren's Song: Selected Essays by Maurice Blanchot*, ed. & intro. Gabriel Josipovici, tr. Sacha Rabinovitch (Brighton: Harvester, 1982): 177.

[23] Blanchot, "Literature and the Right to Death," in *The Work of Fire*, tr. Charlotte Mandell (*La Part du feu*, 1949; Stanford CA: Stanford UP, 1995): 323.

this existential mode seems to do little more than to exclude the utopian from the social domain.

I would suggest, however, that this is precisely what Coetzee seeks to achieve. Like Adorno, he is quite aware that the artwork's implication in its cultural episteme, the fact that it must use the significatory forms of the nature-dominating rational world, precludes it from representing the mimetic mode of subjective experience. Any attempt to imitate the mimetic, and thereby overcome the separation between subject and object, necessarily reproduces it. In other words, Coetzee is mindful that his representation of K's relationship with the environment inevitably replicates the distance between subject and object that it ostensibly seeks to overcome.

This writer's awareness of these problems is apparent in *Life & Times of Michael K*'s acknowledgement of its linguistic evocation of the alinguistic immediacy of K's interaction with natural objects through its juxtaposition of these descriptions with the self-reflexively textual diary section which, in laying bare its linguistic status, exposes that of the novel as a whole. Indeed, by drawing a contrast between the medical officer's entrapment in language and K's proximate mode of being beyond language, the novel must draw attention to its linguistic medium and thus to the fact that it creates the impression that K's life on the farm is free of language in language.[24]

The intentional nature of this self-subversive strategy is apparent from Coetzee's use of the metaphor of the castaway which, in this novel, as in *In the Heart of the Country*, signifies the subject's linguistic and discursive separation from the world. For the most part, this metaphor is generated through allusions to *Robinson Crusoe*. For instance, Michael K's eschewal of language and time is emphasized by his decision not to "keep a record of the passage of the days" or a journal (93). Similarly, the medical officer's location in language is signified by his diary, which announces his status as a castaway. This character, by his own admission, is a "castaway marooned in a pocket of time" (216): unlike K, who we are pointedly told is "not a prisoner or a castaway" (158) but "at home" in his burrow (147), he is sundered from the world of things by language and

---

[24] See Head's discussion of the "self-cancelling aspect of K's story" (*J.M. Coetzee*, 106).

time. In Coetzee's novel, history and language separate the human subject, cast it adrift, from the sensory world of things.

The irony, of course, is that the metaphor of the castaway reflects on its
own tropological status in a linguistic text, thereby signalling the fact that
the novel itself is a sign of a marooned condition. Its linguistic ontology
signals the literary text's distance from the mimetic relationship that it depicts in its evocation of K's life on the farm. By extension, through their
relationship with it, the novel defines the writer and reader as themselves
castaways. On the one hand, the writer, in writing about K's existence on
the farm, writes about that about which he cannot write. On the other,
when s/he reads about K's mimetic behaviour, the reader reads about that
of which s/he cannot read and from which the very activity of reading
excludes him or her.

In their relationship to the novel, then, writer and reader enact their
castaway condition. The implication here seems to be that the text cannot
occupy an "autonomous place," that it inevitably "supplements" the relational modes of the historical domain in which it is ineluctably situated. If
anything, though, this conclusion is as premature and reductive as that
which would claim that Coetzee, through his depiction of K's life on the
farm, renders his writing autonomous. In order better to understand Coetzee's meditation on supplementation and autonomy in *Life & Times of
Michael K*, one has to consider language's failure not only to instantiate
but also to *eliminate* the ineffable: i.e. one must consider that the text, in
describing itself as the loss of the mimetic state it purports to imitate,
nevertheless gestures toward it. In describing itself as the loss of this state,
it inscribes its desire for it.

The argument of *Life & Times of Michael K*, in this regard, emerges in
its implicit inclusion of its writer and reader in its iterative sequence of
birth-scenes, which, cumulatively, stage the failure to account for K's
alterity, the impossibility of controlling it by making it part of a conceptual economy. The sequence is initiated unobtrusively enough by the
opening passage of the novel, in which Anna K gives birth to her son with
the assistance of a midwife (3). A version of the opening scene recurs
when, shortly before being taken to the Jakkalsdrif camp, K is supervised
by a nurse and a state official in the hospital in Prince Albert (97, 99). In
Part II, this iterative pattern again manifests itself in the scene at the
Kenilworth infirmary where K is watched over by the medical officer and
the camp commander, Major Noël van Rensburg (188–92). Further paral-

lels exist between the latter two scenes. In the preamble to each, K is renamed: as "Michael Visagie" in the former (96), and as "Michaels" in the latter (170). The suggestion in both cases, then, is that the state, in creating a new identity for Michael K, attempts to 'give birth' to him.

In Part III of the novel, the sexual encounter of the triad of K, the pimp, and the prostitute enters this sequence of birth-scenes. Moreover, the pimp's name, December, relates him to Major van Rensburg, whose first name, Noël, and red and white tracksuit, connotes Christ's nativity. The prostitute, on the other hand, is affiliated with the medical officer by the white dress she wears (235) – an allusion to the standard uniform of the nursing profession. In addition, she is simply, but pointedly, referred to as "the sister" (236, 238, 239, 242). The scene itself depicts birth more than coitus, as is testified to by the pun on the word "laboured" in the following sentence: "Against his [namely, Michael K's] will the memory returned of [...] the grunting girl as she laboured on him" (246). Finally, in its preamble, the pimp – as part of his attempt "to make a new man" of him (239) – renames Michael K "Mister Treefeller" (237), a name signifying the human subject's separation from the natural world.

The most obviously self-reflexive of these scenes is the one in which the medical officer and camp commander interrogate K. In it, K is referred to as an "unborn creature" (185), and Noël van Rensburg, through his name's etymological link to birth, occupies a maternal position. In the course of the interrogation, the commander and officer attempt to establish the accuracy of the official report, which describes K as an "arsonist" and as an "escapee from a labour camp" who "was running a flourishing garden on an abandoned farm and feeding the local guerilla population when he was captured" (179–80). Being aware of the ironic disjunction between the facts of K's presence on the farm and the state's interpretation of his sojourn there, the reader is able to discern the transformative, indeed creative, nature of identifying thought, the routine manner in which it attempts to subsume the particularity of the object of thought under a universal concept within an already formed system of conceptuality. At the same time, though, the reader's awareness of K's estrangement from the thinking subjects in this scene is also an awareness of their ultimate *failure*, in terms of Coetzee's use of the child-image in this scene and the sequence of which it forms part, to 'give birth' to K, to invest his alterity with form and substance in language.

It is the overtly hermeneutic dimension of the interrogation scene that draws the acts of writing and reading into the novel's iterative sequence of failed birth-scenes. In this passage, both interrogators refer to the account of K's activities as a "story" (177, 180), a metaphor that indicates the tenuous nature of the distinction between creation and interpretation in identifying thought. Indeed, the mix of metaphors in the passage portrays the camp commander and medical officer as writer and reader surrogates "labouring" over K and attempting to "give birth" to his "story." And, in reading of the commander, together with the medical officer as midwife, "labouring at his desk to balance the bodies out against the bodies in" (214), the reader enacts what the scene describes: i.e. s/he unites with Coetzee in an attempt to incorporate into the economy of *Life & Times of Michael K* the ineffable alterity that is figured by Michael K. In other words, the reader's engagement with this novel inevitably becomes part of its sequence of failed birth-scenes.

The hermeneutic dimension of the interrogation scene is, however, most apparent in the reader's awareness of the ironic dissonance between the interrogators' interpretation of K's life on the farm and Coetzee's depiction of this life. Through his use of irony, Coetzee ostensibly places the reader in a position of knowledge from which s/he is able to discern the inaccuracy of the state interrogators' interpretation. This, at least, is what initially appears to be the case. In truth, though, it is precisely such a position of knowledge, one that would serve to establish a contract between reader and author which would distance them from the commander and officer, that is precluded by the novel's admission that it cannot represent K's mimetic behaviour on the farm, that the writer has failed in his attempt to do so. By extension, this admission renders ironic the position of knowledge that writer and reader initially seem to share and, in the process, aligns them with the interrogators in this scene.[25] Like the latter's

---

[25] Attridge's insightful comments on the way in which Coetzee's stylistic choice of point of view distances the narrative voice from K are pertinent here. Even though we learn of K's "though-processes and emotions," our sense of this distance means that we can "never feel that we have assimilated them to our own" (*J.M. Coetzee and the Ethics of Reading*, 50; see also Willem Anker, "Bewaarder van die Stilte: Gedagtes oor J.M. Coetzee se Etiek van Skryf," *Journal of Literary Studies* 22.1–2 [2006]: 130; and Gallagher, *A Story of South Africa*, 161). According to Dick Penner, Coetzee, in response to a question at a writers' workshop in Lexington, commented as follows on his strategic use of point of view in this novel: "there is someone who is telling the story

account, Coetzee's account of K's enigmatic presence on the farm, in the construction of which I as reader collaborate, is a "story," an interpretative construct. It is part of the novel's iterative sequence of failed birth-scenes. Eventually, then, the irony in the interrogation scene doubles back on itself and renders its very premise ironic.

Johan Geertsema's thesis on the ironic relation between representation and otherness is endorsed by the interrogation scene in this novel:[26] what is finally ironic here is not *one* interpretation of K's alterity rather than another, but *all* such interpretations. The infinite distance between his alterity and its interpretations ironizes the latter, thereby signalling the interpreters' loss of control over this otherness. Indeed, Coetzee under-scores this point by indicating that K's *own* account of his otherness, his interpretative construct or "story," is itself inadequate:

> Always when he tried to explain himself to himself, there remained a gap, a hole, a darkness before which his understanding baulked, into which it was useless to pour words. The words were eaten up, the gap remained. (150–51)

Even K is unable to define, possess and so control his alterity. His "story" is incomplete and therefore yet to be told.[27] He is still to be born.

This novel thus develops the prosopopeial image of the child in impor-tant ways. In my reading of *Waiting for the Barbarians*, I made the point that the child-image signifies what has been reduced by the forms of his-tory. History is the loss of the child. I also suggested that the Magistrate attempts to see the barbarian girl in the absence of Empire, its structures of knowledge, its history. Clearly, in *Life & Times of Michael K*, the medical officer, following the interrogation scene, attempts something similar in his relationship with K. Crucially, though, as I have shown, the child-image, in this novel, has a strongly defined metafictional dimension. Indeed, the significance of this work's recursive birth-scenes lies in their self-reflexive articulation of the literary text's relation to an alterity that

---

about Michael K, who looks like an omniscient narrator, but he doesn't actually tell you much." He then went on to add "there's no guarantee that he knows very much." Penner, *Countries of the Mind: The Fiction of J.M. Coetzee* (Westport CT: Green-wood, 1989): 94.

[26] Geertsema, "Irony and Otherness."

[27] See Attwell, *J.M. Coetzee*, 98–99.

ironizes the efforts of both writer and reader to interpret and so construct
it. What is here at stake is a question that I raised in the conclusion to my
previous chapter: how does literary writing respond responsibly to what is
other than history without reducing it, and thereby supplementing history?
I must emphasize that *Life & Times of Michael K*, in posing and responding to this question, is not content simply to stage the other's rendering
ironic of the constitutive enterprises of writing and reading. In signalling a
loss of writerly and readerly control, this irony reveals a failure not only to
instantiate K's alterity but also to eliminate it. What the iterative dimension of the birth-scenes indicates is that, in rendering incomplete the
attempt to explain it, this otherness requires, even demands and so engenders, further explanation and thus *refuses* to be excluded from the
interpretative economy. It *waits* to be included, and waiting is, in this context, quite clearly an ateleological activity.

Owing to its irreducibility, then, K's otherness inspires what it interrupts. By extension, this alterity, of course, ironizes *my* explanation of its
irreducible and therefore inelim	inable nature, a reading which has been
partly prompted, and therefore ironically qualified, by the officer's final,
despairing reading of K as an "an allegory [...] of how scandalously, how
outrageously a meaning can take up residence in a system without becoming a term in it" (228). By further extension, as its erosion of the
difference between reading and writing implies, this novel cannot *not*
ironize its very own staging of its relation to alterity. *Life & Times of
Michael K* is acutely aware that Michael K is a figure for what cannot be
figured. As is suggested by Coetzee's use of the child-image in his portrayal of this character, K is a prosopopeia: a figure, it will be recalled,
that "always buries what it invokes";[28] a "trope of mourning"[29] that signals "a failure of presence."[30]

Ultimately, then, my argument is that this novel's iterative sequence of
failed birth-scenes self-reflexively depicts literature as a space in which
writer and reader encounter an irreducible alterity over which they can
exert no control and which, in fact, acts upon, even masters, them. However, this thesis requires further elaboration and additional support. In the

---

[28] Miller, "Topography and Tropography in Thomas Hardy's *In Front of the Landscape*," 210.

[29] Miller, *Versions of Pygmalion* (Cambridge MA: Harvard UP, 1990): 4.

[30] Simon Critchley, *Very Little ... Almost Nothing: Death, Philosophy, Literature*
(London: Routledge, 1997): 73.

remainder of this chapter, I therefore trace Coetzee's self-reflexive adumbration of these issues in the scene describing the medical officer's final encounter with K on the Cape Flats. My thesis is that the loss of control here dramatized raises the possibility of a tenuous, compromised form of aesthetic autonomy. From its self-conscious argument for such autonomy, it becomes clear that *Life & Times of Michael K* subverts its depiction of K's utopian existence on the farm not simply to exclude the utopian from the social domain but to relocate it to the aesthetic domain. For Coetzee, as for Adorno, the aesthetic's potential for autonomy invests it with a utopian capability.

✍ ༪

One of the consequences of Coetzee's treatment of writing and reading as interrelated activities is a blurring of the distinction between writer-figure and reader-figure in the birth-scenes. The medical officer, who is at first cast as a reader-figure in the interrogation scene, takes over the role of author from the camp commander later in the scene. In the context of the novel's analogy between authorship and maternity, it is also significant that the medical officer is depicted both as a midwife and as a mother. For instance, he notes that K is as "weak as a baby," and feeds him "glucose and milk" with a "feed bottle" (198). Owing to the ambivalence of his depiction, the officer's final encounter with K, which is imaginary and occurs in writing, may be read as a dramatization of the author's loss of control over the other in writing.

Importantly, Coetzee's description of the officer's failed attempt to approach K in this scene evokes Orpheus's loss of Eurydice and thus represents writing as a katabatic descent into the underworld. Indeed, the many allusions to K's ghostly quality and lack of substance place him in the role of Eurydice. After K escapes from the concentration camp, the officer describes him as a "wraith," who is able "to slip through anything" (211). Earlier, he tells K to give himself "some substance" (192), and admonishes him as follows: "And do not think you are simply going to waste away, grow more and more insubstantial till you are all soul and can fly away into the aether" (207). K's lack of substance is explicitly linked to language. When he tells K to give himself substance, the officer is interrogating him, adjuring him to talk. However, as the novel proceeds, it becomes clear that words divest K of substance. Thus, in the imaginary encounter, K finally disappears, rendered insubstantial by the officer's "big, passionate words" (227). Words, it would seem, fail to present K; they fail to do what they are supposed to do. What they in fact signify is the writing subject's complete loss of control over what it seeks to represent: as indicated earlier, while the medical officer cannot instantiate K, nor can he eliminate him. K is a wraith, a ghost, and therefore neither present nor absent. It is for this reason that the officer's diary evinces an indescribable sense of loss. The diary is the loss of K. Just as importantly, though, it is also evidence of the officer's desire for what has been lost. Coetzee is quite aware that desire inscribes a relationship to what the subject does not know. The officer's diary is an effect of a cause that is neither present nor absent; evidence of having been acted upon by something that is yet unknown. Even though K is not, and cannot ever be, present in the diary, neither is he entirely absent from it.

Coetzee's use of the Orpheus myth in this scene bears comparison with Blanchot's description of writing in "The Gaze of Orpheus." In Blanchot's reconstruction of this myth as an analogue of writing, Orpheus, an artist-figure, desires Eurydice, who is the "darkest point" of the "*other* dark."[31] Incidentally, Eurydice is, in this regard, similar to K who, when gazed upon by the medical officer, is described as "a gathering, a thickening of darkness" (227). The "work" of Blanchot's Orpheus is not only to encounter Eurydice in the "*other* dark," but also to possess this exteriority by bringing it, in its nocturnal aspect, to the light of day. Like Coetzee's medical officer, Orpheus must render substantial what is insubstantial, bring it "to the light and, in the light, [give] it form and reality" (177). When Eurydice stands revealed in the daylight, Orpheus's work will have been accomplished.

Through averting his gaze, Orpheus is able to approach the "heart of darkness" and to complete his task (177). In Blanchot's reading, this concession by the gods of the underworld stands for the "law" of the artwork and the necessity of obedience and fidelity to its logic of manifestation (177, 180). In order to satisfy his desire for the "*other* dark," the *il y a*, the presence of things before consciousness, the subject, and the act of writing exist, Orpheus must place himself under the jurisdiction of the "law" of the artwork. That is, the writer must make use of the conventional forms

---

[31] Blanchot, "The Gaze of Orpheus," 177. Unless otherwise indicated, further page references are in the main text.

of writing, must remain faithful to what Blanchot terms their "norms of clarity, for the sake of what is without form and without law."[32] Through these forms, the writer must attempt to reveal what precedes revelation and what revelation destroys.

The impasse of writing that Blanchot here adumbrates is precisely the impasse that the medical officer encounters in his relationship with K: as I have indicated, the officer's attempt to invest him with substance through language robs K of substance. The protocols of writing are unable to perform the task they have been set. It is for this reason that the dominant mood of this section of the novel fluctuates between loss and desire. The medical officer's diary is about its inability to be about what it desires to be about.

In Blanchot's reworking of the myth, Orpheus disregards the gods' prohibition against looking Eurydice in the face, because he desires her "beyond the limits prescribed by the song" (178). By implication, his actual desire is not to render the invisible visible, since the labour here involved would serve merely to betray Eurydice and his desire for her. Instead, it is, impossibly, to see and possess the invisible as invisible in the "heart of darkness." Crucially, his gaze thus signifies the inability of the work to satisfy his desire for Eurydice. It signifies a loss and a desire that exceed the text and, indeed, signal its incompletion. Orpheus is destined to sing not of Eurydice but of her loss, his unsatisfied desire for her. If this is what the song, the literary work, describes, it must always inscribe the trace of its involvement with an unpresentable excess that renders it incomplete.

How does one sing of the loss of what one has never possessed? When placed in the context of Blanchot's account of Orpheus's mournful descent into the underworld, it becomes clear that this is the question scripted by the medical officer's diary in *Life & Times of Michael K*. The diary is not simply the loss of K. It – and this is particularly evident in the officer's imaginary encounter with him – *apostrophizes* K: i.e. it addresses an absent entity; an entity without an address. Although it cannot render K present, the diary is *at the same time* unable to accept his absence. To be sure, the officer's diary is a lament for the loss of what was never present; an attempt to remember what has not been present and

---

[32] Quoted in Critchley, *Very Little … Almost Nothing*, 39.

56   SECRETARY OF THE INVISIBLE ৯

which therefore cannot be recalled, remembered. That is, the diary is evidence that K cannot be forgotten.

It follows that the medical officer's diary is presented as a work of infinite mourning. In establishing the relevance of Derrida's analysis of the work of mourning to Coetzee's writing, Durrant notes that this philosopher distinguishes between healthy mourning – "the assimilation or integration of loss into consciousness" – and unhealthy, inconsolable or infinite mourning, which "is marked by the failure to integrate loss into consciousness."[33] Such a failure of integration goes together with an "encryptment" of the dead within the living: "the dead remain secretly entombed within – internal to but sealed off from – the consciousness of the living, and they also remain enigmatic, coded, untranslated" (31). In Coetzee's novel, the diary evinces precisely K's encryptment in the medical officer's consciousness owing to the latter's inability to comprehend and thus to integrate him into the order of the same. (Tellingly, such encryptment is even more explicit in *The Master of Petersburg*, where Dostoevsky reflects that Pavel, the dead child, is "inside him, a dead baby in an iron box in the frozen earth."[34])

In this argument, the self's inability to name and place the dead means that s/he becomes the host of the dead – indeed, the place or grave of the dead. Unconditional hospitality is infinite mourning. As the following comment by Derrida indicates, it is precisely the failure to name, identify, and so locate and circumscribe the dead that leads to the kind of encryptment that renders mourning infinite:

> Without a fixed place, without a determinable topos, mourning is not allowed. Or, what comes down to the same thing, it is promised without taking place, a determinable place, so thenceforth promised as an interminable mourning, an infinite mourning defying all work, beyond any possible work of mourning.[35]

---

[33] Sam Durrant, *Postcolonial Narrative and the Work of Mourning*, 30.

[34] Coetzee, *The Master of Petersburg*, 52.

[35] Derrida, *Of Hospitality*, 111. Elsewhere in this text, Derrida refers to "The invisibility, the placelessness, the illocality of an 'of no fixed address' for death" (115–17). And he comments elsewhere that "Nothing could be worse, for the work of mourning, than confusion or doubt: one *has to know* who is buried where – and it is *necessary* (to know – to make certain) that, in what remains of him, *he remains there*"; Derrida, *Specters of Marx: The State of the Debt, the Work of Mourning and the New International*, tr. Peggy Kamuf, intro. Bernd Magnus & Stephen Cullenberg (*Spectres de*

The medical officer cannot forget K, because he cannot 'bear' him. In terms of this conjunction of the child motif and the trope of death, the officer must mourn K, the child, because he cannot bear him. Since he cannot name, identify, know K, he cannot recall him in his absence.[36] Nonetheless, his failure to remember K makes it impossible for the officer to forget him. After all, to forget something one must first have remembered it. The failure to name, and so to place, localize, and circumscribe, renders both remembering and forgetting impossible. Given that K must remain unremembered and unforgotten, the medical officer's grief is without term.

Ultimately, K cannot be forgotten because the medical officer can exercise no control over him. Infinite mourning is *not* a work, an action over which a subject can exercise control, a task that a subject can accomplish and complete. If the officer's diary is presented as a work of mourning, it follows that it is presented as a record of his loss of control over K, his inability cognitively to control what he must nonetheless write about. That is, the diary is evidence of the medical officer's failure to maintain himself as a subject in writing. The writer, in writing, loses the ability to say I.[37] In experiencing the "*other* dark," by implication, the officer experiences a condition akin to the *il y a*, the state of passivity concomitant with the divestiture of subjectivity that characterizes K's life on the farm. The difference, though, is that K's passive state on the farm is an effect of the absence of language. Conversely, the medical officer is a castaway: his encounter with the "*other* dark" occurs through language, through an experience of the limits of linguistic conceptuality, of language's inability to signify adequately.

In summary, then, the imaginary encounter between the officer and K presents us with an image of writing in which the subject that writes, in attempting to understand a thing by subsuming its particularity under a universal concept, by relating it to a definite conceptual end, confronts the concept's inadequacy, the fact that, in Adorno's words, it "does not exhaust the thing conceived" but leaves a remainder and, consequently, that

---

Marx: L'État de la dette, le travail du deuil et la nouvelle Internationale, 1993; New York: Routledge, 1994): 9.

[36] See Durrant, *Postcolonial Narrative,* 32.

[37] Maurice Blanchot, "Where Now? Who Now?" in *The Siren's Song,* 194.

"all concepts refer to nonconceptualities."[38] It follows that *Life & Times of Michael K* raises an argument for aesthetic autonomy. Literary writing, by establishing a relation to the remainder or excess of conceptuality, a relation that is not grounded in correlation, straddles the limits of language and history, and constantly gestures towards the limitlessness which they inevitably demarcate. Since it places the writer in relation to what remains unsaid even as s/he attempts to say it, writing may appositely be figured as an Orphic descent into the underworld, into a realm beyond the influence of subjective action and possibility, hence outside history, the cultural episteme and language. To the extent that it is akin to the realm of death, the space of writing is an "autonomous place," something like the Karoo farm which attains a degree of autonomy through K's mimetic relationship to it.

ᘐ ᘐ

It will be remembered that, in the course of the interrogation scene, the camp commander, after failing to make K speak, passes on the "burden" of doing so to the medical officer, who accordingly assumes the role of author (189). Given that this scene serves as a *mise en abyme* of writing *and* reading, the implication is that the reader must author what the writer has failed to say and what therefore still remains to be said. In terms of the analogy between writing and childbirth, s/he must bear what the writer is unable to bear, what is yet to be born. It is precisely in attempting to accomplish this that the reader encounters the literary work's ability to distance itself from itself by pointing to the absence of correspondence between thing and concept, and therefore the remainder which the concept necessarily leaves but seeks to conceal. For Coetzee, as for Adorno,[39] the work is able to evoke what *its* own implication in language, discourse, and thought denies. While it is in the world, its relationship to the non-conceptual divorces it from the world, the language of subsumption, identifying thought and, very importantly, itself. The artwork, as Adorno puts it,

---

[38] Theodor Adorno, *Negative Dialectics*, tr. E.B. Ashton (*Negative Dialektik*, 1966; London: Routledge & Kegan Paul, 1973): 5, 11.
[39] Adorno, *Negative Dialectics*, 5.

has a "twofold essence": it is "an autonomous entity and a social fact,"[40] estranged from history yet unable to take up a position outside it.

For Adorno, it is what Walter Benjamin refers to as the artwork's "aura" that enables the work to point beyond its "givenness" and, in so doing, to inscribe its difference and distance from itself.[41] The reader encounters the auratic capacity of *Life & Times of Michael K* not only in the sense of loss and desire evinced by the medical officer's diary, which gestures toward what the text has failed to name, but also, and far more obviously, in this novel's reflection on its inability to present what it ostensibly presents in its description of K's intercourse with the environment. Here the text points beyond its "givenness" by making its reader aware that when s/he reads of K's intercourse with the environment, s/he is, in fact, reading of the unreadable, that s/he has, in effect, been placed in relation to that of which s/he cannot read.

Through its auratic capacity, then, *Life & Times of Michael K* acts on the reader rather than being acted on by him or her. That is, the reading subject loses control over the literary object. In precluding a determinate reading, the work renders the reader passive and draws him or her into its distance. Indeed, Adorno and Benjamin speak of the work's ability to absorb the viewer or reader into itself.[42] And, when referring to mimetic behaviour as "the trend to lose oneself in the environment instead of playing an active role in it; the tendency to let oneself go and sink back into nature," Adorno and Horkheimer go on to say not only that this "urge," this "yielding attitude to things," underlies "the sublime work of art" but also that, without it, "art cannot exist."[43] If the work succeeds in preventing the reader from identifying it with him-/herself, s/he is identified with it. In a sense, s/he, in the process, becomes *like* the work. Should this happen, it is not the farm of which one reads but *Life & Times of Michael K* that is an "autonomous place," a "pocket outside time." More accurately, this novel becomes an "autonomous place" because it is

[40] *Aesthetic Theory*, 8.

[41] *Aesthetic Theory*, 67. See Walter Benjamin, "The Work of Art in the Age of Mechanical Reproduction" (1936), in *Illuminations*, tr. Harry Zohn, ed. & intro. Hannah Arendt (*Schriften*, 1955; London: Fontana, 1973): 211–44, and "On Some Motifs in Baudelaire" (1939), in *Illuminations*, 152–96.

[42] Adorno, *Aesthetic Theory*, 182; Benjamin, "The Work of Art in the Age of Mechanical Reproduction," 232, and "On Some Motifs in Baudelaire," 196n.17.

[43] Adorno & Horkheimer, *Dialectic of Enlightenment*, 227.

constituted as such in the mimetic moment of reading. What makes the work autonomous is precisely the way in which the reader relates to it.

By implication, aesthetic autonomy is not simply a given. The kind of reading that I have just outlined is only ever a possibility; it may or may not happen in the individual reader's encounter with the novel. Coetzee conceives of the mimetic mode of subjective experience as an *aesthetic* possibility. The important implication here is that aesthetic autonomy is relationally constituted and thus not simply an innate feature of the art-work. While the artwork's capacity to gesture beyond its "givenness" has the potential to induce a mimetic relationship, this potential is always yet to be realized in the reader's reception of the text. Autonomy, that is to say, is a possibility which may or may not be performed in the individual reader's encounter with the individual work.

When it is, though, it will lead to a mimetic relationship in which the subject loses itself in the work. The ethical corollary of this aesthetic is, of course, that the reader, in his or her relationship to it, enacts a respect for the particularity of the work rather than relating it to some or other conceptual end. However, Coetzee, in *Life & Times of Michael K*, takes this ethic a step further in his portrayal of the effect on the medical officer of his failure to comprehend K's otherness – a failure which, it should by now be clear, mirrors that not only of the writer but also of the reader, who must do what the writer has failed to do. As in the case of the Magistrate's relationship to the barbarian girl in *Waiting for the Barbarians*, the medical officer's inability to make sense of K's alterity *concerns* him. This is apparent in K's irritated questions to him, "Why fuss over me, why am I so important?" and "What am I to this man? I ask myself, What is it to this man if I live or die?" (186, 203), which in various permutations recur as a refrain of responsibility throughout the second section of the novel. It is taken up, for instance, by the duty officer, who, nonplussed by the medical officer's anxiety over K's health, his lack of indifference, inquires as follows: "Why are you so interested anyway?" (197). Later, the camp commander, puzzled by the care shown by the medical officer's intercession on K's behalf during the interrogation scene, asks the following question: "Why are you so keen to protect Michaels?" (194). Finally, the aforementioned description of him feeding K with a feed bottle likens the medical officer's overwhelming sense of responsibility for K to that of a mother for her child. The diary section of the novel, it would seem, is a sustained expression of the officer's responsibility for Michael K.

What Coetzee seems to be suggesting here is that the outcome of an encounter with what cannot be identified may entail not only a "yielding attitude to things," a respect for the specificity of what one fails to comprehend, but *responsibility* for it. Although such responsibility is thematized in *Waiting for the Barbarians*, Coetzee, in *Life & Times of Michael K*, intimates that this ethical attitude is a necessary corollary of the excessive nature of the desire that informs the relationship to alterity. The kind of desire for the "*other* dark" of which Blanchot writes not only inspires the subject to invest this alterity with form and substance but also instils a restless dissatisfaction with the insufficiency of form, its inevitable betrayal of the "*other* dark." This is apparent in Blanchot's reading of the Orpheus myth, in which, as I have noted, Orpheus's gaze signifies the failure of the work to satisfy his desire for Eurydice. His gaze, which destroys, indeed betrays, the work is an act of responsibility for Eurydice. So, while the work is a betrayal of Eurydice, the betrayal of the work reduces this original betrayal and therefore constitutes an act of responsibility.[44] In betraying the work, Orpheus's gaze seeks to protect what the work (and therefore he the artist) has betrayed. The desiring subject, in its interminable dissatisfaction with the forms that seek to instantiate the other, its impatient sense of their incompletion, and its resultant betrayal of them, assumes responsibility for the ineliminable other.

Responsibility and desire are therefore inextricably related: the former is an effect of the latter's excessive, transgressive nature, of the dissatisfaction that it engenders with the inadequacy of form – a fretful dissatisfaction that results in new forms which, in their turn, prove to be inadequate and are betrayed. If the medical officer's diary is a lament for the loss of K, it is also a record of his care, of his sense of responsibility

---

[44] See Geertsema, "Irony and Otherness," 72–86. After commenting on Levinas' argument about the other's ability to interrupt the same, and the fact that such interruption becomes part of what it interrupts, Geertsema considers the necessity of reducing "the degree of betrayal of the other" by incessantly interrupting interruption. He maintains that such an "interruption of the interruption of the conceptualization of the other" may be explained in terms of irony.

for him. To care, as the root of the word 'care', *kaera*, signifies, is precisely to lament.[45]

Coetzee's portrayal of the medical officer's obsessive concern for K thus indicates that responsibility is not just a "letting go," a passive dissolution into the otherness of what one has failed to identify, but a substitution of oneself for that otherness. Differently put, the kind of "yielding" involved in responsibility exacts a restructuring of subjectivity: structured as responsibility rather than autonomous freedom, the self becomes an ethical subject. While the ethical subject acts, it acts not out of concern for itself but for the other.

My contention is that Coetzee's account of the medical officer's inability to make sense of K's alterity, followed by the description of the effect of this failure as an inducement to responsibility, is very close to the Levinasian understanding of an ethic rooted in responsibility. The difference, though, is that where Levinas focuses solely on the human subject's encounter with the alterity of the human other in his philosophical ethic, and, indeed, eschews aesthetics,[46] Coetzee emphasizes the ethical potential of the relation to alterity that is established in the writing and reading of literature. This, though, is an argument I develop incrementally in the remaining chapters of this study by tracing the later novels' self-reflexive adumbration of their ability to affect the reader.

For the time being, it is enough to note that Coetzee, in *Life & Times of Michael K*, develops the understanding of ethics implicit in *Waiting for the Barbarians* by suggesting that responsibility derives from the literary work's "twofold essence," its location "both within things and outside them," its essence as a social fact *and* an autonomous artefact. Indeed, the very condition of possibility for such an affective form of responsibility is precisely the aesthetic autonomy that enables the text to place its reader in relation to what is external to history. It is for this reason, then, that Coetzee must subvert his depiction of K's mimetic relationship to the land and thereby locate the utopian in the aesthetic domain. The utopian is not a state that can be projected through Platonic mimesis: its only hope is the aesthetic, the artwork's separation of itself from the cultural episteme and

---

[45] Unless otherwise indicated, all dictionary references in this study are to the *Oxford English Dictionary Online* (http://dictionary.oed.com/).

[46] Emmanuel Levinas, "Reality and its Shadow" (1948), in *Collected Philosophical Papers*, tr. Alphonso Lingis (1948; Dordrecht: Martinus Nijhoff, 1987): 1–13.

therefore from itself. It is the artwork's potential for autonomy that gives it the necessary distance from which to affect the reader by exposing him or her to an otherness beyond history for which s/he cannot but assume responsibility. This is to say that the literary work's potential for autonomy moots the possibility of an affective engagement with history.

Finally, I must emphasize that the kind of autonomy that is self-reflexively outlined in *Life & Times of Michael K* is a function of implication. Far from purporting to be a pure state, it assumes and relies upon implication. When he distinguishes between writing that supplements history and writing that rivals history through its autonomy, Coetzee, in his fiction writing, implies that there is no autonomy without there being something to be autonomous from. The relationship between supplementarity and autonomy is self-evidently dialectical. To be sure, it is precisely the dialectical nature of its autonomy, the fact that the artwork is "both within things and outside them," that invests it with the auratic capacity to inscribe its difference from itself and, in the process, to engage with the social, with history. If *Life & Times of Michael K* affects the reader in the way in which I have described, the very reading of the novel will *determinately* negate society and its identificatory relations.

℗ ঽ

3   A Child Waiting to Be Born
∝   *Foe*

H AD THE MEDICAL OFFICER arrived on the Karoo farm and
thereafter written an account of his sojourn there, together with
K and, perhaps, the old man to whom K refers on the last page
of the novel, the Karoo farm sections of *Life & Times of Michael K* would
have been almost interchangeable with the island section of *Foe*. The
principal difference between these two texts is that, while the farm episode in the earlier novel is presented directly in a way that, initially at
least, suggests an absence of mediation, the island episode in *Foe* is presented from the perspective of Susan Barton in a form that foregrounds
the presence of an active, intending consciousness. In the later novel, the
representational strategy, rather than providing the reader with the illusion
of a direct encounter between observer and observed, is therefore calculated to constantly intimate a mode of being that has been mediated and
transformed by the attempt to know it in and through language.

In terms of representational strategy, then, the island episode in *Foe* is
reminiscent of *Dusklands*, in which Coetzee lays bare the intentionality of
subject-centred consciousness by means of the scenarios that Jacobus
Coetzee constructs on first encountering the Khoi – scenarios, it will be
remembered, that point to the linguistic and discursive separation of the
subject from what it perceives. For instance, Susan Barton's reference to
the discrepancy between her experience of the island and the expectations
generated by "travellers' tales" serves a similar function to these scenarios
in that it foregrounds the mediated nature of this character's encounter
with Friday, the island, and Cruso.[1] To be sure, the intentionality of her

---

[1] J.M. Coetzee, *Foe* (Johannesburg: Ravan, 1986): 7. Unless otherwise indicated,
further page references are in the main text.

consciousness is immediately evident when, on first encountering Friday, she assumes she has "come to an island of cannibals" (6).[2] As with Jacobus Coetzee's encounter with the Khoi in *Dusklands*, Barton positions herself in relation to Friday according to those expectations concerning the 'savage nature' of the 'native' that are generated by colonial discourse which, of course, is partly constituted by travel literature.

Susan Barton makes sense of every aspect of life on the island, no matter how trivial, by integrating it into a pre-existing conceptual framework. For example, she constantly refers to the island birds, which belong to a species with which she is not familiar, as "sparrows" (7, 51), and describes Cruso's strange apparel as follows: "He wore [...] a jerkin, and drawers to below his knees, such as we see watermen wear on the Thames" (8). The first-person-plural pronoun in this sentence, of course, refers to English culture, and thus signals the cultural location of knowledge, the fact that the 'old' world, in terms of which the protagonist as "displaced percipient" describes the 'new' world, functions as centre of absolute meaning and signification.[3] Through the system of knowledge that Susan Barton brings to her encounter with the island, the 'new' is yoked to the 'old' and, in the process, its difference is elided.

By means of his management of point of view, Coetzee from the first thus indicates Barton's implication in culture, thereby exposing both the unreliability of her interpretations and her inability to respond hospitably to difference. What is staged in the novel by way of this presentational strategy is the routine nature with which identifying thought subsumes the particularity of things within an already formed conceptual system. Given its linguistic and discursive separation from the world, the subject is unable to accommodate strangeness, and serves instead, in Levinas' descrip-

---

[2] Laura Wright argues that it is Barton's "ability not to believe" in cannibalism as a "projected justification for colonization" that places her "outside, or at the least, on the boundary of the colonial position" (*Writing "Out of All the Camps,"* 65). This view tends to overlook Coetzee's thematization of this character's (inevitably) mediated perception of island life, what Patrick Hayes refers to as the "interpretative models" that she routinely "extends" to Friday ("'An Author I Have Not Read': Coetzee's *Foe*, Dostoevsky's *Crime and Punishment*, and the Problem of the Novel," *Review of English Studies* 57.230 [2006]: 286). It also ignores the change that Susan Barton undergoes in the course of the novel.

[3] Edward Said, "Orientalism Reconsidered," *Cultural Critique* 1 (1985): 102.

tion, as a "crucible" for the "transmutation of the other into the same."[4] In its interaction with alterity, that is, the subject initiates what Lingis, in his introduction to Levinas' *Otherwise Than Being*, refers to as the "move of Being,"[5] the integrative procedure by which the subject reduces the other to its object in order to achieve full correspondence between its representations and external reality. It is important to note that knowledge, in this Levinasian understanding, involves a movement toward the other followed by a return to the same. In his depiction of Barton's encounter with the island, Coetzee stages just such an integrative procedure. Barton's representations always involve a return to self, the same, 'home'. 'Home', the cultural episteme in which this displaced percipient is located, is always the *telos* of the anamnetic movement that characterizes her relationship to the strangeness of the island.

Earlier in this study, I argued that the castaway condition, in both *In the Heart of the Country* and *Life & Times of Michael K*, serves as a metaphor for the subject's separation from the world by language and history. Tellingly, in this regard, Susan Barton is from the outset characterized as a castaway in *Foe*. On her very first night on the island, she reflects as follows: "Last night I had been bound for home; tonight I was a castaway" (14), and later responds to Cruso's injunction that she remain in the enclosure with the words "I am a castaway, not a prisoner" (20). Significantly, too, this novel conflates castaway and colonizer in Barton's description of herself as "the one who came, the one who witnessed, the one who longed to be gone" (51). In alluding to the words *"Veni, vidi, vici"* with which Julius Caesar is thought to have announced the victory of Zela that concluded the Pontic campaign, these words relate the castaway's desire "to be gone," to return home, to conquest.

It is curious that much criticism of *Foe* disregards the implications of Coetzee's strategic presentation of the story of the island from the perspective of Susan Barton. In the main, readers have taken at face value Barton's impressions of life on the island in general and of Cruso and Friday's relationship in particular. Teresa Dovey, for instance, relies chiefly on Susan Barton's interpretations in order to establish the following

---

[4] Emmanuel Levinas, "Philosophy and the Idea of Infinity" (1957), in *Collected Philosophical Papers*, 49–50.
[5] Alphonso Lingis, "Introduction" to Levinas, *Otherwise Than Being*, xxxiii.

correspondence between the island and the South African political situation during the apartheid era:

> Cruso's rule over his island kingdom represents a form of postcolonial nationalism become neo-colonialism, as the new colonizer, asserting his independence from the mother country, repeats the modes of oppression of the original colonizer. As sole survivors of a wrecked slave ship, both Cruso and Friday are victims of the colonizing enterprise.[6]

Helen Tiffin, too, finds depicted in Cruso's relationship with Friday the "history of European imperialism in Africa and its contemporary South African legacy."[7] Finally, the assumption here that Cruso and Friday's relationship is one of dominance and subservience also emerges in Susan VanZanten Gallagher's references to Cruso's "patriarchal control," and to Friday's position as "the silent slave."[8]

---

[6] Dovey, *The Novels of J.M. Coetzee*, 346–47.

[7] Helen Tiffin, "Post-Colonial Literatures and Counter-Discourse," *Kunapipi* 9.3 (1987): 29.

[8] Gallagher, *A Story of South Africa*, 174, 180. In terms of the routine nature of this assumption, see also Hanjo Beressem, "*Foe*: The Corruption of Words," *Matatu: Journal for African Culture and Society* 2.3–4 (1988): 228–30, Chris Bongie, "'Lost in the Maze of Doubting': J.M. Coetzee's *Foe* and the Politics of (Un)likeness," *Modern Fiction Studies* 39.2 (1993): 273, Graham Huggan, "Philomela's Retold Story: Silence, Music, and the Post-Colonial Text," *Journal of Commonwealth Literature* 25.1 (1990): 18, Brian Macaskill & Jeanne Colleran, "Reading History, Writing Heresy: The Resistance of Representation and the Representation of Resistance in J.M. Coetzee's *Foe*," *Contemporary Literature* 33.3 (1992): 436, Hena Maes–Jelinek, "The Muse's Progress: 'Infinite Rehearsal' in J.M. Coetzee's *Foe*," in *A Shaping of Connections: Commonwealth Literature Studies – Then and Now*, ed. Hena Maes–Jelinek et al. (Sydney: Dangaroo, 1989): 235, Susan Naramore Maher, "Confronting Authority: J.M. Coetzee's *Foe* and the Remaking of *Robinson Crusoe*," *International Fiction Review* 18.1 (1991): 35–36, Kirsten Holst Petersen, "An Elaborate Dead End? A Feminist Reading of Coetzee's *Foe*," in *A Shaping of Connections*, ed. Maes–Jelinek et al., 249–50, Robert M. Post, "The Noise of Freedom: J.M. Coetzee's *Foe*," *Critique: Studies in Contemporary Fiction* 30.3 (1989): 146, and Sheila Roberts, "'Post-Colonialism, or the House of Friday'– J.M. Coetzee's *Foe*," *World Literature Written in English* 31.1 (1991): 88. Three exceptions in this regard are Victoria Carchidi, who points out that, despite the "harsh environment [of the island], Cruso and Friday live in harmony" ("At Sea on a Desert Island: Defoe, Tournier and Coetzee," in *Literature and Quest*, ed. Christine Arkinstall [Amsterdam & Atlanta GA: Rodopi, 1993]: 81), Head, who distinguishes Cruso from his "literary model"

To argue along these lines is to miss the ironic point of Coetzee's fore-grounding of the transformative nature of Barton's identifications: namely, that her understanding of Cruso's relationship with Friday is acquired through conceptual domination, through eliding the difference of what she perceives. Importantly, the assumptive nature of her knowledge of this relationship is exposed very early in the novel: "A mutineer was my first thought: yet another mutineer, set ashore by a merciful captain, with one of the Negroes of the island, whom he has made his servant" (8–9). In itself, the absence of a 'Negro' population on the island casts doubt on this conclusion. Just as significantly, so too does Barton's own interrogation of her initial impressions:

> "What had held Friday back all these years from beating in his master's head with a stone while he slept, so bringing slavehood to an end and inaugurating a reign of idleness? And what held Cruso back from tying Friday to a post every night, like a dog, to sleep the more secure, or from blinding him, as they blind asses in Brazil?" (36–37)

The suggestion here is not simply that Barton may have misunderstood the nature of Cruso's relationship to Friday; it is also that this relationship may perhaps not be premised on power, on the self-consolidating move of Being through which she protects herself against the danger of difference.

Crucially, in this connection, her reflection on the strange stability of Cruso and Friday's relationship, which is later repeated (85), alludes to Hegel's dialectic of recognition. For this philosopher, the real issue of humanity's struggle with nature for cognitive and technological mastery is self-knowledge and independence.[9] In the first chapter of this study, I commented on his argument that an independent individual: i.e. one who has asserted his or her independence by pitting him-/herself against nature, can only receive recognition from an individual whose independence has itself been acknowledged. Such mutual recognition would bring

---

(*J.M. Coetzee,* 114), and Lewis MacLeod, who finds Cruso "a pretty unthreatening, even benevolent character" ("'Do We of Necessity Become Puppets in a Story?' Or Narrating the World: On Speech, Silence, and Discourse in J.M. Coetzee's *Foe,*" *Modern Fiction Studies* 52.1 [2006]: 4).

[9] See Hegel, *Phenomenology of Spirit,* 145–58.

an end to the struggle for affirmation that characterizes the life-and-death struggle and the master–servant relationship.

When read in the context of Hegel's dialectic of recognition, *Foe*'s insistence on the absence of contestation in Cruso's relationship with Friday seems to imply that each of these characters may have acknowledged the other's right to exist, that they, somehow or other, may have achieved an ethical community. There might be more at stake here, though. Upon further reflection, the implication of Coetzee's allusions to the dialectic of recognition in his depiction of this relationship could equally well be that autonomy, independence, and recognition are simply not an issue on the island. Instead of asserting their independence by pitting themselves against nature, Cruso and Friday, in their commerce with the island, have overcome the human separation from the natural world. There is therefore no need for the one to have the other recognize his autonomy.

As in *Life & Times of Michael K*, this suggestion of a utopian reconciliation with nature is developed by means of a number of allusions to *Robinson Crusoe* which cumulatively point to an absence of property relations on the island and to Cruso's forfeiture of self. One such allusion is Barton's description of Cruso's "evening posture" – his habit of standing "on the Bluff with the sun behind him all red and purple, staring out to sea, his staff in his hand and his great conical hat on his head" (37). She concludes her description of Cruso's stance with the following observation: "He is a truly kingly figure; he is the true king of *his* island" (my emphasis, 37). Quite clearly, the description invokes the famous monarch-of-all-I-survey passage in Defoe's *Robinson Crusoe*, in which the protagonist, upon "surveying" the island from an elevated position, and deriving pleasure from thinking that "this was all my own," reflects upon his "right of possession," and regards himself as "king and lord of all this country" (74).[10] Apart from indicating that his notion of kingship is singularly mercantile,[11] this passage renders explicit a marked change in Robinson Crusoe's relationship with the island. A few pages later in the novel, he reminisces as follows:

> Before, as I walk'd about, either on my hunting, or for viewing the
> country, the anguish of my soul at my condition, would break out upon

---

[10] See Hermann Wittenberg's insightful analysis of this passage in "Imperial Space and the Discourse of the Novel," *Journal of Literary Studies* 13.1–2 (1997): 139–41.

[11] See Green, *Dreams of Adventure, Deeds of Empire*, 76.

me on a sudden, and my very heart would die within me, to think of
the woods, the mountains, the desarts I was in; and how I was a
prisoner lock'd up with the eternal bars and bolts of the ocean, in an
uninhabited wilderness, without redemption.[12]

From a Hegelian perspective, the contrast between these two passages
suggests that Crusoe has asserted his independence by pitting himself
against nature. Cognitively and technologically, he has mastered the
island wilderness by possessing it. It is now necessary for him to engage
in a self-fortifying dialectic of recognition with another individual. In
short, he needs a Friday – which is to say, a slave and cannibal.

In *Foe*, Cruso's "evening posture" invokes the monarch-of-all-I-survey
topos, together with its conventional association with power, only to
undermine it. Instead of scanning the terrain with an imperial eye, Cruso,
for instance, looks out to sea. Barton interprets this stance variously. At
first, she assumes that Cruso is on guard for cannibals (12), but later
thinks that he is "searching the horizon for a sail" (38). Eventually,
though, she arrives at the following realization: "His visits to the Bluff
belonged to a practice of losing himself in the contemplation of the wastes
of water and sky" (38). Far from involving a self-constituting process
through which the individual asserts his or her independence and autonomy, as is the case in Defoe's representation, the relation of subject to
space that is here depicted recalls that between Michael K and the Karoo
farm. It echoes K's mimetic behaviour, his "yielding up of himself" to the
environment.

Like the protagonist of *Life & Times of Michael K*, then, Cruso is not in
possession of himself, and is thus incapable of possessing or transforming
the island. In the earlier novel, it will be remembered, K eschews the tools
that he finds in the abandoned homestead on the farm. Again like K, but
unlike Robinson Crusoe, Cruso is simply indifferent to salvaging material
and tools from the wreck of the ship that brought him and Friday to the
island. Barton makes this quite clear:

"It seemed a great pity that from the wreck Cruso should have brought
away no more than a knife. For had he rescued even the simplest of
carpenter's tools, and some spikes and bars and suchlike, he might

---

[12] Defoe, *Robinson Crusoe*, 83–84.

have fashioned better tools, and with better tools contrived a less laborious life, or even built a boat and escaped to civilization." (16)

Later, she suggests to Cruso that they mount a salvaging operation:

> "'If we could dive to the wreck, even now [...] we might save from it tools of the greatest utility. A saw, for instance, or an axe, both of which we lack. Timbers too we might loosen and bring back. Is there no way to explore the wreck?'." (32)

Cruso, however, responds to this suggestion with indifference, even antipathy:

> "'The ship lies on the bed of the ocean, broken by the waves and covered in sand [...]. What has survived the salt and seaworm will not be worth the saving. We have a roof over our heads, made without saw or axe. We sleep, we eat, we live. We have no need of tools'." (32).

That Cruso should dismiss Susan Barton's suggestion and speak of technologically sophisticated tools as if they are "heathenish inventions" indicates more than mere contentment with the rudimentary tools that he does have (see 15–16). As I have already pointed out, Robinson Crusoe, in Defoe's novel, uses the tools that he takes from the wreck to master the island, to turn it into a property and, ultimately, a "little England."[13] By contrast, Cruso's indifference to the wreck, like K's avoidance of the farmhouse, signifies his respect for the openness of terrain.

Not even the terraces and walls that Cruso and Friday build on the island suggest otherwise, notwithstanding Susan Barton's speculation that it may be their intention "to clear the whole island of growth, and turn it into terraces" (33). What is important, both here and elsewhere in the novel, is Barton's inability to make sense of these structures by positioning them in relation to an anterior system of signs: i.e. the system of property relations which imbues with meaning the marks on the *English* landscape. Later in the novel, she considers explaining the significance of precisely these marks to Friday: "Here in England [...] it is our custom to grow hedges to mark the limits of our property. [...] here we grow hedges, and then cut them straight, so that our gardens shall be neatly

---

[13] Rogers, "Crusoe's Home," 390.

marked out" (60). Barton's failure to read the walls and terraces on the
island in terms of this cultural thematic signals the absence of a system of
property relations on the island, one that would enable these structures to
serve as signifiers of the containment and control of space.[14]

Ultimately, then, Cruso's indifference to the wreck, like K's indifference to the abandoned homestead, signifies his refusal, perhaps even inability, to transform the island, both technologically and conceptually.
Judie Newman contends, correctly I believe, that the wreck symbolizes
Cruso's "cultural inheritance,"[15] the episteme in which subjects are
located and through which they make sense of the world. The wreck symbolizes, that is, the epistemological means and procedures through which
the island may be related to 'home,' the centre of meaning and *telos* of
understanding.

In fact, Barton's description of Cruso's "practice of losing himself"
would seem to suggest that this character has ecstatically transcended his
subject position in culture and that he therefore, like K, relates to entities
in the virtual absence of language and discourse. Exactly such an *ek-stasis*
is further connoted by Cruso's preference for silence over speech, which
emerges in Barton's complaint that she is unable to tell him her history
(13). Paradoxically, what he experiences is contingent and therefore not
preceded by the *a priori* forms and categories which, for Kant at least,
constitute the condition of possibility for experience. In his encounter with
it, Cruso does not violate the otherness of the island by integrating it into
the cultural totality of 'home'. Instead, he respects the island's autonomy.
In his relationship with it, the island becomes an "autonomous place."

If this is so, it should follow that Cruso has no wish to leave the island
and return 'home'. It should follow, in short, that he is not a castaway.

---

[14] For Wittenberg, the island in *Robinson Crusoe* "figures as a liminal free space in
which the emerging individualistic middle classes could project their dreams of success and progress through individual endeavour." By contrast, *Foe* may be read "as an
attempt to reconstruct the island as a space to which no such 'value' has yet been
added." The island is "an enigmatic space, inaccessible to the metropolitan imagination." In comparing the representation of space in these two novels, Wittenberg also
points out that, in *Robinson Crusoe*, "there are pages filled with detailed descriptions
of how terrain can be enclosed (by hedges and other means) and thus become valuable
as property" ("Imperial Space and the Discourse of the Novel," 140–44).

[15] Judie Newman, *The Ballistic Bard: Postcolonial Fictions* (London: Arnold,
1995): 96.

Since the castaway condition is a metaphor for the subject's linguistic and discursive separation from the world, precisely this point is implicit in Cruso's aversion to language. Nevertheless, this character's reluctance to be judged a castaway is directly, and repeatedly, emphasized in Barton's account of her stay on the island. Thus, for instance, he reminds her that "not every man who bears the mark of the castaway is a castaway at heart" (33) and she, in turn, is puzzled by his lack of any desire to "escape" the island:

> "Besides, as I later found, the desire to escape had dwindled within him. His heart was set on remaining to his dying day king of his tiny realm. In truth it was not fear of pirates or cannibals that held him from making bonfires or dancing about on the hilltop waving his hat, but indifference to salvation, and habit, and the stubbornness of old age."
> (13–14)

Even when she speaks to him of *her* "desire to be saved," Cruso, according to Barton, "seemed not to hear me. It was as though he wished his story to begin with his arrival on the island, and mine to begin with my arrival, and the story of us together to end on the island too" (34). Upon again telling him of her desire for "salvation," he responds by asserting the autonomy of the island: "I do not wish to hear of your desire [...]. It concerns other things, it does not concern the island, it is not a matter of the island" (36). In Cruso's relationship with it, the island transcends the epistemology of 'home'.

It is therefore hardly surprising that Cruso's story does not end in England. As Barton's words indicate, he chooses to die rather than allow himself to be "saved" by being taken home:

> "On the island I believe Cruso might yet have shaken off the fever, as he had done so often before. For though not a young man, he was vigorous. But now he was dying of woe, the extremest woe. With every passing day he was conveyed farther from the kingdom he pined for, to which he would never find his way again." (43)

It is in his refusal of the *telos* of return, which would, of course, compromise the island's autonomy, that Coetzee's Cruso differs most from his progenitor. The structural corollary of this refusal is that Coetzee's version of the Crusoe story does not possess the tripartite journey structure of

Defoe's novel and the adventure novels which it spawned: i.e. the setting forth of the hero, the exploits of the hero in a strange land, and, finally, the return of the conquering hero as master of two worlds – the known world and the world which has been made known.[16] In Coetzee's reworking of the Crusoe story, the absence of this structure suggests that Cruso's inter-actions with the island are governed by a movement without return from the cultural domain of 'home' to the other.

By presenting the island section of this novel from Barton's uncompre-hending perspective, Coetzee thus juxtaposes two wholly different rela-tional modes. In contrast to the narrator's integrative epistemological procedure, he posits, albeit allusively, Cruso's relationship to the island, which appears to be premissed on an irreversible movement from same to other. In its dehiscence, this relationship evinces what Lingis describes as the distinguishing feature of Levinas' ethical relationship: i.e. a "move-ment of infinition" that precludes the self from foreclosing on difference and thereby obviates the possibility of the other's violent assimilation into the same.[17] Its movement of infinition invests the ethical relationship with a respect for the exteriority of the other relative to the same. In Levinas' terms, it enables a relationship "between separated beings" that "does not totalize them," an "unrelating relation."[18]

For Levinas, such an irreversible movement from the same to the other is only possible if the self gives him-/herself to the other. Although in relation to space rather than the Levinasian human other, it is just such a gift of self to the other that is connoted by the somnolence of island life. Barton, it must be noted, posits sleep as a feature of this life: "How easy it would have been to prolong our slumbers farther and farther into the hours of daylight till at last, locked tight in sleep's embrace, we starved to death" (82). In my discussion of Michael K's somnolence in the previous chapter, I noted that sleep is a state in which the self is not in possession of itself and therefore responsive to the other. Interestingly, Levinas attaches much value to states of un- or semi-consciousness in which the

---

[16] See Percy Adams, *Travel Literature and the Evolution of the Novel* (Lexington: U of Kentucky P, 1983): 50.

[17] Lingis, "Introduction" to Levinas, *Otherwise Than Being*, xxxiii.

[18] Emmanuel Levinas, *Totality and Infinity: An Essay on Exteriority*, tr. Alphonso Lingis (*Totalité et infini: Essai sur l'extériorité*, 1961; Dordrecht: Kluwer Academic, 1991): 295.

subject is not in full possession of self. For example, he imputes to insomnia an "ebbing" of subject-centred consciousness:

> In this anonymous nightwatch where I am completely exposed to
> being[,] all the thoughts which occupy my insomnia are suspended on
> *nothing*. They have no support. I am, one might say, the object rather
> than the subject of an anonymous thought.[19]

Insomnia is, in John Llewelyn's words, a "metacategory": i.e. a category
beyond the categories with which the subject constitutes the world.[20] Differently put, it is a category in which subjective intentionality is arrested.
Not being possessed of self in this state, the subject is ready to be approached by the other.

By relaxing consciousness, then, a condition such as sleep may open
the self out to the other. Just this is implied in *Foe* by Susan Barton's
reflection that the "danger of island life" was not cannibals but "abiding
sleep" (82). While sleep exposes the self to the other in the absence of
intentional consciousness, a cannibal is a category through which the
intending subject constitutes the world. As much emerges in the novel
from the fact that it is Susan Barton who introduces to the island paranoia
about cannibals. It is she who interprets Cruso's habit of staring out to sea
as fear of cannibals (12), an interpretation that is questioned not only by
herself (38) but also in Foe's puzzled reflection on "why a man so fearful
of cannibals should have neglected to arm himself" (53). Just as importantly, her immediate assumption on first encountering Friday, we have
seen, is that he is a cannibal. This construction is a result of projective
intentionality: in intending Friday in this way, Barton consolidates herself,
shields herself against his alterity. By containing his otherness, she is able
to *recognize* Friday and thereby affirm herself and the community of
which she is a part.

Earlier in this chapter, I commented on Robinson Crusoe's need, after
having domesticated the island wilderness, for such recognition. Interestingly, one of this character's first technological accomplishments on the
desert island is the stockade to which I referred in my discussion of *Life &
Times of Michael K*. By means of this stockade, it will be recalled, Robin-

---

[19] Levinas, *Existence and Existents*, 66.
[20] John Llewelyn, *Emmanuel Levinas: The Genealogy of Ethics* (London: Routledge, 1995): 52–53.

son Crusoe is able to "fence" and "fortify" himself "from all the world."[21]
In order to consolidate his self, he must construct cannibals even in the
absence of other human life on the island. As Pearlman argues, "Crusoe's
sense of his psychological boundaries is inadequate; his identity needs to
be buttressed. The wall that he builds is an integument that reinforces the
boundaries of the self – it is a metaphorical psychic skin."[22]

In *Foe*, by contrast, we learn from Susan Barton that the "first and only
piece of furniture" that Cruso "fashioned" is the bed in his hut of poles
and reeds (82). In the context of Robinson Crusoe's fear of difference, of
being engulfed by the other, Cruso's construction of the bed signifies an
openness to otherness. The intertextual juxtaposition is between a self-
fortifying act of hostility to otherness and an act of unconditional hospitality in which the self exposes itself to the other and thereby runs the risk of
forfeiting itself, of being possessed and taken over by the other.

It is tempting to suggest that it is precisely this juxtaposition that is sustained throughout the island section of the novel by Coetzee's presentation of island life from Susan Barton's uncomprehending perspective, a
narrative strategy which, I have argued, lays bare the difference between
the movement of infinition that marks Cruso's commerce with entities and
the assimilative violence of the move of Being that manifests itself in
Barton's projective intentionality. In truth, though, the actual importance
of the contrast inscribed by this narrative strategy lies in its foregrounding
of Barton's ultimate *failure* to elide from her account the otherness of
island life. She is eventually able neither to integrate its strangeness into
her account nor to excise it therefrom. After all, as I have just demon-
strated, the mere fact that the reader detects the flaws and eccentricities in
her narrative of the island testifies to her inability to subsume the
strangeness of the island under the same. Her narrative stages the failure
of the same to *elide* the other. It is to this issue that I now turn.

℘ ঽ

Barton's attitude to language and writing shifts remarkably in the course
of the novel. Initially, she is confident that the story of the island can be

[21] Defoe, *Robinson Crusoe*, 45.
[22] E. Pearlman, "Robinson Crusoe and the Cannibals," *Mosaic* 10 (1976): 52. See
also 47.

told in language and, in fact, shares the eighteenth century's valorization
of the journal as a form that is close to the present of experience and thus
to truth.[23] In suggesting to Cruso that he keep a journal, she argues for a
direct transcription of the reality of lived experience, for the ability of language to capture life's "particularity" (17–18). Once she commences writing, however, it becomes increasingly clear that, rather than confidently
and constatively recording her perceptions, her account of the island documents her doubts and inability to know her experience in language. A
significant part of the narrative, for instance, consists of her reflections on
the "touches of mystery" that were a feature of her experience of the
island: the walls and terraces, Friday's tongue, his apparent submission to
Cruso, the lack of sexual desire on the island, and Friday's scattering of
petals on the water (83–87).

It is also noteworthy that Barton is initially exasperated with these
"touches of mystery" and feels that they mar her story. In Rosemary
Jolly's words, she "desires closure and expects all mysteries to be re-
solved in the course of narrative. In this scheme of things, puzzles or mysteries become 'symptoms' that it is the duty of narrative to 'treat'."[24] Very
importantly, though, and this is apparent from her reaction to Foe's wish
to elide them from his rewriting of her account of her stay on the island,
she comes to believe that these mysteries should be left unexplained.
Quite unconsciously, it seems, she has developed a sense of responsibility
for the otherness of the island.

What we find in Barton's response to the island in this novel is therefore similar to what we found in the medical officer's response to Michael
K in *Life & Times of Michael K* and, to a lesser extent, in the Magistrate's
response to the barbarian girl in *Waiting for the Barbarians*: i.e. a desire
to understand an enigma coupled with a dissatisfaction with the explana-
tions inspired by that desire. It is precisely such a dissatisfaction, one that
requires the subject to protect the other by betraying the forms that betray
it, that is foregrounded in Barton's narrative. Although she does indeed

---

[23] See, for example, this postulation by Arthur Young: "The journal form hath the
advantage of carrying with it a greater degree of credibility; and, of course, more
weight. A traveller who thus registers his observations is detected the moment he
writes of things he has not seen. [...] If he sees little, he must register little" (quoted in
Charles L. Batten, *Pleasurable Instruction: Form and Convention in Eighteenth-Century Travel Literature* [Berkeley: U of California P, 1978]: 33).

[24] Jolly, *Colonization, Violence, and Narration in White South African Writing*, 7.

desire closure, as Jolly maintains, she, just as significantly, is wholly dissatisfied with the forms of closure that narrative provides. As much
emerges in one of her conversations with Foe:

> "The waves picked me up and cast me ashore on an island, and a year
> later the same waves brought a ship to rescue me, and of the true story
> of that year, the story as it should be seen in God's great scheme of
> things, I remain as ignorant as a newborn babe. That is why I cannot
> rest." (126)

Barton's responsibility for the strangeness of the island manifests itself in
her *restless* dissatisfaction with the forms through which she, and indeed
Foe, attempts to make sense of it.

Ultimately, Barton's letters to Foe are a record of a self-consuming,
parental sense of responsibility for the "true story" of the island. If she is
"ignorant" of the "true story," it follows that it is effectively lost and must
therefore be found. Perversely, though, it also follows that her attempts to
find it – the narratives that emanate from her quest – will be found want-
ing. It is for this reason that the motif of the lost child features so promi-
nently in this novel. In her quest to find the child she has lost, Barton must
reject, and so abandon and betray, those impostors, such as the girl who
claims to be her daughter, she encounters along the way. She must trust
what she cannot but doubt: namely, that when, or if, her true daughter is
eventually found, she will recognize her. In terms of the analogy between
story and child in this novel, Barton must trust that, should the "true
story," of which she is ignorant, ever be written, she would recognize it.
Part of Coetzee's point here is that Barton's quest is without term, that her
responsibility is infinite. Her quest is, in fact, ateleological: because she
awaits what she does not know, hence will not be able to identify should it
arrive, her search can have no conclusion. So possessed by the desire to be
reunited with her actual daughter, or, analogously, to recognize the "true
story" of the island, is she, that she cannot help but reject what she encounters along the way. Whatever is "born," in terms of Coetzee's metaphor, will always be "stillborn or perhaps stifled," like the "dead babe"
she and Friday encounter on their journey to Bristol (104–105).[25]

---

[25] See Gayatri Chakravorty Spivak's discussion of the mother–daughter subplot in
"Theory in the Margin: Coetzee's *Foe* Reading Defoe's *Crusoe/Roxana*," *English in
Africa* 17.2 (1990): 1–23.

In testifying to her responsibility for the island, Barton's letters, of course, testify to her loss of control over its strangeness. Coetzee, in a development of the birth-metaphor in *Life & Times of Michael K*, uses a sequence of three sex-scenes to figure this character's possession by, and consequent obsession with, the truth, or radical otherness, of the island.

In the first of these scenes, Susan Barton awakens to find Cruso caressing her body. After having sexual intercourse with him, she reflects with some surprise on her response to his unsolicited advances:

> "We yield to a stranger's embrace or give ourselves to the waves; for the blink of an eyelid our vigilance relaxes; we are asleep; and when we awake, we have lost the direction of our lives. What are these blinks of an eyelid, against which the only defence is an eternal and inhuman wakefulness? Might they not be the cracks and chinks through which another voice, other voices, speak in our lives? By what right do we close our ears to them? The questions echoed in my head without answer." (30)

Through its imbrication with the sleep-motif, sexual intercourse here connotes an ebbing of subject-centred consciousness and therefore the self's exposure to the other's otherness. In the absence of intentional consciousness, the self receives the stranger, becomes a home for him in being unhomed by his otherness. Initially Cruso's guest on the island, as she herself points out (30), Barton becomes his host. She does so with unconditional hospitality: i.e. by "yielding" to him in being possessed by his strangeness. So, ultimately, as her reference to the waves implies, what happens to Barton in this encounter is very similar to what happens to Cruso in his evening meditations on the Bluff.

In terms of the complex of metaphors in this passage, Barton's account of the island is inspired by her unexpected sexual encounter with Cruso. From the "embrace" of this "stranger," she conceives a child, the story of the island. A further corollary of this metaphoric equation of insemination, inspiration, gestation, labour, maternity, and writing is that her attempt to write this narrative is a wholly involuntary response to her contact with the alterity of island life. Like a woman with child, she cannot but try to "bear" – write – the story. As she tells Friday, "I must assume the burden of our story" (81). Both the obsolete sense of the word "burden": namely, a child in the womb, and its primary sense: namely, a load or a weight, which it is difficult, even oppressive to bear, are here invoked. By playing on these senses of the word, Coetzee also introduces the idea that the writer as parent is oppressed, even mastered, by the story as child. Earlier, for instance, Barton reflects as follows on Foe writing or, in her word, "labouring," in his attic: "I think of you [...] as a beast of burden, and your house as a great wagon you are condemned to haul, a wagon full of tables and chairs and wardrobes" (52). To be inspired by the other's alterity is not only to be invaded, but also mastered, by it. As the house-motif in this passage indicates, it is to make of oneself a home for the other and then to be burdened by that home.

But the writer's real burden is not so much writing itself as the imperative of responding responsibly to the other in writing. Indeed, writing is an attempt to ease the burden by enabling the other to enter culture, history, the same. Barton's wariness about language, though, amounts to a suspicion that writing cannot accomplish this task. Hence her concern for the mysteries of the island. Her ultimate allegiance is to the strangeness of the island rather than to the narrative through which she attempts to invest it with form. Metaphorically, her responsibility is to the unborn child who is always yet to be born.

Levinas' description of the effect of the human other on the self as "maternity, gestation of the other in the same" has an obvious relevance to Coetzee's depiction of Barton's inspiration by the alterity of the island.[26] While it cannot enter the same, the other demands to be born. It is because this "gestation" – and the roots of this word signify 'to bear', 'to carry' – is without term that Levinas characterizes it as a "persecution," "suffering," and "obsession."[27] Levinas' basic point here is one that Coetzee, as

---

[26] Levinas, *Otherwise Than Being*, 75.

[27] It is worth quoting in full Levinas' description of the effect on the self of its overwhelming responsibility for the other:

> It is being torn up from oneself, being less than nothing, a rejection into the negative, behind nothingness; it is maternity, gestation of the other in the same. Is not the restlessness of someone persecuted but a modification of maternity, the groaning of the wounded entrails by those it will bear or has borne? In maternity what signifies is a responsibility for others, to the point of substitution for others and suffering both from the effect of persecution and from the persecuting itself in which the persecutor sinks. Maternity, which is bearing par excellence, bears even responsibility for the persecuting by the persecutor. (*Otherwise Than Being*, 75)

we have seen, hints at in *In the Heart of the Country* and thereafter develops in *Waiting for the Barbarians* and *Life & Times of Michael K* – that responsibility is an unequal relationship. In responsibility, the self is subordinated to the other, even mastered by him or her. Where this hierarchical relationship differs from the Hegelian master–servant relationship, however, is in the fact that it is not premissed on a dialectic of recognition but on the self's unconditional hospitality. It is through his or her forfeiture of self that the self invests the other person with authority.

If not already clear, the relevance of Levinasian responsibility to Coetzee's understanding of literary inspiration is further evident in his depiction of Barton's relationship to Friday. If she is to tell the story of the island, she must make Friday's silence speak. After all, his silence is the principal mystery of the island. Tellingly, in this respect, she describes Friday as "the child of his silence, a child unborn, a child waiting to be born that cannot be born" (122). Her burden, then, is precisely to bear the unbearable; hence her complaint to Foe: "I must have my freedom! [...] It is becoming more than I can bear!" (147). To explain her sense of oppression, Barton hereafter recounts the story of Sinbad's encounter with the old man of the river:

> "There was once a fellow who took pity on an old man waiting at the riverside, and offered to carry him across. Having borne him safely through the flood, he knelt to set him down on the other side. But the old man would not leave his shoulders: no, he tightened his knees about his deliverer's neck and beat him on his flanks and, to be short, turned him into a beast of burden. He took the very food from his mouth, and would have ridden him to death had he not saved himself by a ruse." (147–48).

Clearly, the burden image in this passage signifies more than a reversal of the terms in a relation of dominance and subservience. Barton's oppression by Friday is an effect of her surrender of her freedom and autonomy. It is an epiphenomenon of her hospitality, of the fact that she has become his host, a home for him. Thus she continues her complaint with the words: "I walk with him, I eat with him, he watches me while I sleep. If I cannot be free of him I will stifle" (148). In referring to the stranger's

---

He goes on to describe the responsible subject as being "bent under the charge of an immemorial weight" (76).

invasion of the self, the sudden *proximity* of his or her strangeness, its gestation *in* the same, Levinas makes the point that "there is nothing more burdensome than a neighbour."[28] Having become a home for him, Barton is burdened with Friday: she is condemned, like Foe, to haul her house around like a "great wagon."

Notwithstanding their similar conceptions of responsibility, it should again be noted that where Levinas focuses on the subject's relation to the human other, Coetzee explores the relation that is established with alterity in literary writing. Importantly, this relationship involves both writer and reader. It will be remembered that, in the interrogation scene in *Life & Times of Michael K*, the camp commander passes the "burden" of making K's silence speak to the medical officer (189). In my discussion of this scene, I pointed out that the writer's failure to speak the unspeakable makes it incumbent on the reader to do so. The incompleteness of the text *demands* that the reader complete it. In *Foe*, this requirement is figured by Barton's relationship with Foe, who, like the medical officer in the earlier novel, is ambivalently depicted as both writer and reader. Barton, we are told, has "entrusted" Foe with "the story of the island" (81). Fittingly, this point is developed through a repetition, with variation, of the sex-scene that describes Barton's inspiration by Cruso's otherness. In fact, this later scene, which depicts Barton's sexual involvement with Foe, announces its relation to the first in Barton's sense that she "might have thought [her] self in Cruso's arms again" (139). The second of these scenes self-consciously takes up the refrain, or burden, of the first.

When Barton mounts Foe, she does so with the words "This is the manner of the Muse when she visits her poets" (139), thereby implementing her theory that she "was intended not to be the mother of [her] story, but to beget it" (126). Quite explicitly, then, she assumes the role of muse, that is, a "goddess," as she earlier explains to Foe, "who visits poets in the night and begets stories upon them" (126). Nonetheless, what is at issue here is the inspiration not only of an author but also of a reader. Hence Barton's words to Foe shortly before she straddles him: "I pursue you with my own dull story, visiting it upon you in your uttermost refuge" (139). Indeed, earlier in the novel, the story of the island, written in the form of a letter from Susan Barton to Foe, is depicted as her attempt to inspire this reader:

---

[28] Levinas, *Otherwise Than Being*, 88.

> "How I wish it were in my power to help you, Mr Foe! Closing my
> eyes, I gather my strength and send out a vision of the island to hang
> before you like a substantial body, with birds and fleas and fish of all
> hues and lizards basking in the sun, flicking out their black tongues,
> and rocks covered in barnacles, and rain drumming on the roof-fronds,
> and wind, unceasing wind: so that it will be there for you to draw on
> whenever you have need." (53)

Foe is *visited* by the vision that Barton visits upon him through her narrative. The suggestion is that, owing to its non-completion, its inability
both to capture and to exclude the strangeness of the island, this "dull
story" may infiltrate Foe's consciousness and make of him a host who
receives it with unconditional hospitality. This point is further clarified by
Barton's expression of gratitude to Foe: "Am I to damn you as a whore
for welcoming me and embracing me and receiving my story?" (152). In
terms of the metaphor of hospitality, it is obviously significant that Barton
and Friday quite literally enter and take over Foe's house, to which Barton, in yet another invocation of the sleep-motif, refers as "a house of
sleepers," and likens to "the cave where men close their eyes in one reign
and wake up in another with long white beards" (93–94). Like Cruso's
island, Foe's house, it would seem, is a place of sleepers and thus a site of
unconditional hospitality.

Through its allusions to his hospitality, the novel suggests that Foe
loses control over the alterity to which he is exposed in reading Barton's
narrative, and that it is now *his* responsibility to invest it with substance. It
is his Orphic duty to render visible what is invisible. The distinction between writing and reading in the novel therefore collapses. In fact, as
much is indicated toward the end of the protracted conversation between
Barton and Foe in Part III by the description of Friday sitting at Foe's
desk, in his robes, pen in hand (151). The real author, Coetzee implies, is
neither Barton nor Foe but the otherness of the other which visits itself
upon *both* of them, inspiring them to give it substance in the language and
forms of the same. Both are enthralled by the authority of Friday's otherness. Like Barton, Foe is, again to use Elizabeth Costello's term for a
writer, a "secretary of the invisible," acted upon by an alterity which the
same can neither include nor exclude.

While it is Foe's responsibility to author the alterity of the island, to
make Friday's silence speak, he cannot help failing. Barton has "entrusted"

with this responsibility a castaway, a purveyor of words and forms that are a foe to the other. Tellingly, she eventually comes to realize that she has placed her trust in the untrustworthy:

> And might not Foe be a kind of captive too? I had thought him dilatory. But might the truth not be instead that he had laboured all those months to move a rock so heavy no man alive could budge it; that the pages I saw issuing from his pen were not idle tales of courtesans and grenadiers, as I supposed, but the same story over and over, in version after version, stillborn every time: the story of the island, as lifeless from his hand as from mine? (151)

Like Barton, Foe is wholly incapable of telling the "true story" of the island. But, even as he inevitably betrays her trust, his betrayal attests to both his assumption of responsibility for the other and the interminable nature of this responsibility. Crucially, in this regard, his inability, metaphorically speaking, to give birth to the island's alterity does not suspend the attempt to do so. Instead of lapsing into silence, he, as Barton's words indicate, continues to write, to "labour." What is here suggested is that Foe, in failing to present this alterity, also fails to negate it. Not having been eliminated, the invisible continues to wait, and demand, to be rendered visible. To appropriate Barton's description of Friday, the alterity in question is "a child unborn, a child waiting to be born that cannot be born" (122). Foe thus betrays Barton's trust out of an overwhelming sense of responsibility for the other. In fact, Barton's description above of Foe's writing suggests that responsibility must lead to betrayal, which, in its turn, ensures a continuance of responsibility. While the other must be accommodated in the language of the same, the attempt to do so to which this imperative leads necessarily betrays the other and must therefore itself be betrayed. The quest for the lost child is without term.

℘ ঽ

Foe's self-reflexive preoccupation with the literary work's relation to alterity and the implications of this relationship for writing and reading obviously reflect on its own reception by the actual reader. It is therefore now necessary to examine the manner in which this novel both anticipates and comments on the ways in which its reader may respond to it.

From the first, *Foe* locates its reader as letter-reader within its structure. Part I is addressed to a reader who is referred to as "you" (7, 9, 11, 14, 38), and whose identity is only revealed to be Foe at the end of this section (45). In Part IV, the deliberate nature of this retention of information is laid bare through the repetition of the first sentence of the novel, but this time together with the salutation "Dear Mr Foe" (155). The implications of this strategic alignment of the text's actual reader with its internal reader are manifold. As *I* read the opening paragraphs of the novel, I ostensibly read of a transaction between Susan Barton and Foe, of her passing of the burden of rendering visible the invisible to Foe. In actual fact, though, and this seems to be the chief point of the novel's alignment of internal and external reader, it is *I* who am receiving this burden from J.M. Coetzee, the author of *Foe*. Through its reading, its relationship with me, the novel thus enacts the ontogenetic anxiety that it thematizes in its depiction of the Barton–Foe relationship. It is incumbent on me, and me alone, to do what Coetzee has failed to do, a failure that is implicit in my very act of reading.

A further implication of Coetzee's alignment of me with Foe is that he deems me untrustworthy, likely to betray the responsibility with which he has entrusted me. Owing to my location in language, the same, I am a foe of alterity, a castaway, and therefore bound to betray his trust. Nevertheless, his responsibility for the other, his servitude to it, means that he is compelled to trust the untrustworthy: the very fact that I am reading this novel means that silence is not a choice that is open to him. He must write. It is his responsibility to render me responsible. To subside into silence would be a betrayal of this responsibility.

In order to render the reader responsible, Coetzee must ensure that his novel interrupts the move of Being that informs recuperative reading practices. If it is to secure a hospitable reception for the alterity that it has failed both to exclude and to include, the text must evade the reader's intentional consciousness. *Foe* must affect him or her unbeknownst to him or her. As with *Life & Times of Michael K*, this novel relies on the auratic potential of the work of art, its ability to gesture beyond its "givenness,"[29] its location in the cultural episteme, to achieve this end.

Foe's aura, which is more pronounced than that of *Life & Times of Michael K*, is largely an effect of Coetzee's presentation of the island

---

[29] Adorno, *Aesthetic Theory*, 67.

community from Susan Barton's uncomprehending perspective. It should be noted that this presentational strategy does not simply distance the reader from the narrator by foregrounding her unreliability. In presenting the reader with Barton's epistemological failure, the novel confronts him or her with his or her own. What I have omitted from my reading of Barton's reading of the island is the critical point that Coetzee relativizes, without ever correcting, her interpretations. In focusing on a set of allusions to, among others, Hegel, Levinas, Defoe, colonial discourse, I have been able to piece together, to create, a wholly different story from that provided by Barton. Where I have erred, though, is in neglecting to say that Coetzee refuses to legitimize this alternative story. Instead, he relativizes it, too, by ensuring that it co-exists alongside Barton's story and various others. For instance, while the allusions to Hegel do indeed question whether or not Cruso's relationship with Friday is premissed on power, this is all they do. The fact remains that Friday cooks and carries firewood for Cruso. What we have is two contrasting interpretations of this relationship, each of which renders the other provisional and thereby precludes the possibility of a teleological reading. Similarly, although Cruso evinces no fear of cannibals, he, according to Barton, recounts stories of cannibals and tells her that Friday was once one (12).

My point is that *Foe* steadfastly refuses to provide the reader with a position of certitude from which to determine the truth, the "true story" of the island. For example, the stories that Cruso tells Barton are, by her own admission, "so various, and so hard to reconcile one with another," that she is unable to distinguish between "truth" and "fancy" (11–12). Besides, Barton is not merely an unreliable narrator because she fails to understand the "strange island": in places, she quite blatantly contradicts herself. While initially telling us that Cruso has green eyes, she later states that they are yellow (8, 30). The reader is simply given too much material for a teleological interpretation of the "strange island." Accordingly, my story of the island, like Barton's and those critical interpretations that simply take her story at face value, is the wrong story.

All in all, then, Coetzee's auratic presentation of life on the island not only places the reader in relation to what has *not* been recognized and identified; it also seeks to prevent him or her from subsuming it under a concept. *Foe* quite literally points beyond what it says, thereby inscribing distance between itself and the reader. Nevertheless, the nature of this distance requires clarification. Through it, this work both resists *and* exacts interpretation. In the very process of precluding the possibility of a determinate reading, the novel's aura inspires the desire to know. Its distance, by implication, engenders proximity. In encountering the absence of something determinate, the reader cannot but sense the uncanny presence of something indeterminate. Should s/he gain such a sense, the reader will have been rendered passive in his or her encounter with the novel's aura. S/he will have been drawn into the work's distance and, rather than identifying the work with him-/herself, have been identified with it. In yielding his or her thought to the text, s/he will have overcome the separation between reading subject and literary object.

It would thus seem that *Foe*'s aura holds out the possibility of the sort of mimetic relation that is connoted by Coetzee's allusive depiction of Cruso's bond with the island (a depiction, I must now add, that is relativized by this character's killing of the apes on the island). That is, the space of reading becomes an "autonomous place," cut off from history, identifying thought, the same. My contention, though, is that there is more at stake in this novel than simply the possibility of a mimetic relation. The fact that the distance produced by its aura is also a proximity means, for instance, that I have had to question the reading of the island that I provide in the first section of this chapter, that I have had to supplement it with the present reading, which, I suspect, is itself not the full story. In other words, the novel's aura acts upon me; it inspires more readings even as it makes me realize that each of these is inadequate, not the "true story," and therefore has to be betrayed and abandoned.

Simply put, *Foe*'s aura invests it with a certain power. To employ Barton's distinction between Friday's silence and that of her story, this novel's aura does not produce a "helpless silence" (122). Instead of allowing the reader to make of the text what s/he wishes, it protects what Coetzee has failed to present. What is more, its aura, in evading intentional consciousness and thereby suspending the move of Being, may enable the novel to infiltrate the reader's consciousness and thereby become his or her uninvited visitor. It is just this possibility of reading as a form of unconditional hospitality that is mooted by this novel's ending, which is also the last of its sex-scenes.

ॐ ॐ

The novel concludes with two companion passages describing two visits
by an anonymous first-person narrator to Foe's house. In the course of
both these visits, s/he encounters a scene from the novel that the reader
has recently read – the section of Part III in which Barton and Friday pay
an unannounced visit to Foe's second house. During this visit, Barton,
after having engaged in sexual intercourse with him, discusses with Foe
the importance of making Friday's silence "speak" (142). Foe, having
referred to the "silence" of the story of the island, its "heart" or "eye,"
which he likens to the sea, argues that he, together with Barton, must
undertake "the task of descending into that eye" (141). To this, Barton
responds with the questions:

> "But who will do it? [...] It is easy enough to lie in bed and say what
> must be done, but who will dive into the wreck? On the island I told
> Cruso it should be Friday, with a rope about his middle for safety. But
> if Friday cannot tell us what he sees, is Friday in my story any more
> than a figuring (or prefiguring) of another diver?" (142)

The fact that its ending attempts to answer these questions by, in its turn,
prefiguring what would happen should the actual reader encounter the
silence of the story by "diving" into the wreck, indicates that *Foe* per-
petually awaits its reception by the reader.

Tellingly, in this regard, the anonymous narrator, in the first of the ending's two passages, on arriving at Foe's house, enters a textualized space
and encounters various of the novel's characters in postures of sleep.
Clearly, Foe's second house, like both the first and the island, is a locus of
sleep, a "house of sleepers." Given that sleep signifies a state of openness
to the other, the suggestion here is that *Foe* waits without assumption or
expectation for this uninvited visitor. Indeed, s/he arrives unannounced.

Both passages conclude with the narrator, on opening Friday's mouth,
being reduced to a state of passivity akin to sleep; what Barton earlier
refers to as a "waking slumber" (17). In the first, the narrator thinks that
s/he "might even have been asleep" during his or her encounter with
Friday (154). In the second, though, the meeting with Friday only takes
place after the reader-figure starts reading a manuscript s/he finds, the
first sentence of which, with the addition of the salutation "Dear Mr Foe"
(155), is also the opening sentence of the novel. On reading this passage,
s/he enters the text and seems to identify with Barton. Just as Barton
"gives herself to the waves," the reader-figure immerses him-/herself in

the text. Transported by the narrative, s/he is embraced by, in Newman's words, "a sexualised sea," and moves "through a 'great bed' of seaweed, where something 'gropes' a leg, 'caresses' an arm."[30] The diver then descends the "trunks," goes below deck and "enter[s]" a dark "hole" in the wreck off the island (156). This is where s/he encounters Friday.

In questioning Friday and opening his mouth, the diver is rendered passive:

> From inside him comes a slow stream, without breath, without interruption. It flows up through his body and out upon me; it passes through the cabin, through the wreck; washing the cliffs and shores of the island, it runs northward and southward to the ends of the earth. Soft and cold, dark and unending, it beats against my eyelids, against the skin of my face. (157)

As is evident from the fact that the reader-figure's eyes are closed, the attempt to make Friday's silence speak gives way to a passive waiting without expectation. What is here suggested is an overcoming of intentional consciousness; a state in which the reader-figure encounters the text without expectation and is therefore able to receive with unconditional hospitality the strangeness it harbours.

In assuming the "task" of descending into the wreck and making Friday's silence speak, the reader-figure is thus inspired by, even impregnated with, the novel's otherness. It is noteworthy, in this regard, that both this passage and the sentence that concludes the description of the first encounter with Friday, "From his mouth, without breath, issue the sounds of the island" (154), allude to the Mount Snowdon episode of Wordsworth's *The Prelude*, in which the quietening of the poet's external eye and consequent openness to the world are imaged by his listening to the invisible subterranean stream:

> There I beheld the emblem of a mind
> That feeds upon infinity, that broods
> Over the dark abyss, intent to hear
> Its voices issuing forth to silent light
> In one continuous stream [...].[31]

---

[30] Newman, *The Ballistic Bard*, 9–10.

[31] William Wordsworth, *The Prelude*, ed. J.C. Maxwell (Harmondsworth: Penguin, 1971): 14, ll. 70–77.

Foe ends with the suggestion that its reader, in reading its opening lines, may assume the "burden" of Friday's silence.

Interestingly, though, the novel, through this suggestion, indicates that *it*, in fact, expects a certain kind of reader. In prefiguring its reading, its author's passing of the burden of making Friday's silence speak to its reader, *Foe* inevitably intends a certain kind of reading. It does so notwithstanding its representation of the reader-figure's entry into Foe's house, which connotes the text's openness to its guest. In this scene, it will be recalled, the narrator is unnamed, a stranger, who enters a "house of sleepers"; the implication being that his or her host waits for him or her without expectation. If anything, this representation of unconditional hospitality betrays what it seeks to present.

The novel's apparent contradiction of itself is, however, self-reflexively foregrounded by Coetzee's location of the reader-figure's second encounter with Friday on the wreck, which, as is intimated by the allusion to Defoe's writing in the diver's reference to "the mud of Flanders, in which generations of grenadiers now lie dead" (156), symbolizes not only Cruso's, but also Coetzee's, "cultural inheritance," the literary intertext which has enabled the writing of this novel. In a foetal position in the most remote part of this wreck, "In the last corner, under the transoms, half buried in sand" (157), the reader-figure finds Friday. When s/he questions him, it turns out that "this is not a place of words" (157). The implication is, once again, that the literary tradition of which *Foe* forms part cannot eliminate the otherness that it has failed to integrate into its intertextual economy. In fact, what we have is a gestation of the other in this economy. The further implication is therefore that the works that form the literary tradition have all been inspired by a desire for this otherness. Coetzee's placement of the narrator's encounter with Friday's silence on the wreck off the island signifies, in the words of the medical officer to K in *Life & Times of Michael K*, how scandalously "a meaning can take up residence in a system without becoming a term in it" (228).

It follows that although the novel addresses its reader from its location in the same and must therefore have expectations of him or her, the ineliminable otherness that inhabits the text waits for him or her without expectation. Were the encounter that it attempts to project to take place, it would do so despite the work and its various expectations of the reader. As much is connoted by the immensely ironic description of the reader-figure's meeting with Friday in a locale outside language, a description which draws attention to the fact that what is described cannot be described, that the "figure[] of alterity"[32] encountered by the narrator is a prosopopeia, a figure for what cannot be figured. What this ending ultimately figures, then, is its inevitable failure to prefigure the kind of reading that it seeks to prefigure.

Strictly speaking, what the novel expects cannot be expected. It expects a reader who, in reading the novel, may encounter that which is not a part of the novel, a term in its economy. As its subversion of its prefiguring of its reading indicates, the work prepares for an encounter which, if it were to take place, would do so despite its intentions. In fact, were a reader to arrive such as the one it expects, the novel's success would have been brought about by its failure. The paradox here is that the text, in its attempt to expose the reader to the other, *relies* on its implication in the same, and therefore on its inevitable loss of control over the other, its failure either to present or to eliminate it.

What is ultimately indicated by *Foe*'s ending, then, is Coetzee's desire to control the uncontrollable. He *depends* on the fact that the other cannot be controlled in his bid to expose the reader to it. That is, he hopes that his inability to instantiate it will enable the other to invade his text. By implication, he tries to put to use the other that may inhabit the novel as a result of his loss of control over it. He seeks to expose the reader who visits his novel to its uninvited visitors; to visit on his reader the work's uninvited visitors. In this way, to use the text's metaphoric vocabulary, this writer tries to pass to the reader the burden of giving birth to the unborn child, the child that cannot be born.

So, although Attridge is quite right when he says that the literary relation to otherness cannot serve as part of a political programme,[33] I would argue that Coetzee nonetheless does try to use the other to alter the social domain. His entire notion of aesthetic autonomy is premised on a relationship that comes into being in reading, one that will then affect the reader's social relations. This writer's intention is that the reader should assume the burden of responsibility for the other and that this, in turn, will alter his or her relations in society. In this regard, it is noteworthy that the parallel between the island and the novel aligns the reader with Susan

---

[32] Attridge, *J.M. Coetzee and the Ethics of Reading*, 12.
[33] Attridge, *The Singularity of Literature*, 4.

Barton. Should s/he be affected by the text in the way impossibly pre-figured by the novel's ending, the reader's return to the world from the work will have been prefigured by Barton's return from the island to England. Like Barton, s/he will be the site of a gestation of the other in the same: i.e. the reader will be mastered and persecuted by the over-whelming desire to bring the other into being, and by a restless dissatis-faction with the social forms that exclude it. Like Susan Barton, s/he will be a protector of the other.

Since this novel was written during the apartheid period, it goes with-out saying that the dissatisfaction felt by the reader of that period with totalizing discourses would inevitably have extended to the forms of apartheid. Nevertheless, the kind of political action to which an exposure to alterity may lead is quite obviously wholly unpredictable and by its very nature impossible to quantify and determine. My point, however, is that although Attridge is justifiably suspicious of any suggestion that the other may be put to use, *Foe* does, in fact, quite outrageously and with remarkable ingenuity, attempt to make a possibility of this impossibility. If anything, this self-consciously paradoxical endeavour is even more pro-nounced in *Age of Iron.* Whereas *Foe* confines its speculation about the possibility of an affective engagement with the discourses of apartheid to a loose alignment of the reader with Susan Barton, *Age of Iron* provides a detailed, albeit figurative, exposition of the nature, and potential efficacy, of such an engagement.

✍ ৡ

4 From the Standpoint of Redemption
∅   *Age of Iron*

M Y ULTIMATE PURPOSE in this chapter is to outline Coetzee's self-reflexive articulation, in *Age of Iron*, of the possibility of interrupting apartheid history by opening out the
literary text to a source beyond history. The question raised in this novel is
thus identical to the one posited in *Waiting for the Barbarians*, *Life &
Times of Michael K*, and *Foe*: how can that which is hostile to the other be
made into a home for it? My reading of this work, which focuses on its
interlacing of metaphors and motifs, shows the increasing subtlety with
which Coetzee negotiates this impasse.

In *Age of Iron*, the protagonist's location in culture is articulated more
directly than is the case with the protagonists of the earlier novels. This is
simply because Mrs Curren is quite aware of, and deeply dissatisfied with,
her implication in South Africa's colonial history:

> A crime was committed long ago. [...] So long ago that I was born
> into it. It is part of my inheritance. It is part of me, I am part of it. [...]
> Though it was not a crime I asked to be committed, it was committed
> in my name. I raged at times against the men who did the dirty work
> [...] but I accepted too that, in a sense, they lived inside me. So that
> when in my rages I wished them dead, I wished death on myself too.[1]

As in the earlier fiction, Coetzee's contention here is that the world constructs the subject, that knowledge of the world cannot be separated from
being *in* the world. In a companion passage, Mrs Curren again makes this
point when, after telling Vercueil that she wants "to rage against the men

---

[1] Coetzee, *Age of Iron* (London: Secker & Warburg, 1990): 149–50. Unless otherwise indicated, further page references are in the main text.

who have created these times," she concludes that "It is childish [...] to point fingers and blame others," and that "Power is power, after all. It invades. That is its nature. It invades one's life" (107). This is far more than merely a liberal English South African's expression of distaste for apartheid ideology. Mrs Curren is aware that her consciousness is an *historical* consciousness, that she has been interpellated as a subject in a society whose insensible systems of relations locate her attitudes to life in general.

Like Magda in *In the Heart of the Country*, this character's knowledge that she has been shaped by the times accounts for her profound dis-ease with her present identity: "From the cradle a theft took place: a child was taken and a doll left in its place to be nursed and reared, and that doll is what I call I" (100).[2] Her awareness of the contextual nature of her identity is an awareness of the extent to which the apartheid state's structures of power shape identities in ways that preclude other possibilities of self-hood. More than this, though, her intense dissatisfaction with the forms of her society signifies her responsibility for what is not ontologically present, for what has not yet emerged. As the presence of the child-motif in this passage indicates, Mrs Curren, like Susan Barton, is in search of the lost child. The difference is that she realizes that her contextualized identity is, in fact, the loss of that child. What she is, is a deformation of the child; what she calls 'I' renders the child unborn.

Not surprisingly, then, the apartheid state is figured, in *Age of Iron*, as an author or, more accurately, a muse that inspires the individual to construct him-/herself in certain ways. In the novel, the metaphor of the message plays an important part in this portrayal. Already in *Foe*, it should be remembered, the word "message" is associated with inspiration: Susan Barton attempts to inspire Foe by sending him her story of the island in the form of a message. In the following passage, Mrs Curren describes the effect on the individual of the state's "message":

> Television. Why do I watch it? The parade of politicians every evening [...]. What absorbs them is power and the stupor of power. Eating and talking, munching lives, belching. Slow, heavy-bellied talk. Sitting in a circle, debating ponderously, issuing decrees like hammer-blows:

---

[2] See Head's insightful discussion of the doll and child metaphors in this novel (*J.M. Coetzee*, 134ff.).

> death, death, death. Untroubled by the stench. Heavy eyelids, piggish
> eyes, shrewd with the shrewdness of generations of peasants. [...]
> And their message stupidly unchanging, stupidly forever the same.
> Their feat, after years of etymological meditation on the word, to have
> raised stupidity to a virtue. To stupefy: to deprive of feeling; to be-
> numb, deaden; to stun with amazement. Stupor: insensibility, apathy,
> torpor of mind. Stupid: dulled in the faculties, indifferent, destitute of
> thought or feeling. From *stupere* to be stunned, astounded. A gradient
> from *stupid* to *stunned* to *astonished*, to be turned to stone. The mes-
> sage: that the message never changes. A message that turns people to
> stone.
>   We watch as birds watch snakes, fascinated by what is about to
> devour us. [...] A thanatophany: showing us our death. *Viva la*
> *muerte!* their cry, their threat. Death to the young. Death to life. Boars
> that devour their offspring. The Boar War. (25–26)

The passage alludes to the story of the Gorgons in Greek mythology, a
myth according to which Medusa had such a frightful aspect that whoever
looked upon her was turned to stone.[3] This myth, in *Age of Iron*, serves as
an analogue for the deforming influence of the state's "message." In fact,
the equation is made even more apparent by the pun in the passage on
'*boer*', an Afrikaner nationalist, and 'boar': the Gorgons were represented
with heads entwined with snakes and with huge tusks like those of a
boar.[4]

Elsewhere in the novel, a set of allusions to the myth of Circe further
stresses the deforming influence of the state's discourses of power. While
in Guguletu, Mrs Curren describes the effect on Mr Thabane of the state-
instigated violence she has witnessed:

> His look had grown uglier. No doubt I grow uglier too by the day.
> Metamorphosis, that thickens our speech, dulls our feelings, turns us
> into beasts. Where on these shores does the herb grow that will pre-
> serve us from it? (95)

---

[3] See Robert Graves, *The Greek Myths* (Harmondsworth: Penguin, 2nd ed. 1960),
vol. 1: 127–29.
[4] See Pierre Grimal, *The Dictionary of Classical Mythology*, tr. A.P. Maxwell–
Hyslop (*Dictionnaire de la mythologie grecque et romaine*, 1951; Oxford: Blackwell,
1986): 174.

Like Circe's spell, which metamorphosed Odysseus's men into swine, the
state's power structures deform and brutalize whoever is exposed to them.
It is for this reason that, throughout the novel, South Africans are described as ugly – as, for instance, when Mrs Curren exclaims "How ugly
we are growing, from being unable to think well of ourselves!" (121).

Alluding as it does to Hesiod's description of the "age of the iron race,"
in which "The father will quarrel with his sons, the sons with their / father,
/ guest will quarrel with host," and "Might will be justice,"[5] the title of this
novel, of course, foregrounds the debasement of South African society by
the insensible system of power relations established under colonialism. In
fact, Coetzee, in his Jerusalem Prize acceptance speech, refers to precisely
this phenomenon when he observes that "The deformed and stunted relations between human beings that were created under colonialism and
exacerbated under what is loosely called apartheid have their psychic representation in a deformed and stunted inner life."[6]

In *Age of Iron*, the metaphor of sickness and disease further signifies
such deformation.[7] Tellingly, Mrs Curren who, as we have seen, is conscious of having been invaded and shaped by the state's structures of
power, refers, in the opening page of the novel, to the "news" that she has
received of her cancer (3). Later, she describes this "news" as a message
that has been "sent by Saturn" – the archetypal Political Father (59). In a
significant development of the metaphor of hospitality, Coetzee here depicts Mrs Curren as not only the receiver but also the host of the state's
message. Through this message, history invades her and takes her over. In
fact, this point is made by Coetzee's use of the same analogy between self

---

[5] *The Poems of Hesiod*, tr. R.M. Frazer (Norman: U of Oklahoma P, 1983): 103–
104.

[6] Coetzee, "Jerusalem Prize Acceptance Speech," in *Doubling the Point*, 97–98.

[7] One of the images of the state's debasement of the individual that I do not examine
in this chapter is that of sleep. In *Age of Iron*, unlike the earlier novels in which it
usually connotes the self's receptivity to otherness, sleep, for the most part, intersects
with the "stupor," the "insensibility, apathy, torpor of mind" induced by the state's
"message." By implication, "the sleep of worldliness" connotes the subject's indifference to difference (153). Early in the novel, Mrs Curren describes the "soul-stunted"
white South African children as "spinning themselves tighter and tighter into their
sleepy cocoons" (6), and comments on their "Slumbrous" souls (7). Later, after remarking on her "childhood slumber," she asks the following question: "Have I ever
been fully awake?" (100).

and house that we find in *In the Heart of the Country* and *Foe*. Like her, Mrs Curren's house is in a state of decay:

> This house is [...] tired of holding itself together. The floorboards have lost their spring. The insulation of the wiring is dry, friable, the pipes clogged with grit. The gutters sag where screws have rusted away or pulled loose from the rotten wood. The rooftiles are heavy with moss. (13)

Significantly, too, the novel contains a description of the installation of burglar bars on the windows of the house (24–25). The only points of access to the world beyond this "cage" are now through the "wires"; i.e. "the telephone wire," "the television wire," and "the aerial wire" (25). It is noteworthy that this description is followed directly by the passage in which Mrs Curren describes television as the medium through which the state sends its "message that turns people to stone." By means of this medium, history possesses the subject and, in the process, excludes the other.

This point requires some elaboration, however. What the analogy between house and self in this passage suggests is that the self is inspired – which is to say, acted upon – by the state's discourses to construct itself through indifference to the particularity of others. Through perpetuating colonial power relations, the apartheid state inspires the individual to conceive of other individuals in its generic terms. In turn, this precludes the individual from being exposed to singularity, difference, otherness. The description of Mrs Curren's house suggests that her location in the cultural domain has fortified her against difference and, in the process, has rendered her indifferent both to others and to their suffering. She has already begun to change when, later in the novel, upon witnessing the violence that is elided by state television during her visit to Guguletu, she entreats Mr Thabane to "listen" to her and then adds: "I am not indifferent to this ... this war. How can I be? No bars are thick enough to keep it out" (95).

Initially, though, it is quite clear that the effect of the state's message is precisely to inspire such indifference. It is worth mentioning, in this connection, that the analogue for Coetzee's depiction of Mrs Curren's relationship with Vercueil is the myth of Circe and Odysseus. While Vercueil, who claims to have once been a sailor (170–71), is associated with Odysseus (77), Mrs Curren directly refers to herself as Circe (77).

Also, her house is an island of sorts and Vercueil a castaway, as is implied by the novel's opening description of her discovery of him outside her house, which reverses the gender roles in Susan Barton's description, at the beginning of *Foe*, of her discovery by Friday after having been washed up on the island. The medium of transformation in Mrs Curren's relationship with Vercueil is, however, not magic but discourse or, perhaps, the magic of discourse. Although in a different context, her later words to Vercueil are germane in this regard: "We half perceive but we also half create" (153). Shortly after having met him, she positions Vercueil, hence herself, in a relationship of dominance and subservience premissed on race and class by putting him to work in her garden. As her protestations to the contrary indicate, she thereby transforms him into something that he is not: "I know you are not a gardener [...] and I don't want to turn you into what you are not. But we can't proceed on a basis of charity" (19). Her actions are, of course, reminiscent of Magda's "dance" with Hendrik, of Visagie's attempt to turn Michael K into a manservant, and, indeed, of all the other Hegelian master–slave relationships that one finds in Coetzee's fiction. At this point in the novel, then, Mrs Curren's behaviour is clearly inspired by the discourses of history. Through them, she presumes to identify Vercueil, and this identification inspires her to treat him as she does.

The important point, however, is that, in reducing Vercueil to a term in a power relationship, Mrs Curren does the same to herself. In turning him into a servant, she turns herself into a white madam. Accordingly, in reading of the relationship between Mrs Curren and Vercueil, which is focalized by the former, we are throughout aware not only that Vercueil is not what Mrs Curren assumes he is,[8] but also that she, in constructing and defining herself in relation to what he is not, makes of herself what she despises. She deforms the child. Coetzee's point is not the relatively banal one that the apartheid state debases its citizenry, but that, itself a construct of colonial history, it inspires the individual to deform him-/herself. When Mrs Curren expresses her sense that she is the loss or deformation of the child, she does so through agentless constructions: "a theft took place: a child was taken and a doll left in its place." The omission of agents from these formulations renders both the implied subject and the

---

[8] See Gilbert Yeoh, "Love and Indifference in J.M. Coetzee's *Age of Iron*," *Journal of Commonwealth Literature* 38.3 (2003): 117–25.

nature of the action to which they refer ambiguous.[9] In turn, this ambiguity suggests that *both* the state and Mrs Curren are responsible for the loss of the child. Mrs Curren, under inspiration by the state, has authored herself in a way that has deformed the child. The child is stolen by the state in being abandoned by her.

Through her treatment of Vercueil, Mrs Curren thus exemplifies her later argument that she is a part of the apartheid society that she resists. The additional point that emerges from her behaviour towards Vercueil is that she is not only shaped by the times in which she lives, but also shapes them in her relations with others. In the process, she shapes herself. Crucially, it is she, and not the state, who is imaged as Circe in this scene. Although described as a doll, a puppet, she is more like an author who acts in being acted upon, and who is therefore never quite an agent in full control of his or her actions.

Inspired by history, then, Mrs Curren is initially unable to respond to Vercueil's particularity. Only much later in the novel does she finally express a desire to do so: "I want to see you as you really are" (165). Just as importantly, in not responding to his particularity, she is unable to particularize herself. In this regard, it is clearly significant that Vercueil is depicted as her visitor in the novel. Since he arrives outside Mrs Curren's house, her treatment of him invites being read in terms of the ethic of hospitality. In having named and identified this stranger, who she wishes would leave, she renders herself incapable of responding generously to his strangeness. By her own admission, she cannot give unconditionally:

> He needs socks. He needs shoes. He needs a bath. He needs a bath
> every day; he needs clean underwear; he needs a bed, he needs a roof
> over his head, he needs three meals a day, he needs money in the bank.
> Too much to give [...]. (17)

This passage is causally connected to the scene in which Mrs Curren puts Vercueil to work in her overgrown garden on the grounds that they cannot "proceed on a basis of charity," and then relates the word "care," etymologically, to charity: "Care: the true root of charity" (20). The implication is that she is unable *not* to transform Vercueil *because* she *cannot*

---

[9] See Coetzee, "The Agentless Sentence as Rhetorical Device," in *Doubling the Point,* 170–80.

care enough. Only through caring sufficiently will she be able to respond
to his particularity. In terms of the metaphoric equation of self and house,
it is important that she should describe her house as one that was built
"without love," a house that is "cold, inert," and which "even the African
sun has never succeeded in warming" (13).

If anything, this failure to care well enough is even more pronounced in
Mrs Curren's relationship with John. Having assisted John after the police
attack, she complains as follows to Florence and Bheki:

> 'Why did you leave me alone to look after him? Why didn't you
> stay and help?'
> I sounded querulous, certainly, but for once was I not in the right?
> 'I do not want to be involved with the police,' said Florence.
> 'That is not the question. You leave me alone to take care of your
> son's friend. Why must I be the one to take care of him? He is nothing
> to me.' (60)

The question which Mrs Curren asks here is a variant of Cain's response
to God's question concerning the whereabouts of Abel: "Am I my
brother's keeper?"[10] In commenting on Cain's response, Levinas makes
the point that it is grounded in the lack of ethics: "Cain's response is
sincere. Only the ethical is absent there; the answer is solely from ontology; I am I and he is he. We are beings ontologically separate."[11] Seen
from this perspective, Mrs Curren's indifference to John suggests the self-
interested (indeed, self-fortifying) and therefore conditional nature of her
hospitality. As in the case of her treatment of Vercueil, she places John at
a distance by naming and conceptualizing him from her subject position
in South African society, and this enables her to respond with a degree of
indifference to his plight.

So, ultimately, Coetzee's portrayal of Mrs Curren's indifference to
Vercueil and John suggests that what is absent from the South Africa
depicted in this novel is an ethic of generous hospitality. In his Jerusalem
Prize acceptance speech, Coetzee ascribes the debasement of human relations in South Africa to precisely a failure to care generously: "At the
heart of the unfreedom of the hereditary masters of South Africa is a

---

[10] *Authorised King James Version of the Holy Bible* (London: Collins, n.d.), Gen.
4:9.
[11] Quoted in Zygmunt Bauman, *Postmodern Ethics* (Oxford: Blackwell, 1993): 70.

failure of love. To be blunt: their love is not enough today and has not been enough since they arrived on the continent."[12] Being an order that tolerates the particular only as an example of the universal, South African society is characterized by the absence of the kind of love of which Coetzee speaks.

What one finds in *Age of Iron*, then, is a stark, yet full, depiction of the indigence and distortion of life under apartheid. It should be added that this novel, in its detailed evocation of South African society, is quite unusual in Coetzee's oeuvre. Probably for this reason, Jean–Philippe Wade, in commenting on *Age of Iron*'s realism, concludes that it is "free of any metafictional 'laying bare' of its devices."[13] To me, this seems a rather hasty inference, however. In depicting a society that has been brutalized by power relations, *Age of Iron* inevitably raises the deeply self-reflexive question of how to respond responsibly to what Adorno calls "damaged life."[14] After all, by reflecting "damaged life," the novel cannot but reflect on its position relative to that life; it must reflect on whether or not it reflects "damaged life" *from* "damaged life." In other words, the problem that Coetzee confronts in writing this novel is quite similar to the one that Adorno raises when he argues, in *Minima Moralia*, that, after the Holocaust, philosophy must view life from a messianic perspective: i.e. as damaged and deformed. "The only philosophy which can be responsibly practised in face of despair," he says, "is the attempt to contemplate all things as they would present themselves from the standpoint of redemption."[15] Adorno's argument appears to be that one can only really talk about what is "indigent and distorted" from a perspective that has not been contaminated by indigence and distortion.[16] In other words, thought must become autonomous; it must transcend what it thinks if it is truly to present the world as "indigent and distorted." But, as Adorno understands full well, thought is always already contaminated by the damaged life of

---

[12] Coetzee, "Jerusalem Prize Acceptance Speech," 97.

[13] Jean–Philippe Wade, "Doubling Back on J.M. Coetzee," *English in Africa* 21.1–2 (1994): 212.

[14] Theodor Adorno, *Minima Moralia: Reflections from Damaged Life*, tr. E.F.N. Jephcott (*Minima Moralia: Reflexionen aus dem beschädigten Leben*, 1951; London: Verso, 1978).

[15] Adorno, *Minima Moralia*, 247.

[16] *Minima Moralia*, 247.

which it thinks. Knowledge is part of the damaged life that must be revealed from the redemptive standpoint.

It seems to me that Coetzee was acutely aware of such problems in his writing of the late-apartheid period. Indeed, in his Jerusalem Prize acceptance speech, he comments on the implications for literary production of the deformation of the "inner life" of South Africans by the colonial "relations of contestation" in apartheid society:

> All expressions of that inner life, no matter how intense, no matter how pierced with exultation or despair, suffer from the same stuntedness and deformity. I make this observation with due deliberation, and in the fullest awareness that it applies to myself and my own writing as much as to anyone else. South African literature is a literature in bondage, as it reveals in even its highest moments, shot through as they are with feelings of homelessness and yearnings for a nameless liberation. It is a less than fully human literature, unnaturally preoccupied with power and the torsions of power, unable to move from elementary relations of contestation, domination, and subjugation to the vast and complex human world that lies beyond them. It is exactly the kind of literature you would expect people to write from a prison.[17]

The question that *Age of Iron* raises by the mere fact of its material existence is whether or not it is able to reflect damaged life from damaged life. My attempt to show how Coetzee scripts and then attempts to negotiate this issue forms the substance of the remainder of this chapter.

℘ ॰

Coetzee's concern with the inevitable deformity of his representation of damaged life is allusively staged in the development that Mrs Curren undergoes once she realizes that her identity has been inspired by the state and, accordingly, becomes increasingly dissatisfied with the forms of identification inscribed in history. Her response to this realization is directly articulated in the novel: "I want to sell myself, redeem myself, but am full of confusion about how to do it" (107). A little earlier, she expresses her desire to "rise above the times" (107) and, elsewhere, says that she does "not want to die in the state [she is] in, in a state of ugliness"

---

[17] Coetzee, "Jerusalem Prize Acceptance Speech," 98.

(124). The novel's meta-representational debate is related to this desire for self-redemption: indeed, as I proceed it will become clear that there is a very close analogy between self and text in this novel.

Initially, Mrs Curren considers committing suicide by self-immolation outside the Houses of Parliament in Cape Town. Her choice of the "House of Lies" as the locus for this gesture of protest indicates that her proposed suicide is a means of destroying the false self that she has been inspired to create by history (128), and of recovering the lost "child" that has been replaced with the "doll" that she calls "I" (100). For her, it would seem, suicide is not merely an act of self-annihilation, but one of self-redemption; it is part of her quest for the lost child. It is therefore understandable that once she starts planning this act of self-affirmation a "faint glow of pride" begins "to return" to her body, and "The crab" stops "gnawing" (106). As the following words by Mrs Curren indicate, the image of the crab is directly related to that of the doll, which signifies the artificiality of her state-inspired sense of self: "Were I to be opened up they would find me hollow as a doll, a doll with a crab sitting inside licking its lips" (103). Since the word 'cancer', in Latin, means 'crab', the suggestion is again that her illness should be construed as a metaphor for the contextual nature of her identity, the fact that the identity she has created has been inspired by history in the form of the state's "message."

Although Mrs Curren does not in the end burn herself to death, she has the following dream about it:

> I have had a dream of Florence, a dream or vision. In the dream I see her striding again down Government Avenue holding Hope by the hand and carrying Beauty on her back. All three of them wear masks. I am there too, with a crowd of people of all kinds and conditions gathered around me. The air is festive. I am to provide a show.
>
> But Florence does not stop to watch. Gaze fixed ahead, she passes as if through a congregation of wraiths.
>
> The eyes of her mask are like eyes in pictures from the ancient Mediterranean: large, oval, with the pupil in the centre: the almond eyes of a goddess.
>
> I stand in the middle of the avenue opposite the Parliament buildings, circled by people, doing my tricks with fire. Over me tower great oaks. But my mind is not on my tricks. I am intent on Florence. Her dark coat, her dull dress have fallen away. In a white slip ruffled by the wind, her feet bare, her head bare, her right breast bare, she strides

past, the one child, masked, naked, trotting quickly beside her, the
other stretching an arm out over her shoulder, pointing.

Who is this goddess who comes in a vision with uncovered breast
cutting the air? It is Aphrodite, but not smile-loving Aphrodite, patron-
ess of pleasures: an older figure, a figure of urgency, of cries in the
dark, short and sharp, of blood and earth, emerging for an instant,
showing herself, passing.

From the goddess comes no call, no signal. Her eye is open and is
blank. She sees and does not see.

Burning, doing my show, I stand transfixed. The flames flowing
from me are blue as ice. I feel no pain.

It is a vision from last night's dream-time but also from outside
time. Forever the goddess is passing, forever, caught in a posture of
surprise and regret, I do not follow. Though I peer and peer into the
vortex from which the visions come, the wake of the goddess and her
god-children remains empty, the woman who should follow behind not
there, the woman with serpents of flame in her hair who beats her arms
and cries and dances. (163–64)

The dream suggests the impossibility of redeeming self through this strategy. In it, Mrs Curren positions her "show" in relation to both Florence,
who is described as a goddess of war, and the South African parliament,
the implication being that her mode of self-redemption is itself inspired by
history and the conflictual relations that inform it. An important signal in
this regard is Mrs Curren's reflection that her act may be thought to have
been inspired by madness (105). In this context, madness is a metaphor
for the individual's possession by history. Before this reflection, on her
visit to Guguletu, where she witnesses the violent confrontation between
black township dwellers and the state, the same metaphor appears in the
following observation by her: "All of us running mad, possessed by
devils. When madness climbs the throne, who in the land escapes conta-
gion?" (97). And, a little later, after discussing with Vercueil her strategy
of self-redemption, she again refers to madness: "That, if you like, is the
craziness that has got into me. [...] You know this country. There is madness in the air here" (107). The suggestion is quite clear: having been
inspired by history, Mrs Curren's mode of self-redemption would not
recover her lost self, the abandoned child, but simply affirm, and so consolidate, her present self. Instead of distancing her from and protesting

against the "unnatural structures of power that define the South African state,"[18] it would merely confirm her implication in these structures.

Already implicit in Mrs Curren's desire for self-redemption, the novel's meta-representational debate on its worldliness emerges quite clearly in the above portrayal of her intended act of self-immolation as a "show." Earlier, she describes the act as one of "These public shows" (105), and likens her role in it to that of "a juggler, a clown, an entertainer" (129). This motif, together with a pointed allusion to Nathaniel Hawthorne's *The Scarlet Letter* and the suggestion that, like a literary work, the "show" will be open to multiple interpretations (105), indicates that the content of the dream should be seen as an image of literary production. If the "spectacle" is seen as such (129), then the relation, in the above passage, between it and both the mythological tableau representing Aphrodite in her aspect as a goddess of war and the Houses of Parliament should be construed as a figure for the relation of fiction to South Africa's political history during the 1980s.[19]

The point of this metafictional meditation emerges in Mrs Curren's inability to "follow" or pursue Florence and her children in her dream. She "stands transfixed," we read, and is "caught in a posture of surprise and regret," a description that echoes the earlier depiction of the impact on the individual of the message that the Gorgon-like state transmits through the medium of television. It will be remembered that this message is described as being able to "stupefy," to "stun with amazement" or, punningly, to "astonish" the individual: i.e. to turn him or her to stone. The parallels here imply that South African literature has been deformed by the state's structures of power. However, this literature is not simply the victim of the state's deforming drive. Since the portrayal of Mrs Curren as "the woman with serpents of flame in her hair" also associates her with the Gorgon Medusa,[20] the suggestion is that, having been deformed by the state's structures of power, South African literature, in its turn, proceeds to deform by reproducing the power relations installed by these structures. In so doing, it is both victim and perpetrator and therefore, despite its intention to the contrary, propagates the state's discourses by endorsing the

---

[18] Coetzee, "Jerusalem Prize Acceptance Speech," 97.
[19] See Brian Macaskill & Jeanne Colleran, "Interfering with 'The Mind of Apartheid'," *Pretexts* 4.1 (1992): 72.
[20] See Graves, *The Greek Myths*, 127.

stunted relations which they inscribe in society. Accordingly, this literature actively participates in its own deformation. It is part of the state's
"message."

It is because of South African literature's role in supplementing history
that its analogue in *Age of Iron*, Mrs Curren's show, is likened to trivial
forms of entertainment such as juggling. The fact that Florence ignores
the show indicates that this literature fails successfully to intervene in history. Its protest is not heeded because, ironically, it unintentionally pro-
motes rather than rivals the violence of history. A further implication of
Coetzee's critique here is that the novel *should* intervene in history but
that it should do so by changing rather than reproducing its deformed relations. This suggestion of an alternative role that literature might fulfil is
evident in the ambiguous description of Mrs Curren as having "serpents
of flame" in her hair. Apart from associating her with the Gorgon, this
depiction also alludes to the Furies, who, in Greek mythology, were represented as crones with snakes for hair. According to Robert Graves, it
was the Furies' task to hunt down perpetrators of crimes against society
and, in particular, to protect the filial bond: i.e. the very relationship
whose perversion is a feature of Hesiod's age of the iron race:

> Their task is to hear complaints brought by mortals against the in-
> solence of the young to the aged, of children to parents, of hosts to
> guests, and of householders or city councils to suppliants – and to
> punish such crimes by hounding the culprits relentlessly, without rest
> or pause, from city to city and from country to country.[21]

The description of Mrs Curren as "the woman who should follow behind" Florence and her daughters must be read in the context of this myth.
From these allusions, it may be inferred that, although the social role of
the novel in the South African age of iron should be to preserve the filial
bond and to promote hospitality by following, in the sense of pursuing,
the violators of these relations, it cannot perform this function, because it
follows history by supplementing the contestatory relations that have
generated it. Like Mrs Curren, it "stands transfixed," "caught in a posture
of surprise and regret."

---

[21] Graves, *The Greek Myths*, 122; see also 37–38.

How, then, to respond responsibly to damaged life? In "Into the Dark Chamber," Coetzee discusses the problem that faces the South African writer in representing violence in general and torture in particular. He makes the point that "there is something tawdry about *following* the state" in producing representations of its violence and thereby "making its vile mysteries the occasion of fantasy."[22] The obvious alternative to "looking on in horrified fascination as the blows fall" is, of course, "turning one's eyes away."[23] However, as he argues, this is not really a choice but a dilemma. The actual problem, he maintains, is "how to treat something that, in truth, because it is offered like the Gorgon's head to terrorize the populace and paralyze resistance, deserves to be ignored."[24] In order to negotiate this problem, the writer must work out how "*not* to allow himself to be impaled on the dilemma proposed by the state, namely, either to ignore its obscenities or else to produce representations of them." S/he must recognize the "true challenge": i.e. "how not to play the game by the rules of the state, how to establish one's own authority, how to imagine torture and death on one's own terms."[25]

It is, of course, precisely this representational problem of treating "something" which, "like the Gorgon's head," "paralyze[s] resistance" that is staged in *Age of Iron* in Mrs Curren's attempt to redeem herself. The scene that describes her visit to Guguletu self-reflexively presents the issue of representing violence that Coetzee addresses in "Into the Dark Chamber." On the one hand, the fact that she baulks at what she sees and expresses her desire to "go home" (90) articulates the possibility of ignoring the violence. On the other hand, Mr Thabane's question, "What sort of crime is it that you see? What is its name?" (90), asserts the apparently indubitable imperative to represent the violence. However, the seemingly fixed choice articulated by these two possible responses is complicated by Mrs Curren's answer to Mr Thabane's question: "These are terrible sights [...]. They are to be condemned. But I cannot denounce them in other

---

[22] Coetzee, "Into the Dark Chamber," 364.

[23] "Into the Dark Chamber," 368.

[24] "Into the Dark Chamber," 366.

[25] "Into the Dark Chamber," 364. This distinction between "following" the political and the "challenge" or imperative to discover "one's own terms" obviously rearticulates, albeit in a subtler form, the crude opposition, in "The Novel Today," between supplementing history and rivalling it through finding an autonomous place from which to speak with a degree of authority.

people's words. I must find my own words, from myself. Otherwise it is not the truth. [...] To speak of this [...] you would need the tongue of a god" (91). To invoke Adorno once more, Mrs Curren would have to speak "from the standpoint of redemption."

Being doubtful about philosophy's ability to contemplate "things" from such a standpoint, Adorno devoted much attention to the possibility of aesthetic autonomy offered by art. "Aesthetic identity," he states in the opening pages of *Aesthetic Theory*, "is meant to assist the non-identical in its struggle against the repressive identification compulsion that rules the outside world."[26] Being true to the opacity of an object, to the misalignment of thing and concept, the artwork can offer such assistance despite the fact that it is in the world.[27] For Adorno, as I have shown in this study, it is this "twofold essence" of the artwork,[28] its ambivalent position within and outside things, that invests it with a precarious autonomy which, in turn, enables it to criticize society. In the next two sections of this chapter, I again dwell on the importance of the notion of aesthetic autonomy to Coetzee's fictional project. In doing so, I do not try to argue that Coetzee speaks with "the tongue of a god," that he occupies the "standpoint of redemption." Nor do I even seek to counter Parry's argument that Coetzee fails to subvert the domination of European textual power in colonial discourse.[29] I merely show that the aesthetic's ability to relate to alterity, and thus to distance the work from itself and therefore from the "administered world," enables *Age of Iron* to attempt a responsible response to damaged life from its position within damaged life.

ᘒ ᘒ

In *Age of Iron*, the alternative to Mrs Curren's "show," which, as I have indicated, has been inspired by history, is her letter. The letter adumbrates the possibility of a mode of writing that, while located in history, tries to operate "in terms of its own procedures and issues."[30] Significantly, in this

---

[26] Adorno, *Aesthetic Theory*, 6.
[27] *Aesthetic Theory*, 8.
[28] *Aesthetic Theory*, 8.
[29] Benita Parry, "Speech and Silence in the Fictions of J.M. Coetzee," in *Writing South Africa: Literature, Apartheid, and Democracy*, ed. Derek Attridge & Rosemary Jolly (New York: Cambridge UP, 1998): 151.
[30] Coetzee, "The Novel Today," 3.

regard, the novel, and therefore the letter, opens with a passage containing images of childbirth. The first of these is found in Mrs Curren's description of her reaction to the "news" of her terminal condition:

> The news was not good, but it was mine, for me, mine only, not to be refused. It was for me to take in my arms and fold to my chest and take home, without headshaking, without tears. (3)

This unusual account is then followed by her equally strange description of her first encounter with Vercueil as "this other annunciation," which, of course, alludes to the angel Gabriel's annunciation of Christ's birth to the Virgin Mary (4). It is noteworthy that, in this instance, the metaphor of childbirth is accompanied by a set of allusions to the approach of the other. Mrs Curren describes Vercueil as homeless, a stranger, and "A visitor, visiting himself on me" (3) – in other words, in language similar to what Levinas and, later, Derrida, use to talk about the advent of the stranger.

Given the conjunction of conception and inspiration in Coetzee's writing, it is plausible to conclude that this passage juxtaposes two wholly different forms of inspiration. On the one hand, as I have already mentioned, the "news" that Mrs Curren receives of her cancerous condition signifies her inspiration and, in terms of the metaphor of madness, possession by history. The fact that this "news," and thereafter the tumours (59), is associated with childbirth implies that the product of this inspiration is her show. On the other hand, the encounter with the stranger alludes to inspiration from a source beyond history. The suggestion here is that "this other annunciation" is the cause of which her letter is the effect. To be sure, Mrs Curren starts her letter the day after she discovers Vercueil. Later, she says, "There is not only death inside me. There is life too," and elaborates as follows: "What is living inside me is something else, another word. And I am fighting for it, in my manner, fighting for it not to be stifled" (133). The letter is her attempt to bear this immaculately conceived word, to speak her own words, from herself. Importantly, this labour is directly related to her attempt to redeem herself, as is evident in the association of the stranger with the birth of Jesus Christ. Somehow or other, it seems, her encounter with Vercueil may save her by enabling her to "rise above the times," rather than "die in the state" she is in, "in a state of ugliness" (124). The suggestion is that, somehow or other, she may find it possible to respond to his particularity, to see him as he "really" is (165), and thereby particularize herself. From the first, then, Mrs Curren's letter-writing is directly related to her desire for salvation, her desire to reconstitute herself or, in terms of the dominant metaphor in this novel, to find the abandoned child.

The contrast that I have just drawn between history and autonomy, show and letter, in my reading of this passage is far too stark, however. Elsewhere, for instance, Mrs Curren, in describing her letter, refers to "Words vomited up from the belly of the whale, misshapen, mysterious" (128). They are "The *issue* of a shrunken heart" (my emphasis, 125), "tracings of the movements of *crabbed* digits over the page" (my emphasis, 120). In applying the motif of deformity and cancer to Mrs Curren's writing, Coetzee qualifies the distinction between letter and show. While the letter she writes may be inspired by a source outside history, the words in which it is couched are a part of history, part of the domain of the same which, in this novel, is figured as an age of iron: i.e. an order characterized by precisely its deformation of the other. Not surprisingly, then, the problem in *Age of Iron*, as in *Life & Times of Michael K* and *Foe*, is how to bear what is yet unborn. Mrs Curren suggests as much in this remark to Vercueil: "I have a child inside that I cannot give birth to. Cannot because it will not be born. Because it cannot live outside me. [...] It beats on the gate but it cannot leave" (75). Instead of a rigid opposition, what one finds in the novel's opening passage is a tension between the same and the other in which the first of these terms constantly threatens to engulf the second.

This, though, is an issue to which I return later in this chapter. Since the novel's opening passage suggests that Mrs Curren's relationship with Vercueil inspires her attempt to redeem herself and that this bid for salvation is directly related to her letter-writing, I must now elaborate on what I said earlier about this relationship. Although it is true that the hospitality she extends to Vercueil is at first conditional, Coetzee's subsequent depiction of this relationship indicates that, despite her various reservations about him, and the degree to which they limit her generosity, Mrs Curren is eventually deeply affected, and therefore changed, by her encounter with this stranger. Initially reserved, her hospitality becomes unconditional. The most obvious signal in this regard is her ultimate failure to turn Vercueil into a gardener. Importantly, this failure is implied by her comparison of herself to Circe and of Vercueil to Odysseus: in the myth, Circe is of course unable to turn Odysseus into a pig, because Hermes has provided him with an antidote to her spell in the form of the herb moly. The question raised by Coetzee's use of this mythological analogue is why it should be that Mrs Curren is unable to transform Vercueil. How does he resist her spell? What is his moly?

Age of Iron answers this indirect question obliquely through a web of references and allusions to Leo Tolstoy's "What Men Live By," a story about a poor shoemaker who provides sustenance to a naked stranger who eventually turns out to be an angel.[31] Vercueil, as we have seen, is from the first associated with angels, and this characterization is sustained throughout the novel. Shortly before referring to the Tolstoy story, Mrs Curren remarks of Vercueil, "Not an angel, certainly" (12), and a little later elaborates:

> What chance is there, if I take a walk down Mill Street, of finding my own angel to bring home and succour? None, I think. Perhaps in the countryside there are still one or two sitting against milestones in the heat of the sun, dozing, waiting for what chance will bring. Perhaps in the squatter camps. But not in Mill Street, not in the suburbs. The suburbs, deserted by the angels. When a ragged stranger comes knocking at the door he is never anything but a derelict, an alcoholic, a lost soul. Yet how, in our hearts, we long for these sedate homes of ours to tremble, as in the story, with angelic chanting! (13)

It should be noted that this passage alludes not only to "What Men Live By" but also to its intertextual antecedent, the famous Pauline injunction on hospitality: "Be not forgetful to entertain strangers: for thereby some have entertained angels unawares."[32] Coetzee's interest in Tolstoy's story is clearly related to its thematizing of unconditional hospitality.

In "What Men Live By," the purpose of the angel's visit is to *learn* what it is that sustains humankind. His encounter with the shoemaker teaches him that "though it seems to men that they live by care for themselves, in truth it is love alone by which they live."[33] On the one hand, the allusions to this short story in Coetzee's novel point to the difference be-

---

[31] See Yeoh, "Love and Indifference in J.M. Coetzee's *Age of Iron.*"
[32] *Authorised King James Version of the Holy Bible,* Heb. 13:2.
[33] Leo Tolstoy, "What Men Live By" (1885), in *Twenty-Three Tales,* tr. Louise & Aylmer Maude (London: Oxford UP, 1906): 81.

tween Tolstoy's shoemaker's selfless generosity and Mrs Curren's grudg-
ing charity in their respective encounters with a stranger. Initially, at least,
as I have already shown, the encounter between Mrs Curren and Vercueil
indicates the former's seeming inability to love and care unconditionally.
Unlike the house in Tolstoy's story, hers, we have seen, is "without love."
In terms of the Pauline injunction, Mrs Curren is guilty of poor hospitality.

On the other hand, the intertextual contrast between these two narratives may function proleptically by suggesting that Mrs Curren *will* ultimately learn what it is that "men live by." If this is so, Coetzee's novel
will have altered the teacher–student relationship in Tolstoy's story by
suggesting that it is Mrs Curren who learns from the stranger and not
simply the stranger who learns from her. In the process, the novel's
allusive substructure will have indicated why it is that Mrs Curren does
not, or cannot, transform Vercueil. That is, it will have indicated that she
learns from him a lesson of love that precludes her from foreclosing on his
difference.

In my view, Coetzee's allusions to the Tolstoy story serve precisely
such a proleptic purpose. After returning home from a visit to the hospital,
Mrs Curren is followed into her house by Vercueil. We read that he enters
her home "Uninvited" (74), a description that later recurs in her reference
to him as "A man who came without being invited" (165). The house in
question is, of course, the very one that has previously only been entered
by the state's message. I have shown that this, together with Mrs Curren's
installation of burglar bars, metaphorizes the way in which the self's location in the cultural domain secures it from the danger of difference. What
is at stake here is the integument or uncrossable boundary formed by
intentional consciousness between the culturally embedded subject and
difference. At one point in the novel, Mrs Curren, in pondering the paradox of the ugliness of a "not unattractive" woman she sees, ascribes the
person's ugliness to "A thickening of the membrane between the world
and the self inside," an integument that has been erected out of fear "that
light, air, life itself were going to gather and strike her" (116). It is just this
fear of exposure to otherness that is symbolized by Mrs Curren's fortifi-
cation of her home.

Proceeding as it does from the expectations attendant on her location in
the cultural domain, the kind of hospitality that Mrs Curren initially offers
Vercueil can only ever be conditional. As I have indicated, she knows him

in advance. It is precisely owing to the conditional nature of hospitality that Levinas frequently associates the other with a burglar. It will be recalled that, in the first chapter of this study, I indicated that, according to Levinas, the other, to approach "me," must not "knock," but "assign[] me before I designate him" or her.[34] Indeed, "my" "assignation" by the other "is entry into me by burglary." The other's otherness "slips into me 'like a thief' through the outstretched nets of consciousness." Possession by the other, Levinas continues, is "non-phenomenal," "beyond representation," "unbeknownst to myself, 'slipping into me like a thief'."[35]

When read in the context of Levinas' description of the approach of the other, Vercueil's uninvited entry into Mrs Curren's house connotes the opening-up of the self to the otherness of the other person, its infiltration of the self's consciousness. This is further implied by Mrs Curren's thought on watching Vercueil eat the bread she has given him: "My mind like a pool, which his finger enters and stirs. Without that finger stillness, stagnation. [...] His dirty fingernail entering me" (74). In entering her house, Vercueil enters Mrs Curren. Indeed, the sexual innuendo in the passage suggests the usual confluence in Coetzee's writing of sexual activity and inspiration. What is figured here is the self's assignation and possession by the other.

In being invaded and possessed by Vercueil's otherness, Mrs Curren is dispossessed of self. It is through this forfeiture or surrender of self that she learns to love. Her experience with Vercueil, as is implied by the following words to her daughter, involves a form of *ek-stasis*: "Letting go of myself, letting go of you, letting go of a house still alive with memories: a hard task, but I am learning" (119). This reference to a "letting go" of self, of course, brings to mind the strong emphasis on "yielding" and "losing" self in *Waiting for the Barbarians, Life & Times of Michael K*, and *Foe*. That is, it connotes the form of responsibility that comes with an effacement of self before the other. Just such a generous substitution of self for the other person is implicit in Mrs Curren's gift of bread to Vercueil. The allusion here to the Eucharist is, of course, apposite: the kind of generosity at stake in responsibility involves precisely a *sacrifice* of self. In *Otherwise Than Being*, Levinas resorts to similar imagery in making this point: "To give, to-be-for-another, despite oneself, [...] is to take the bread out

---

[34] Levinas, *Otherwise Than Being*, 102, 87.
[35] *Otherwise Than Being*, 145, 148, 150.

of one's own mouth, to nourish the hunger of another with one's fasting" (56; see also 142). Since it is done "despite oneself," the willing offering of bread is an act of self-effacement, even self-sacrifice.

Coetzee's allusions to Tolstoy's story therefore do finally suggest that Mrs Curren learns from the stranger.[36] In the process, they also indicate the nature of the latter's moly: Mrs Curren is finally unable to metamorphose Vercueil because she is inspired by his otherness. Her attempt to transform him is resisted by his alterity, which, through its possession of her, enables love – here conceived of as a movement of infinition from same to other. Ironically, then, she changes in trying to change Vercueil. What is more, this change takes the form of a liberation: through her encounter with Vercueil's alterity, she is freed from her claustrophobic imprisonment in herself, the same, history. In *Age of Iron*, as in *In the Heart of the Country*, the figure for this self-entrapment is the house: as I have noted, Mrs Curren refers to her house as a "cage" in which she is "locked up" (25), and later describes herself as "a woman in a burning house running from window to window, calling through the bars for help" (170).

Importantly, too, Mrs Curren's liberation is not the result of a conscious decision: it comes unbidden. One of the ways in which Coetzee makes this point is through his allusive presentation of this character's development. She, the narrator and focalizer of the novel, does not know that Vercueil has affected her in the manner I have described and, consequently, cannot narrate the event of her inspiration. Her inability to do so is precisely the point. Since she is not conscious of (indeed, cannot be conscious of) having been possessed by Vercueil's alterity, she cannot know, rationally grasp, what has happened to her. By means of his management of point of view, then, Coetzee dramatizes this character's loss of control over her visitor's otherness.

A further way in which Coetzee indicates the unconscious nature of the change that Mrs Curren undergoes is through his ironic emphasis (an emphasis that is equally strong in his later works) on the notion of learning. Mrs Curren 'learns' to love; she undertakes the 'task' of "letting go." Nevertheless, the kind of learning here at stake is obviously not a rational process, one over which the self can exercise control. After all, one cannot control one's 'letting-go' of self, one's loss of control over self. Mrs Curren learns *despite herself*. While learning is certainly an action, it is de-

---

[36] Cf. Yeoh, "Love and Indifference in J.M. Coetzee's *Age of Iron*," 107.

picted in *Age of Iron* as an action attendant on the self's forfeiture of self. In a sense, it is an action that refuses the possessive case; one that results from precisely the passivity to which the self is reduced in its encounter with the other.

Finally, as in *Waiting for the Barbarians*, where the Magistrate's relationship to the barbarian girl mediates his other relations, we find in this novel that the lesson of love which Mrs Curren learns is not limited to her relationship with Vercueil but also affects her interactions with the other characters in the novel. In assuming responsibility for Vercueil, it seems, she assumes responsibility for all. Significantly, in this regard, her attitude to John changes dramatically in the course of the narrative. Her initial resentment at having had to "take care" of him after the first police attack gives way to what sounds very much like an ethical imperative:

> I must love, first of all, the unlovable. I must love, for instance, this child. Not bright little Bheki, but this one. He is here for a reason. He is part of my salvation. I must love him. But I do not love him. Nor do I want to love him enough to love him despite myself.
>
> It is because I do not with a full enough heart want to be otherwise that I am still wandering in a fog.
>
> I cannot find it in my heart to love, to want to love, to want to want to love. (125)

The movement of love is an irreversible one from the self to the other.[37] Accordingly, as Mrs Curren here intuits, *her* feelings for John are entirely inconsequential. If anything, she must love him *because* she finds him unlovable. She must love her neighbour not as herself, but despite herself. Tellingly, Mrs Curren does find it in her heart to love John. A little later in the novel, while trying to protect him from yet another police attack, she reflects as follows: "He was lost [...]. I ached to embrace him, to protect him" (139).

By the end of *Age of Iron*, Mrs Curren's relationship with Vercueil in her dilapidated old house has come to enact the conclusion reached by Tolstoy's angel that "men" live not by care for themselves but by "love alone." It should be noted, in this respect, that it is not simply Mrs Curren

---

[37] See Attridge, *J.M. Coetzee and the Ethics of Reading*, 93.

but Vercueil, too, who 'learns' to love in the course of the novel.[38] When
Mrs Curren is at her most vulnerable: i.e. about to be violated by the street
children under a flyover, she is rescued by Vercueil, who then carries her
to safety (146). In a manner reminiscent of the Sinbad image in *Foe*, the
burden-image here signifies Vercueil's assumption of responsibility for
the weak and helpless other. He becomes his sister's keeper. A little later,
Mrs Curren suggests as much in explaining the nature of their relationship
to a policeman: "Mr Vercueil takes care of me" (157). Through being
affected by her, Vercueil 'learns' to love. Mrs Curren, who for much of
the novel has wondered why it should be that Vercueil has "chosen" her,
now realizes that he did not "choose" her and neither did she "choose"
him – that it is, in fact, the alterity of each that has affected the other:

> It is not he who fell under my care when he arrived, I now understand,
> nor I who fell under his: we fell under each other, and have tumbled
> and risen since then in the flights and swoops of that mutual election.
> (179).

So, even though it does not quite ring with "angelic chanting" (13), Mrs
Curren's house does ultimately becomes a house of love, a locus of selfless hospitality in a society at war. In short, it is an island of sorts, an
"autonomous place" insulated from the war in the society in which it is
nonetheless located. Although very similar in this respect to the island settings in *Life & Times of Michael K* and *Foe*, the image of the house in *Age
of Iron* is, if anything, more effective because of its location *in* a society in
the throes of civil war. Given its suburban location, the house is a potent
image not only of what is not yet in South African society, but also of
what is not outside this society, of what the age of iron has not been able
to exclude.

ᛟ ॐ

My argument is that *Age of Iron* seeks to contrive a relationship with the
reader that is mirrored from within the novel by the image of Mrs Curren's house. If it manages to do so, this text will reflect the damaged life
of apartheid society from a position that is both within (i.e. implicated in)

---

[38] Cf. Yeoh "Love and Indifference in J.M. Coetzee's *Age of Iron*," 107; and Attridge, *J.M. Coetzee and the Ethics of Reading*, 101.

and outside (i.e. independent of) that life. This novel's self-reflexive meditation on the way in which such an autonomous position would afford it the possibility of engaging, albeit affectively, with the distorted relations that have shaped South African society is the subject of the rest of this chapter. While my argument in this respect harks back to my discussion of *Foe*'s prefiguring of its reception by the reader, my emphasis now falls on how Coetzee, in *Age of Iron*, develops the idea of an affective engagement with apartheid history.

The house in *Age of Iron* is an image both of the self and of Mrs Curren's letter, which, in turn, seeks to become an image not so much of the novel as of an encounter between it and the reader which takes the form of an "event" in which the reader not only acts but is acted upon by the text.[39] Mrs Curren, I have pointed out, takes up the letter to her daughter in response to having been inspired by her encounter with Vercueil's otherness. Her letter-writing, as is connoted by the metaphors of birth and maternity, is an attempt to bear the alterity of which she has become host. It is, in fact, her attempt to find the lost child, the one that, to use her figure, was stolen from the cradle, and of which she is merely a distorted representation. Like Susan Barton's writing in *Foe*, Mrs Curren's epistolary endeavour is imaged as a labour, an attempt to bring the other into being, to accommodate it in the same, in history. As I have noted, however, Mrs Curren reflects on the deformity of her words, is suspicious of language's ability to achieve this end. Notwithstanding these reservations, her responsibility for the other obliges her to make a home for it of the language of her letter. To be responsible for the other obliges one to ensure that the same accommodates it. Mrs Curren's letter must therefore host the visitor of which she is the host.

This character must do more than this, however. In addition to questioning the ability of language to accommodate the other, the device of the letter self-reflexively points to its own reception. A letter, after all, presupposes a reader. Mrs Curren's obligation to make her letter accommodate the other thus involves making sure that the reader of the letter responds responsibly to the otherness that it may accommodate. The problem here is, of course, that the reader is located in the same, the age of iron, which, by definition, excludes the other, is capable only of condi-

---

[39] See Attridge, *The Singularity of Literature*, 58–62; and his *J.M Coetzee and the Ethics of Reading*, xii, 39–40.

tional hospitality. It is for this reason that Coetzee depicts the reader of the letter somewhat ambiguously: indeed, Mrs Curren's daughter is portrayed as both the "beloved" (118) and "like iron" (68), caught up in the deformed relations in the country she has left. She has "grown strange" (127), and has abandoned her mother. In terms of this depiction, the intended recipient of the letter is uncomfortably close to its unintended recipients: namely, the police who read it on raiding Mrs Curren's house. When she reflects on this "visit" (154), Mrs Curren imagines "Soiled fingers turning the pages, eyes without love going over the naked words" (154). In fact, the uninvited visit these strangers pay the text is likened to rape: "The true purpose the touching, the fingering. The spirit malevolent. Like rape: a way of filthying a woman" (154). Being located in the same, its reader is incapable of responding responsibly to the otherness that the letter desires to host. Strictly speaking, then, Mrs Curren can have no such expectation of her reader. On the contrary, what she *can* expect is violence.

Why, then, does she go on? "The rest," as she says, in an allusion to *Hamlet*, "should be silence" (149). The obvious answer to this question is that this character's responsibility for the other she bears means that she has no choice but to continue. She is a "secretary of the invisible." Acted upon by this alterity, she must "follow the pen," go "where it takes" her (99; see also 102). There is, however, more at stake here. At one point in the novel, Mrs Curren addresses her daughter not as she is in her present state, but as she was before being deformed by the relations of power in history, and as she may yet become, were she to transcend this context:

> you are with me not as you are today in America, not as you were
> when you left, but as you are in some deeper and unchanging form: as
> the beloved, as that which does not die. (118)

Although addressed to its reader in the present of reading, the letter *apostrophizes* her other possible self, the invisible one that has yet to come into being. The letter is addressed not just to the child of iron, but to what the child of iron prevents from emerging and, in fact, deforms. It is addressed to what cannot be born but refuses to die. By extension, the letter is addressed to what its reader would be, were she to "rise above the times." The "beloved" apostrophized by the letter is this stranger, the stranger that Mrs Curren's daughter may become.

It follows that the letter is inspired not simply by Vercueil's otherness but by the alterity of its addressee. As it happens, Mrs Curren's daughter and Vercueil are closely aligned throughout the novel. In a particularly insightful reading of *Age of Iron*, Thangam Ravindranathan points out that "Mrs Curren's rationale for accepting him [namely, Vercueil] in her house": i.e. to nurse and nurture him, "is one that makes of him a surrogate child."[40] Also, when Vercueil arrives, it is in the alley where her daughter used to play, "In the place hitherto occupied by the daughter."[41] To some extent, then, Vercueil and Mrs Curren's daughter are interchangeable. They – which is to say, the invisible child – inspire Mrs Curren's letter. To be sure, the letter is a reply or response to this alterity. So, for instance, it is depicted as Mrs Curren's performance of her responsibility to her reader – her gift of her self to her daughter. What this portrayal, in turn, suggests is that Mrs Curren has been invaded and taken over by this stranger. In the following passage, she describes her metamorphosis into the letter she gives her daughter:

> So day by day I render myself into words and pack the words into the page like sweets: like sweets for my daughter, for her birthday, for the day of her birth. Words out of my body, drops of myself, for her to unpack in her own time, to take in, to suck, to absorb. As they say on the bottle: old-fashioned drops, drops fashioned by the old, fashioned and packed with love, the love we have no alternative but to feel toward those to whom we give ourselves to devour or discard. (8)

The generous "giving of self" to the other here evident is also implicit in Mrs Curren's aforementioned statement: "This is my life, these words, these tracings of the movement of crabbed digits over the page" (120). Since it serves as a *mise en abyme* of Coetzee's relationship with his reader, Mrs Curren's relationship with her daughter suggests that the novel is structured as the writer's generous substitution of himself for the reader. It is the very medium through which this substitution takes place, and thus the means by which the writer structures himself as responsibility for the reader.

---

[40] Thangam Ravindranathan, "*Amor Matris*: Language and Loss in J.M. Coetzee's *Age of Iron*," *Safundi: The Journal of South African and American Studies* 8.4 (2007): 398.

[41] Ravindranathan, "*Amor Matris*," 398.

The act of radical self-effacement figured by the structuring of the novel as a gift to the reader is also alluded to by the latent image of bread in the above quotation. The sentence, "This is my life, these words," invokes Christ's words at the Last Supper and the liturgical formulae of the Eucharist. In so doing, this sentence also echoes Mrs Curren's gift of bread to Vercueil. What is here at stake is again the notion of unconditional care. In fact, the etymological root of 'Eucharist', which derives in part from *caris* 'to care', suggests as much; to care is to love *despite oneself*, to sacrifice oneself without calculation or expectation of recompense or return. To care is to sacrifice oneself beyond an economy of sacrifice.[42] In this regard, it should be recalled that Mrs Curren's gift is addressed to an otherness within her daughter that is waiting to come into being. From this potential recipient, who is yet to come, she cannot expect anything in return. As it is, her gift, can only be received by this stranger after her death. The letter, and by extension the novel, is thus presented as a site of unconditional hospitality: it signifies the writer's forfeiture of self in being taken over by the reader's otherness.

Coetzee, however, takes this logic of responsibility a step further. After equating her life with the words of her letter, Mrs Curren continues as follows: "These words, as you read them, if you read them, enter you and draw breath again" (120). In entering the text, the reader: i.e. the child "like iron," may be exposed to, and thus entered by, the strangeness of the stranger that Mrs Curren has *become* and which the text hosts *despite itself*. This expectation of the letter, hence of the novel, is further apparent in the motif of inspiration. Before her invocation of the Eucharist, Mrs Curren writes the following to her daughter:

> Like a moth from its case emerging, fanning its wings: that is what, reading, I hope you will glimpse: my soul readying itself for further flight. [...] And after that, after the dying? Never fear, I will not haunt you. There will be no need to close the windows and seal the chimney to keep the white moth from flapping in during the night and settling on your brow or on the brow of one of the children. The moth is simply what will brush your cheek ever so lightly as you put down the

---

[42] See Derrida's discussion of the economy of sacrifice in *The Gift of Death*, tr. David Wills (*Donner la mort in L'ethique du don: Jacques Derrida et la pensée du don*, 1992; Chicago: U of Chicago P, 1995): 82–115. A sacrifice beyond an economy of sacrifice would, of course, involve a movement of infinition from same to other.

> last page of this letter, before it flutters off on its next journey. It is not
> my soul that will remain with you but the spirit of my soul, the breath,
> the stirring of the air about these words, the faintest of turbulence
> traced in the air by the ghostly passage of my pen over the paper your
> fingers now hold. (118–19)

In this passage, the self that is becoming text is further metaphorized as spirit, breath. The allusion here to the representation in Greek mythology of the soul as a butterfly emerging from a dying person's mouth is made quite explicit by Mrs Curren's reference to "A white moth, a ghost emerging from the mouth of the figure on the deathbed" (118), and recurs in the final sentence of the novel, in which Mrs Curren, quite impossibly, records her death: "[Vercueil] took me in his arms and held me with mighty force, so that the breath went out of me in a rush" (181). With her death, Mrs Curren metamorphoses into spirit, breath, text. Indeed, this association is drawn clearly enough in her description of herself in bed together with Vercueil: "We share a bed, folded one upon the other like a page folded in two, like two wings folded" (173). By expiring: i.e. being metamorphosed into a moth and therefore breath, Mrs Curren, the text, is able to inspire her reader.

In reading the novel, the reader is exposed to what is invisible, "the stirring of the air" about the words. S/he is exposed to the caress of the air disturbed by the pages of the text. What Coetzee seems to be suggesting is that, although hostile to the other, and therefore to love, language may, despite itself, serve as an attenuated vehicle thereof. Although wholly unreliable, it may, again despite itself, become the messenger of the writer's message of love. When she decides to write her letter of love to her daughter, Mrs Curren draws the following distinction:

> In another world I would not need words. I would appear on your
> doorstep. 'I have come for a visit,' I would say, and that would be the
> end of words: I would embrace you and be embraced. (8)

"But in this world, in this time," she continues, "I must reach out to you in words" (8). In this passage, we find not a mutually exclusive opposition between caress and language, but a recognition that the latter, although ill-equipped to do so, may impart a sense of the former. After all, Mrs Curren still attempts to "reach out" to her daughter: i.e. to embrace her, even though she has to do so through the distancing medium of language.

Notwithstanding the fact that the "current of love" which "course[d]" through the hand with which she once caressed her daughter has been reduced to the "love" which "flickers and trembles like St Elmo's fire" in "every *you*" written by the hand of the writing subject (53, 118), it is still liminally there. Through its insubstantial, ghostly, spiritual nature, the fact that it is, properly speaking, neither present in nor absent from the text, this gift of love may inspire the reader when s/he reads *Age of Iron*. Should the reader be exposed to this otherness upon visiting the text, s/he will, quite involuntarily, become its host. The text will have achieved or, more accurately, become the occasion of "a mutual election" (179): in opening itself to the reader's otherness, it will have exposed the reader to the otherness of which it is the involuntary host.

Age of Iron thus seeks to achieve what cannot be achieved, what could only happen despite itself, irrespective of its intentions. That is, this novel strives to become the site of a "mutual election" in its relationship with the reader: it attempts to expose the reader to what is beyond the same and thereby save him or her from claustrophobic self-entrapment. Put in terms of the child-motif, the text tries to pass the burden of the unborn to the reader and thereby engender in him or her the kind of restless dissatisfaction with his or her present construction of self that Mrs Curren evinces throughout the novel. Like Mrs Curren, the reader thus inspired will not wish to die in "a state of ugliness": his or her desire for the unborn will lead to a constant betrayal of the forms in history through which s/he has constructed him-/herself. And, in restlessly attempting to bear the unborn, to find forms more adequate to that task, s/he will attempt to redeem and save him-/herself. The child "like iron" will "want to be otherwise" (125), to become the beloved stranger to whom Mrs Curren's letter, and therefore the novel, is addressed. Should the novel manage to inspire in the reader such a desire for an other self, one that is yet to emerge, it will have inspired love, which is to say, responsibility for the unborn. The text will have been, and this, too, is, of course, suggested by the image of the Eucharist, a saviour of sorts: in sacrificing himself to what the reader is not yet, the writer will have inspired the reader to sacrifice him-/herself as well.

The social effect of such a "mutual election" is allusively projected by the novel's stock of metaphors. For example, the text itself, it now becomes clear, is the moly that could preserve the reader from the Circe-like state's brutalizing spell, its "message" of power. I pointed out earlier in this chapter that Mrs Curren, on observing the metamorphic effect of the state-induced violence in Guguletu, wonders where "the herb" may be found "that will preserve us" from this spell (95). The novel seeks not only to perform this function but also to reverse the spell. By extension, the text aspires to have the same effect on the reader that Vercueil has on Mrs Curren: in inspiring love, it will make him or her act against the deformed and deforming relations of history. Simply put, the novel attempts to rival history.

Coetzee's depiction of Mrs Curren's letter as a Fury develops this idea. In an allusion to the Fury's task of accusing and persecuting the violators of filial piety and inadequate hospitality by, again to quote Graves, pursuing them "relentlessly, without rest or pause, from city to city and from country to country," Mrs Curren first "accuses" her daughter of filial impiety and then anticipates her response to her letter: "*I do not need this* you say to yourself through gritted teeth: *this is what I came here to get away from, why does it have to follow me?*" (127, 178). Earlier, I showed that the South African literature that supplements history by producing representations of the state's violent actions is represented in the novel by the ambiguous portrayal of Mrs Curren as a Gorgon or Fury *manqué* who is unable to "follow" Florence and her children. By contrast, *Age of Iron*, as the self-representational device of the letter indicates, is able not only to follow but also to pursue and harass those who follow the state in having been deformed by its "message." In invading and possessing the reader, this novel, like the Furies, persecutes and maddens the children of iron. In fact, it cannot *not* do this: possessed as it is by the reader it has possessed, the novel both obediently follows *and* despotically persecutes him or her. In terms of the notion of a "mutual election," it is mastered and burdened by what it masters and burdens. Its intervention in history is therefore not by design but by *a*ffect. The image of the Furies, that is to say, points to the performative nature of Coetzee's text's engagement with history: its rivalry with the state's message is grounded in the event of possession which makes of it, and indeed the reader, a protector of the unborn, of what the forms of history deform.

Collectively, these images seem to express the novel's refusal to posit history as an *a priori* structure, and its desire, instead, to rival history by mediating and justifying the distorted relations of power in the social domain. Yet, even as they moot the possibility of such an affective engagement with history, these metaphors, thanks to their ambivalence and ambiguity, query it.

Presented as a message, *Age of Iron* is a novel about messages and messengers. It is also about the possibility of the messenger's betraying the message. Mrs Curren entrusts her letter to Vercueil, who is depicted not just as Odysseus but also as Hermes, the messenger of the gods and bearer of moly. Besides, as I have shown, Vercueil is throughout the text likened to angels: i.e. divine messengers. Nevertheless, Mrs Curren herself calls this characterization into question when she decides that he is "No Odysseus, no Hermes, perhaps not even a messenger" (128). In the process, she considers the nature of the trust that she must place in him: "I give my life to Vercueil, because I do not trust Vercueil. [...] Because he is the weak reed I lean upon him" (120). Mrs Curren must trust the untrustworthy.[43]

Like Vercueil, the novel itself, which, I have noted, is not so much a message as a messenger of sorts, cannot be trusted. In placing his trust in the text, Coetzee questions its trustworthiness, its ability to do what he trusts it to do, by bathetically associating it with winged creatures of a rather different order from angels and Furies. While the novel *should* be like Hermes, the bearer of moly, an angel announcing the birth of a saviour, a Fury persecuting those guilty of filial impiety and poor hospitality, it turns out to be more like a moth. Accordingly, whenever the word "hover" is used, this ambiguity intrudes and so questions the novel's ability to protect the unborn, to be its guardian angel. Such a moment may be found in the scene in which Mrs Curren, after having attempted unsuccessfully to protect John from the police, one of whom she turns on "in a fury" (139), imagines following John and being with him in his final moments (159–60). She "hovers" over him, attempting to protect him; but the child is already dead.[44]

Coetzee's point, in foregrounding this ambivalence, is that the novel's engagement with history is not premised on action. While "The times call for heroism" (151), for heroic deeds, the novel does not possess

---

[43] See Attridge's insightful discussion of the form of trust that is staged in this novel in *J.M. Coetzee and the Ethics of Reading*, 91–112.

[44] See Ravindranathan, *"Amor Matris*," 399; and Ian Duncan, "Narrative Authority in J.M. Coetzee's *Age of Iron*," *Tydskrif vir Letterkunde* 43.2 (2006): 180.

"heroic status" (151). Like Mrs Curren, in her abortive attempt to "protect" John, it has "no power" to "save" and "protect" (139). Instead, it must rely on the possibility of an affective engagement with the times. Its only way of intervening in history, in other words, is through its 'ability', despite itself, to affect the reader, despite him-/herself. Its intervention, this is to say, is grounded in precisely a *loss* of power, of ability.

When Coetzee places his trust in the novel's 'ability' to convey his message of love, he is therefore quite literally trusting its untrustworthiness. He is trusting that its *inability* either to instantiate or to eliminate the message of love with which it has been entrusted will result in the reader's being exposed to this message on reading the novel. What is more, he trusts that, through this exposure, should it take place, the reader will be affected in the way projected in the text. This is the "wager on trust" on which the entire novel is premissed (119). As in *Foe*, Coetzee, in this novel, attempts to predict the unpredictable, to calculate the incalculable, to control the uncontrollable. Even as he does so, however, he is eminently aware of the keen irony involved: he invests *Age of Iron* with the knowledge that it expects what it, in fact, desires, that desire, unlike expectation which is grounded in a degree of foreknowledge, inscribes a relation to the unknown and therefore to what is ultimately uncontrollable and unpredictable. If what this novel desires should happen, it will have been unexpected.

In *Age of Iron*, one encounters Coetzee's fullest exposition of the notion of an affective engagement with damaged life under apartheid. More so than any of its predecessors, this novel explores, albeit cautiously, the potential social effects of such an engagement. At the same time, as I have just emphasized, the text questions what it suggests: at best, it presents the possibility of an affective engagement with apartheid history as an impossible possibility, a possibility that could only arise by default. Still, we once more find Coetzee, in this work, attempting to use the other, to put to use the other that he has, in fact, attempted to lay a trap for in his writing. Since the effects of this strategy are simply not empirically verifiable, this writer can only rely on trust and the rueful knowledge that even if his plan were to work, he would not know that it had.

When I say that *Age of Iron* provides us with a detailed reflection on the possibility of an affective engagement with apartheid history, it may sound as though I am claiming that the ethic of writing that I have outlined thus far in this study is peculiar only to Coetzee's writing of the apartheid period. This is not what I wish to imply. While the ethic in question is one that was developed in this period, there is no particular reason why it should have changed with the end of apartheid. Given the nature of Coetzee's understanding of ethics and aesthetics, history is by definition conceived of fairly generally as the realm of language, the order of the same, the domain of subjective possibility and action. Although configurations of the same certainly do change, these new configurations must in turn be interrupted. The same is thus in constant need of interruption. If this is so, it should follow that Coetzee's post-apartheid writing will be not substantially different from his apartheid-era or Australian writing. We should find in, say, *Slow Man*, the same restless responsibility that is thematized in *Age of Iron* and, indeed, even earlier in *Waiting for the Barbarians*. In the next chapter, I begin to test this thesis in a reading of *The Master of Petersburg*, which was written after the release of Nelson Mandela and the unbanning of the African National Congress and published in 1994: i.e. the year in which South Africa held its first democratic elections.

ᘖ ᘛ

5 The Writing of a Madman
⚭ *The Master of Petersburg*

I N *THE MASTER OF PETERSBURG*, the character Dostoevsky is
torn between the demands of history and those of a 'force' that
exceeds history and which is represented by the trope of death. As is
apparent in the parallel between his meeting with Councillor Maximov,
the state functionary,[1] and his various meetings with Sergei Nechaev, the
revolutionary (95–107, 117–22, 174–203), the realm of history is shaped
by an economy of contestation, of the reciprocity of retribution. Ostensibly, the choice with which Dostoevsky is presented in these encounters
is a relatively straightforward one: i.e. between endorsing state oppression
and supporting revolutionary change.[2] However, in a manner reminiscent
of Mrs Curren's decision not to immolate herself in protest against the
apartheid government in *Age of Iron*, Dostoevsky declines this choice.

He explains his reluctance to continue his association with the revolutionaries in terms of a desire to resist being "poisoned by vengefulness"
and thus to maintain a degree of autonomy (111). The implication here is
that he does not wish to occupy a position of rivalry in a binary opposition, one that would predispose him to respond to others in generic terms
and, by extension, predispose others to respond to him similarly. Simply
put, he does not want to be a term in one of the conflictual relations out of
which history "erects" itself.[3] Instead, it seems, he desires something beyond the reach of history. Just such a wish is articulated when, after

---

[1] Coetzee, *The Master of Petersburg*, 31–49. Unless otherwise indicated, further
page references are in the main text.

[2] See Monica Popescu, "Waiting for the Russians: Coetzee's *The Master of Petersburg* and the Logic of Late Postcolonialism," *Current Writing: Text and Reception in
Southern Africa* 19.1 (2007): 3.

[3] Coetzee, "The Novel Today," 3.

noting that Anna Sergeyevna sees his "lack of zeal" about meeting with Nechaev as "apathy," Dostoevsky reflects as follows:

> To make her understand he would have to speak in a voice from under the waters, a boy's clear bell-voice pleading out of the deep dark. 'Sing to me, dear father!' the voice would have to call, and she would have to hear. Somewhere within himself he would have to find not only that voice but the words, the true words. Here and now he does not have the words. Perhaps – he has an intimation – they may be waiting for him in one of the old ballads. But the ballad is in no book: it is somewhere in the breast of the Russian people, where he cannot reach it. Or perhaps in the breast of a child. (110–11)

Dostoevsky's words at this point in the novel, of course, echo Mrs Curren's response, in *Age of Iron*, to Mr Thabane's injunction that she should "name" the atrocity that she witnesses in Guguletu: "I must find my own words, from myself" (91). If anything, this parallel between the two novels is even clearer in Nechaev's repeated admonition to Dostoevsky to represent the violence of the Russian state. After remarking that the activists "in the forefront of the struggle continue to be hunted down and tortured and killed" and that this reality is occluded by the "shameful Russian press," Nechaev remonstrates with Dostoevsky as follows: "I would have expected you to know this and write about it" (103). Later, he again reproves Dostoevsky with the question "How can you ignore a spectacle like this [...] a spectacle that can be multiplied a thousandfold, a millionfold across this country?" (180), and enjoins him to "Make a start! Tell them about your stepson and why he was sacrificed!" (181).

Like Mrs Curren, Dostoevsky responds to this historical imperative by arguing for a language that somehow transcends the opposition between state and revolutionary. What we have in this novel is thus, once more, the articulation of a desire not to evade history but to engage with it, as Coetzee argues in "Into the Dark Chamber," in a different language (364), in a manner that does not supplement the relational structures that determine the form it assumes.

In this respect, the child-metaphor in the passage in which Dostoevsky expresses his desire for his own, autonomous voice is particularly telling. Like the protagonists of *Life & Times of Michael K*, *Waiting for the Barbarians*, *Foe*, and *Age of Iron*, this character must find the lost child if he is to speak on, and in, his own terms. Crucially, though, the child he is to find is one of whom history, the domain of the same, is not simply the deformation but death.[4] In this regard, it should be noted that, even though Dostoevsky is apparently in Petersburg to ascertain the circumstances surrounding the death of his stepson, Pavel, the novel never does clarify these circumstances. It never makes it clear whether or not Pavel has been killed by the state or by the nihilists, thus suggesting that he is a victim of the conflict between the two, and therefore of history.

Dostoevsky is actually in Petersburg to raise Pavel from the dead (17, 19). Throughout this novel, the emphasis falls on the enormity, indeed impossibility, of this task, as emerges, for instance, in this reflection by Dostoevsky: "A gate has closed behind his son, a gate bound sevenfold with bands of iron. To open that gate is the labour laid upon him" (19). What is also emphasized is that, if this character is to resurrect Pavel, he will have to transcend himself: the crucial irony in this novel, as in *Age of Iron*, is that the protagonist is implicated in the history that he wishes to transcend and is thus himself partly responsible for the loss of the child he seeks.

Although Coetzee, in *The Master of Petersburg*, again uses the trope of madness to convey the notion of the subject's situatedness in history, he develops this metaphor extensively by drawing on the historical Dostoevsky's literary response to revolutionary nihilism in *The Devils* (sometimes entitled *The Possessed*), a novel that centres on the biblical story of the unclean devils which, having been exorcized from a "sick" or "mad" man by Christ, enter a herd of swine which then rushes headlong down a steep bank into the sea.[5] In *The Devils*, the tale of the Gadarene swine serves as a structural metaphor through which the historical Dostoevsky

---

[4] The intriguing, if slightly peripheral, question that here suggests itself is one that is also implicit in my discussion of birth, death, and mourning in *Life & Times of Michael K*: is there a difference between waiting to be born and waiting to be resurrected? Ultimately, I suppose, the further question is whether or not one can distinguish between the forms of responsibility concomitant with the Levinasian "gestation of the other in the same" and the Derridean notion of the encryptment of the dead in the living. Evidently not for Coetzee, who, in this novel, seems to imply that both gestation without term and infinite mourning involve responsibility for that which has not emerged, cannot emerge, and yet insists on emerging. So, for example, as I show later in this chapter, Dostoevsky is depicted as labouring to bear Pavel. At the same time, though, and this I noted in my discussion of the relevance of the notion of mourning to Coetzee's *Life & Times of Michael K*, this character also conceives of himself as Pavel's grave, the "frozen earth," containing an "iron box" containing a "dead baby" (52).

[5] *Authorised King James Version of the Holy Bible*, Mark 5:2–20.

explores and ultimately condemns political nihilism. As the following comparisons drawn by one of the nihilists in the novel indicate, this story generates a series of analogies which suggest that Russia is a "sick" or "mad" man possessed by devils, and that the swine which the devils enter upon being exorcized are the revolutionaries:

> These devils who go out of the sick man and enter the swine – those are all the sores, all the poisonous exhalations, all the impurities, all the big and little devils, that have accumulated in our great and beloved invalid, in our Russia, for centuries, for centuries! [...] But a great idea and a great Will shield her from on high, as with that madman possessed of the devils, and all those devils, all those impurities, all those abominations that were festering on the surface – all of them will themselves ask to enter into swine. [...] They are we [...] and we shall cast ourselves down, the raving and the possessed, from the cliff into the sea and shall all be drowned, and serves us right, for that is all we are good for.[6]

In his novel, however, Coetzee applies the story of the Gadarene swine not only to Russia and the phenomenon of revolutionary nihilism but also to the character Dostoevsky himself.[7] The protagonist is thus depicted as a "sick man" possessed by devils, the outward sign of this affliction being his epilepsy, a malady which the novel relates to demon-possession. Besides, this character speculates that not "seizure" but "possession" would be "the right word" to describe the fits from which he suffers (213).

Coetzee's reworking of the story of the Gadarene swine in *The Master of Petersburg* thus clearly comments on the subject's location in the power dynamics or "sickness" of its society. By applying this story to Dostoevsky, he suggests that it is not just the nihilists who have been "contaminated" by the "sickness" of Russia: Dostoevsky is a part of Russia and is therefore also "sick." It is thus hardly surprising that, as the novel develops, the boundaries between this character and his social context are increasingly blurred. Indeed, he refers to epilepsy as "the emblematic sickness of the age" (235) and earlier, without realizing the implica-

---

[6] Fyodor Dostoevsky, *The Devils*, tr. & intro. David Magarshack (*Besy*, 1871; Harmondsworth: Penguin, 2nd ed. 1971): 647–48.

[7] See Head's argument that "if Dostoevsky parodies the Nechaevites in *Demons*, Coetzee subverts that parody into a debate about writing" (*J.M. Coetzee*, 147).

tions of his words, equates himself with Russia, "I am required to live
[…] a Russian life: a life inside Russia, or with Russia inside me" (221).

The irony that follows from Coetzee's emphasis on his writer-figure's
being-in-the-world is that, notwithstanding Dostoevsky's reluctance to
assume an oppositional position within history, he *already* occupies such
a position. After all, the decision not to assume a position is itself a position. If he is to articulate the "true words," to find the lost child, he must
respond not to history but to what has been excluded by history and consequently by himself. Midway through the novel, this becomes quite clear
when, after shaking his head "as if to rid it of a plague of devils," he
muses as follows:

> Somewhere inside him truth has lost its way. As if in the labyrinth of
> his brain, but also in the labyrinth of his body – veins, bones,
> intestines, organs – a tiny child is wandering, searching for the light,
> searching to emerge. How can he find the child lost within himself,
> allow him a voice to sing his sad song? (126)

From the first, Dostoevsky is implicated in the loss of his stepson. Already implicit in the fact that Pavel is, strictly speaking, an orphan, bereft
of a father and a mother, and in Dostoevsky's "exile" in Dresden, this
point is stressed by the protagonist's recollection of his promise to Pavel
on taking him to school "for his first term": "*You will not be abandoned.*
And abandoned him" (5). Later, it is directly articulated in Anna Sergeyevna's accusation, "You ran away from him" (138), and in Sergei Nechaev's charge of desertion: "You went abroad and left him behind. You lost
touch with him, you became a stranger to him" (119).

Dostoevsky is therefore himself the loss of what he seeks. If he is to
recover the lost child, to resurrect him, he will have to transcend history
and thus himself. It will be remembered that, in *Age of Iron*, Mrs Curren's
possession by history is eventually countered by her inspiration by Vercueil's otherness. By contrast, in this novel, Dostoevsky is throughout
simultaneously acted upon by history and by the otherness that it precludes from coming into being. He is the site of an irreducible tension between these two 'forces'. Significantly, the novel opens with an image of
hospitality. A stranger, only later identified as Dostoevsky,[8] arrives un-

---

[8] Rachel Lawlan, "*The Master of Petersburg*: Confession and Double Thoughts in
Coetzee and Dostoevsky," 132.

announced outside a house in Petersburg, is taken to the room previously
occupied by his recently deceased stepson, finds his suit, presses it to his
forehead, and inhales deeply: "Faintly the smell of his son comes to him.
He breathes in deeply, again and again, thinking: his ghost, entering me"
(3–4). In this scene of inspiration, the visitor is visited by the ghost of the
dead child and therefore becomes its host. Dostoevsky is captivated by
what he seeks to capture.

The Master of Petersburg is therefore a novel about its protagonist's
possession by both history and the other. Haunted by these two 'forces',
this character is never entirely in control of his actions. In fact, the theme
of the individual's dispossession of self is, in this novel, far more pronounced than in the preceding ones. In the opening chapters, for instance,
it emerges that Dostoevsky's very identity is constituted by the forces that
possess him. He is constantly acted upon by impulses, urges, desires, and
dreams that *come* unbidden to him. Apart from Pavel's "smell," the
"news" of his death also comes to Dostoevsky (19). Seeing Anna Sergeyevna's hands, "A memory comes back to him" (10). When he "falls"
asleep: i.e. when sleep 'comes', "He imagines himself plunging down a
long waterfall into a pool, and gives himself over to the plunge" (6).
"During the night," we read, "a dream comes to him" (17). Upon suddenly
and inexplicably desiring Anna Sergeyevna at Pavel's graveside, he asks
himself: "Where does his desire come from?" (10). The point that is emphasized here is that things *happen* to Dostoevsky: urges, impulses,
dreams, and words *arrive* uninvited and unannounced. He is at the mercy
of, even mastered by, memory, dream, desire, and revenants. In his words,
"wherever impulse leads he is ready to follow" (19).[9]

Dostoevsky's wholly ambivalent response to Matryona, the daughter of
Pavel's landlady, Anna Sergeyevna, most clearly illustrates the extent to
which his actions are simultaneously inspired by history and the otherness
that it excludes. The opening chapters of the novel establish a strong
affinity between Matryona and Pavel. Apart from learning from Anna
Sergeyevna that they were close (14), we also read Dostoevsky's thought
that "Somewhere in" Matryona, Pavel "still lives, breathing the warm,
sweet breath of youth" (14). Since the suggestion here is that Matryona
hosts Pavel, Dostoevsky's antipathy to her is striking. Alongside his son's

---

[9] Attridge reads this dimension of the novel in terms of the Derridean *arrivant*: i.e.
the unexpected visitor (*J.M. Coetzee and the Ethics of Reading*, 122–24, 125).

grave, having observed this child observing his grief, he stares back at her with naked malice:

> A terrible malice streams out of him toward the living, and most of all toward living children. If there were a newborn babe here at this moment, he would pluck it from its mother's arms and dash it against a rock. Herod, he thinks: now I understand Herod! Let breeding come to an end! (9–10)

The reference here is not only to Herod's slaughter of the innocents in his bid to destroy the infant Jesus[10] but also to this figure's association with madness and anger on the medieval stage.

Later, when Matryona "encounters" Dostoevsky's "gaze" exploring her, "An angry impulse rises in him. He wants to grip her arm and shake her" (13). He is "in a rage against everyone who is alive when his child is dead," we read, but "most of all against this child, whom for her very meekness he would like to tear limb from limb" (16). In these sentences, the child is again associated with Jesus Christ and therefore salvation; Dostoevsky is again associated with Herod and the madness, anger, and vengefulness that, in this novel, characterize the realm of history.

Possessed by both the other and history, Dostoevsky tries to find and destroy the lost child. In the following passage, in which he once more catches Matryona watching him, this conflict is finally directly articulated: "There is a rush of feeling in him, contradictory, like two waves slapping against each other: an urge to protect her, an urge to lash out at her because she is alive" (23). If he is to succeed in his Herculean "labour" of opening the "gates of death" that have shut behind Pavel (242), he must resist history's logic of vengeance. That is, he has to resist the logic for which he, ironically, provides a home and which defines his identity. He must respond to what is not yet in history, which history has killed, but which nonetheless haunts history – indeed, this is a novel about ghosts, about that which returns after having been killed.

In short, Dostoevsky must respond to that of which history is the death and which therefore cannot be responded to in the terms of history. To do this, he must transcend history and therefore himself. He must become other than himself. In the logic of the metaphor of demon-possession, this would entail exorcizing the devils, the *spirit* of vengefulness that charac-

---

[10] *Authorised King James Version of the Holy Bible,* Matt. 2:3–19.

terizes Russian history. Following the scene in which he wishes to "rage" against Matryona, he retires to his room and attempts precisely such an exorcism:

> He lies down on the bed, his arms tight across his chest, breathing fast, trying to expel the demon that is taking him over. He knows that he resembles nothing so much as a corpse laid out, and that what he calls a demon may be nothing but his own soul flailing its wings. (16)

If he is to open the "gates of death," Dostoevsky must become a different person, a stranger to himself.

ॐ ॐ

A corollary of having to respond to what is outside history and refractory to its terms from a position within history is that it is impossible to identify it and so know whether or not this exteriority has arrived. Dostoevsky simply cannot be sure that he will recognize Pavel, were he to come. For this reason, *The Master of Petersburg* is dominated by the confusion and doubt that beset Dostoevsky's work of mourning, his attempts not only to summon the dead child but also to locate him, to place him. At first, when he walks the streets of Petersburg, he constantly looks out for Pavel:

> The sky is low and grey, a cold wind blows; there is ice on the ground and the footing is slippery. A gloomy day, a day for trudging with the head lowered. Yet he cannot stop himself, his eyes move restlessly from one passing figure to the next, searching for the set of the shoulders, the lilt to the walk, that belongs to his lost son. By the walk he will recognize him: first the walk, then the form. (48–49)

Possessed by that for which he searches, he cannot help searching; he cannot control the desire to identify and so locate the revenant.

Later, though, Dostoevsky realizes that there is no guarantee whatever that he would in fact recognize Pavel if he were to arrive. He must therefore "answer to what he does not expect" (80), which means that he cannot even expect the unexpected. Since every creature might, or equally well might not, be Pavel, he has to respond responsibly to all. What is more, such responsibility is without term: he can never know finally that Pavel has, in fact, arrived, and hence despairingly wonders whether he is required to spend the remainder of his life "peering into the eyes of dogs and beggars" (81). His possession by Pavel thus directly affects his interactions with other beings: in relating to them, he must relate to what they may unwittingly host – must relate to what is not phenomenally apparent.

In his reading of this novel, Attridge questions the feasibility of infinite responsibility and refers to Derrida's conclusion, in *The Gift of Death*, that Levinas' phrase "every other (one) is every (bit) other" makes an impossible demand.[11] It is precisely the impossibility of such responsibility, Attridge then points out, that enables ethics. According to Derrida, responsibility *starts* when the individual has to respond to two, incompatible injunctions. He elaborates on this point as follows in an interview:

> Now, although I think, at least I obviously think, that no finite being can remember every thing and every injunction, so cannot be infinitely responsible, I also think that, nevertheless, that's another contradiction, that responsibility must be infinite. That's why I always feel not responsible enough, because I'm finite and because there are an infinite number of others to whom or for whom or from whom I should be responsible. I'm always not responsible enough, and responsibility is infinite or it *is* not; but I cannot be responsible *to some extent* in the strict sense of "responsibility." There *is* a field in which responsibility might be, can be, limited, such as trade, or commerce; but, in ethics the responsibility to the other is infinite *or* it is not. That's why I always feel guilty. Not because I cultivate bad conscience – I don't like bad conscience – but because of the structure of responsibility, its infinity, although I am a finite being. That is why I'm always unequal to my responsibility, always disproportionate to my own finitude and the field of responsibility that I have – infinite responsibility towards the other, towards God, and so on and so forth.[12]

---

[11] Attridge, *J.M. Coetzee and the Ethics of Reading*, 122–24. Cf. Lucy Graham's account of Derrida's reflections on Levinas' phrase in "'Yes, I am giving him up': Sacrificial Responsibility and Likeness with Dogs in J.M. Coetzee's Recent Fiction," *Scrutiny2* 7.1 (2000): 4–15. Graham maintains that Derrida dismisses the notion of responsibility for all. For some insight into the intersection between Derrida and Levinas' thinking on responsibility, see the former's farewell to the latter ("Adieu," in *The Work of Mourning*, ed. & tr. Pascale–Anne Brault & Michael Naas (*Chaque fois unique, la fin du monde*, 1996; Chicago: U of Chicago P, 2001): 200–209.

[12] Derrida, "Following Theory: Jacques Derrida," interview, in *life. after. theory*, ed. Michael Payne & John Schad (London: Continuum, 2003): 48–49.

For Derrida, it is precisely its infinite nature that makes of responsibility a burden, a persecution.

In *The Master of Petersburg*, Coetzee's understanding of the aporetic nature of infinite responsibility is most apparent in the scene in which Dostoevsky hears the dog "calling" in the night and realizes that he must answer: "*Because* it is not his son he must not go back to bed but must get dressed and answer the call" (80). The impossibility of placing Pavel, of identifying him, thus precludes the possibility of responding indifferently to the dog and, indeed, all other beings. Dostoevsky realizes as much:

> Pavel will not be saved till he has freed the dog and brought it into his bed, brought the least thing, the beggarman and the beggarwoman too, and much else he does not yet know of; and even then there will be no certainty. (82)

The uncertainty and doubt attendant on his ateleological work of mourning would seem to have the potential to invest his relations with others with what Levinas refers to as "non-indifference."[13]

Dostoevsky is also aware of this: after asking himself "must every beggar then be treated as a prodigal son, embraced, welcomed into the home, feasted?" he responds as follows: "Yes, that is what Pascal would say: bet on everyone, every beggar, every mangy dog; only thus will you be sure that the One, the true son, the thief in the night, will not slip through the net" (84). Potentially, at least, every being is the lost child. Significantly, in this regard, Dostoevsky refers to the howling dog as a "gross, smelly child" (80), and notes that Ivanov, whom he does welcome home and to whom he offers his bed, has lips that are "small and pink as a baby's" (88). To respond indifferently to anyone or anything is to stand accused of abandonment. Hence, after failing to release and succour the dog, Dostoevsky feels guilty of having "abandoned" it (82). When everyone may be the lost child, or the host of the "true son," the saviour, responsibility for one becomes responsibility for all. Despite its different *telos*, this logic, Dostoevsky realizes, is remarkably similar to Herod's: "And Herod would agree: make sure – slay all the children without exception" (84).

Coetzee develops this ethic through a sequence of scenes that establish a close affinity, bordering on identity, between Pavel and Sergei Nechaev.

---

[13] Levinas, *Otherwise Than Being*, 97.

In terms of the logic of infinite responsibility, Dostoevsky must care unconditionally for Nechaev, whom he hates and even suspects of having murdered Pavel. If he fails to do so, it follows that he does not love his son well enough, even that he has abandoned him. In the first of these scenes, Dostoevsky attempts to call up Pavel's face in his mind, only to find that the image of Nechaev appears instead. He then tries to "dismiss the image" with the words "Go away!" (49). Crucially, this action adversely affects his attempt to "summon up Pavel's face," to restore the filial bond: "'Pavel!' he whispers, conjuring his son in vain" (49). In a later scene, he again tries to "conjure" up his stepson: "*Pavel!* he whispers over and over, using the word as a charm. But what comes to him inexorably is the form not of Pavel but of the other one, Sergei Nechaev" (60). This experience forces him to conclude that "a gap is opening between himself and the dead boy" (60).

When he does eventually reappear in a vision, Pavel is together with a bride who Dostoevsky thinks may be one of the women who lured him to the garret. Importantly, it later transpires that the woman in question is Nechaev in disguise (96). Eventually, Dostoevsky asks himself the obvious question: "Is that what he must learn: that in God's eyes there is no difference between the two of them, Pavel Isaev and Sergei Nechaev, sparrows of equal weight?" (238). In being haunted by Pavel, he is haunted by Nechaev, as is, of course, implicit in his very attempt to dismiss the latter's image. Like Mrs Curren, who recognizes that her ability to love her daughter is contingent on loving the unlovable John, Dostoevsky here begins to realize that he can only love Pavel if he loves Nechaev, the "unloved and unlovely young man" (61). He must learn to love Nechaev despite himself.

If Dostoevsky's desire for Pavel were to lead to infinite responsibility, it would bring about an exorcism of sorts. Acted upon by this desire, he would care for the other being, despite his and its positions in history and the names and identities that these positions ascribe. At one point in the novel, Anna Sergeyevna responds as follows to his intense antipathy towards Nechaev: "If you were not here there would be no Nechaev" (173). Just as Dostoevsky constructs his identity by assuming an oppositional stance in relation to Nechaev, Nechaev defines his identity relative to Dostoevsky. Just as Nechaev is a disfigurement of Pavel, so too is Dostoevsky. Both are versions of the unlovable. If Dostoevsky is to find Pavel, he has to learn to relate to others "ecstatically": i.e. notwithstanding himself. Were he to do this, his relationships would exceed what Derrida refers to as "the strict economy of exchange, of payback, of giving and giving back, of the 'one lent for every one borrowed,' of that hateful form of circulation that involves reprisal, vengeance, returning blow for blow, settling scores."[14] That is to say, Dostoevsky would define himself through his responsibility for what is other than history, for what has not yet emerged.

Since such responsibility would require Dostoevsky to admit to himself what is different from himself, and so redefine the border or threshold between his interior and exterior, it would exact a sacrifice of his present identity. Responsibility, thus conceived, is precisely an exorcism of the self as it is; it requires the self to become other than itself. Significantly, Levinas, in discussing the other's "accusation" of the self, frequently refers to responsibility as precisely an emptying-out of the self:

> To revert to oneself is not to establish oneself at home, even if stripped of all one's acquisitions. It is to be like a stranger, hunted down even in one's home, contested in one's own identity and one's very poverty, which, like a skin, still enclosing the self, would set it up in an inwardness, already settled on itself, already a substance. It is always to empty oneself anew of oneself [...]. It is to be on the hither side of one's own nuclear unity, still identifiable and protected; it is to be emptied even of the quasi-formal identity of a being someone.[15]

In *The Master of Petersburg*, Dostoevsky points to the form of exorcism enabled by responsibility when, after "abandoning" the dog, he realizes that he has forfeited a chance of abandoning himself, "that an opportunity for leaving himself as he is behind and becoming what he might yet be has passed" (82). Through not responding hospitably to the dog, i.e. in closing the door on it, he closes "the door upon himself," imprisons himself in himself, "manacles" himself to himself (82). Clearly, the suggestion here is that he squanders an opportunity for saving himself. Had he saved the dog, through sacrificing himself – by annihilating himself as he presently is – he would have saved himself in becoming other than himself.

As in *Age of Iron*, then, salvation is in this novel depicted as an epiphenomenon of unconditional care, of hospitality. This form of salvation,

---

[14] Derrida, *The Gift of Death*, 102.
[15] Levinas, *Otherwise Than Being*, 92.

it must be added, is deeply paradoxical, in that it is precisely not a reward or some form of return that the self receives in exchange for its sacrifice. One saves oneself by forfeiting one's self and thereby rendering it impossible for the self that gives to receive anything in return for its gift. Since the gift concerned is, in fact, the self, the self that gives is, as it were, no longer there to receive any reward. One is therefore saved not in the sense of being protected, preserved, or spared from something or other, but precisely through being delivered over to the other being and, in the process, losing one's prior identity. Dostoevsky can thus only save himself by losing himself, by assuming responsibility for all and, in the process, becoming a stranger unto himself. What is required of him, if he is to save Pavel, is to sacrifice himself without any hope or expectation of receiving any form of recompense. In other words, he must sacrifice himself without expecting as reward the salvation of either Pavel or himself.

It is difficult not to see in this depiction of a relationship between a father and a son premised on sacrifice an allusion to Abraham's readiness to sacrifice Isaac to God.[16] Unlike Abraham, though, Dostoevsky is, in this narrative, required to sacrifice *himself* in order to save Isaev, his son. The problem with the form of sacrifice that is required of Dostoevsky, however, is that it cannot be a willed action. Throughout this study, I have argued that, for Coetzee, responsibility is not a matter of choice, a task that a willing and able subject, acting in a world of possibility, has the power to undertake, perform, and complete. Given that what he must do is not a possibility open to an agent, Dostoevsky cannot simply *assume* responsibility and, in the process, predict the outcome of having done so. Should he 'assume' responsibility for all – if such responsibility should arrive or, to use Coetzee's term, "come" – it will have happened unbeknownst to him.

Not surprisingly, then, Dostoevsky, in the scenes involving the dog and Ivanov, proves quite incapable of such a disinterested form of love. Cain's disavowal of responsibility for his brother, "Am I my brother's keeper?" which I discussed in the previous chapter, is repeatedly alluded to. When

---

[16] *Authorised King James Version of the Holy Bible,* Gen. 22:1–19. After referring to Coetzee's "underlying allusions to the Bible," Sue Kossew points out that "The father/son motif, where the son is sacrificed in order to save the father and the rest of humanity, underlies the entire story" (*Pen and Power,* 217). See also Derrida's discussion of this archetypal sacrifice and the exchange economy it implies (*The Gift of Death,* 82–115). My ensuing discussion draws on several of Derrida's insights.

he decides against sheltering the dog, Dostoevsky thinks: "Why me? [...]
Why should I bear all the world's burdens?" (91), and: "*What is it to me?*"
(82). Later, when he cannot find Ivanov, "He sighs with relief," and
thinks "I have done what I can" (93). As I argued in my discussion of Mrs
Curren's abnegation of responsibility in her initial interactions with John,
what is signified by such variants of Cain's question is precisely a failure
to love well enough – to love despite oneself.

Moreover, Dostoevsky, although required in these scenes to sacrifice
himself without expectation of recompense, without calculation, expects a
sign of sorts. He is prepared to abandon the dog because, in his calculus,
the dog is not the "true son":

> He suspects he will not save the dog, not this night nor even the next
> night, if there is to be a next night. He is waiting for a sign, and he is
> betting (there is no grander word he dare use) that the dog is not the
> sign, is not a sign at all, is just a dog among many dogs howling in the
> night. But he knows too that as long as he tries by cunning to dis-
> tinguish things that are things from things that are signs he will not be
> saved. (83)

In other words, he would only be prepared to sacrifice himself for the dog
if he thought it likely that he would receive something in return for this
action.

Even when he offers succour to Ivanov, Dostoevsky is once more
gambling; he is hoping for a sign that this stranger is the "true son." In
fact, he is bargaining with God:

> There is no sign of Ivanov when he goes out later in the afternoon, nor
> when he returns. Should he care? [...] Even if, in the present charade,
> Ivanov is the one playing the part of God's angel – an angel only by
> virtue of being no angel at all – why should it be his role to seek out
> the angel? Let the angel come knocking at my door, he tells himself,
> and I will not fail, I will give him shelter: that is enough for the bargain
> to hold. Yet even as he says so he is aware that he is lying to himself,
> that it is in his power to deliver Ivanov wholly and absolutely from his
> cold watchpost. (92–93)

This passage, which alludes to the Pauline injunction on hospitality that
forms the subtext to Mrs Curren's treatment of Vercueil in *Age of Iron*,
points to the conditional nature of Dostoevsky's generosity to Ivanov.

Once again, his hospitality is calculated: he requires something in exchange, some form of payment or reward, for his sacrifice. His responsibility for Pavel is grounded on the assumption that God will reward him for his sacrificial gift.

Dostoevsky thus fails in his attempt at assuming responsibility for the other being. His sacrifice – and this he intuits – is finally too self-interested, aimed at consolidating, rather than forfeiting, his self, and thus, ironically, modulates into a search for personal salvation; Pavel's death is "turned into the occasion of his father's reformation" (81). In terms of the archetypal Abraham story, Dostoevsky, the father, in failing to sacrifice himself, evinces Abraham's readiness to sacrifice, and so abandon, his son. And, in terms of the other archetype for infanticide invoked in these passages, he, in trying to redirect Herod's logic, merely aligns himself with its *telos*. To all intents and purposes, Dostoevsky's actions are still inspired by history and its economy of reprisal and vengeance.

These ironies, it must be emphasized, point not so much to Dostoevsky's personal failings as to the deeply aporetic nature of his task. The sacrifice that he has to perform cannot take place in an economy of exchange. The intentionality of his act of giving, its willed nature, inevitably destroys the gift. Derrida, in a discussion of Baudelaire's "The Pagan School," explains the aporia at work here:

> The moment the gift, however generous it be, is infected with the slightest hint of calculation, the moment it takes account of knowledge or recognition, it falls within the ambit of an economy: it exchanges, in short it gives counterfeit money, since it gives in exchange for payment. Even if it gives "true" money, the alteration of the gift into a form of calculation immediately destroys the value of the very thing that is given; it destroys it as if from the inside. The money may keep its value but it is no longer given *as such*. Once it is tied to remuneration, it is counterfeit because it is mercenary and mercantile; even if it is real. [...] as soon as it is calculated (starting from the simple intention of giving as such, starting from sense, knowledge, and whatever takes recognition into account), the gift suppresses the object (of the gift).[17]

---

[17] Derrida, *The Gift of Death*, 112.

If Dostoevsky is to save Pavel, he must learn to sacrifice himself unconditionally: i.e. without intention. Indeed, in order to avoid betraying the gift,
Derrida explains, "One must give without knowing, without knowledge or
recognition, without *thanks*: without anything, or at least without any
object."[18]

But how is one to learn to give in this way? In *The Master of Petersburg*, as in *Age of Iron*, the notion of learning is treated with some irony.
Dostoevsky, for instance, berates himself for lacking "the will" to save
Pavel (52). It is, of course, precisely its willed nature that thwarts any
such enterprise. If he is to learn to love, he must, ironically, sacrifice the
will to learn. If he does ever learn this lesson, it will have been despite
himself.

ॐ ॐ

The only way in which Dostoevsky may perhaps learn to love despite
himself, and thereby render an impossibility possible, is through writing.
In this study, I have maintained that, for Coetzee, to write is to act in
being acted upon. It is to become "a secretary of the invisible," to be inspired by what is not yet in history, the domain of the same. In *Age of
Iron*, as I have shown, writing is figured as precisely Mrs Curren's sacrifice despite herself. With the hindsight afforded by a reading of *The Master of Petersburg*, it could even be argued that writing in the earlier novel
is figured as the means by which Mrs Curren exorcizes from herself the
madness of history and gains a degree of autonomy in her relations with
others.

I started this chapter by showing that Dostoevsky, in refusing to side
with either the state or the nihilists, indicates his desire for autonomy by
reflecting on the necessity of speaking in a boy's voice "from under the
waters" (110). He must find the "true words" – the language that transcends history's economy of vengeance – which he feels may be located
"in the breast of a child" (111). Earlier in the novel, he has already intuited
how this may be achieved: "Poetry might bring back his son. He has a
sense of the poem that would be required, a sense of its music" (17). If he
is to exorcize the spirit of history by which he is possessed, Dostoevsky
must sacrifice himself in writing.

---

[18] *The Gift of Death*, 112.

Writing, in this novel, is linked to this character's efforts to summon the dead Pavel. In the opening chapter, we are provided with the following description of Dostoevsky's attempt to hunt the ghost by which he is haunted and which therefore inhabits him:

> He is there: he stands by the door, hardly breathing, concentrating his gaze on the chair in the corner, waiting for the darkness to thicken, to turn into another kind of darkness, a darkness of presence. Silently he forms his lips over his son's name, three times, four times.
>
> He is trying to cast a spell. But over whom: over a ghost or over himself? He thinks of Orpheus walking backwards step by step, whispering the dead woman's name, coaxing her out of the entrails of hell; of the wife in graveclothes with the blind, dead eyes following him, holding out limp hands before her like a sleepwalker. No flute, no lyre, just the word, the one word, over and over. (5)

A little later, in a dream, Dostoevsky, in the form of a turtle, tries to re-establish contact with Pavel:

> As he swims he sometimes opens his mouth and gives what he thinks of as a cry or call. With each cry or call water enters his mouth; each syllable is replaced by a syllable of water. He grows more and more ponderous, till his breastbone is brushing the silt of the river-bed.
>
> Pavel is lying on his back. His eyes are closed. His hair, wafted by the current, is as soft as a baby's
>
> From his turtle-throat he gives a last cry, which seems to him more like a bark, and plunges toward the boy. He wants to kiss the face; but when he touches his hard lips to it, he is not sure he is not biting. (17–18)

Both these descriptions of Dostoevsky's attempts to gain access to Pavel, in effect to open the "gates of death," are linked to writing by means of the Orpheus myth. The lyre, the instrument with which Orpheus played the music of love that enabled him to enter the underworld, is believed to have once been made from the shell of a tortoise, a belief still evident in one of the words for the lyre used by Greek authors, *chelys* 'tortoise'.[19]

---

[19] Anthony Baines, "Lyre," in *The New Oxford Companion to Music,* ed. Denis Arnold (Oxford: Oxford UP, 1983), vol. 2: 1106.

When this is borne in mind, the following description of Dostoevsky's posture at his writing desk gains an obvious significance:

> The task left to me: to gather the hoard, put together the scattered parts. Poet, lyre-player, enchanter, lord of resurrection, that is what I am called to be. And the truth? Stiff shoulders humped over the writing table, and the ache of a heart slow to move. A tortoise heart. (152–53)

Much later in the novel, shortly before he commences writing, this image recurs when "he catches a quick glimpse of himself hunched over the table" (236). Through the turtle–tortoise motif, then, writing is related to love. It is the means by which Dostoevsky must accomplish the task he has been assigned.

When Dostoevsky finally sits down to write, toward the end of the novel, it is to follow a "shade" into "the jaws of hell" (241), to pass "through the gates of death" (242). Writing is thus depicted as an entry into the realm of death in which the subject and language can exert no power. This description of writing as a katabasis cannot but evoke Blanchot's reading of the Orpheus myth as an allegory of the writer's task. In "Orpheus' Gaze," it will be remembered, Blanchot maintains that Orpheus is inspired by his overwhelming desire for Eurydice, the "*other* dark."[20] Acted upon by the invisible, the writer cannot *not* write. Significantly, the "shade" that Dostoevsky follows when he sets out to write is the obscure image of himself that he sees in the mirror and which, earlier in this scene, he describes in terms that bring to mind the "*other* dark": i.e. as "excessive" (236), a "stranger" (238), veiled (236, 237), and obscured by a "cloak of darkness" (238). Dostoevsky *follows* this shade (241): he is mastered by it, enthralled by his desire for it. And, in following it, "naked as a babe" (241), he answers the questions that he earlier asks himself in contemplating the image in the mirror:

> Is he required [...] to put aside all that he himself is, all he has become, down to his very features, and become a babe again? Is the thing before him the one that does the fathering, and must he give himself to being fathered by it? (240–41)

---

[20] Blanchot, "Orpheus' Gaze," 177.

Dostoevsky therefore writes because he loses himself in giving himself to the "*other* dark." Writing is not so much an activity as an event that happens to him, that comes to him.

Nevertheless, it would be premature to conclude that this character, through writing, leaves "himself as he is" behind, sacrifices himself and thereby re-creates himself. That is, it would be presumptuous to suggest that Dostoevsky "become[s] a babe again," that he resurrects the child buried within him, the one of which he is the death. My reading has so far ignored the sheer ambivalence with which this novel depicts writing. In the first place, the turtle–tortoise motif is deeply ambiguous: even as it associates writing with the self-sacrificing love that will enable Dostoevsky to transcend the order of the same, it dissociates it from this kind of love. Various of the words and phrases in the passages in which this motif occurs, such as "stiff," humped," "hunched," "slow to move," and "tortoise heart," connote a paucity, even distortion, of the generous love that is called for if Dostoevsky is to complete his task. Furthermore, these passages clearly distinguish between lyre and language. It is through the lyre's music of love that Orpheus charmed the gods of the underworld and extracted from them the concession of the averted gaze that enabled him to approach Eurydice.[21] By contrast, Dostoevsky is not a lyre-player; his artistic medium is language. While the "plea" of the boy from "under the waters," in one of the previously cited passages, is "Sing to me, dear father!" (110), he must use words, the syllables of which are replaced with water even as he tries to articulate them (17). The watery underworld in this novel, like the one in the ending of *Foe*, is "not a place of words."[22]

Coetzee's point, yet again, is that language is part of the domain of the same and therefore hostile to the other. From my discussion of the allusions, in *Life & Times of Michael K*, to Blanchot's reading of the Orpheus myth, it will be recalled that the "*other* dark" is not only what inspires writing but also what, owing to its refractoriness to language, eventually destroys the work by rendering it radically incomplete. In Blanchot's hands, the myth becomes a reflection on the impasse in which the writer finds him-/herself owing to the incommensurability of his or her desire for what exceeds language with the linguistic and literary means with

---

[21] Ovid, *Metamorphoses*, tr. Rolfe Humphries (Bloomington: Indiana UP, 1955): 234–35.
[22] See Coetzee, *Foe*, 157, and Head, *J.M. Coetzee*, 154–56.

which s/he must attempt to realize this desire. It is noteworthy, in this
context, that Dostoevsky, in pondering the excessive, unknowable, nature
of the image in the mirror, wonders what its name is and, after having
tried to find a name for it, concludes that the reason he has failed to do so
may be "because the figure is indifferent to all names, all words, anything
that might be said about it" (238).

In *The Master of Petersburg*, Coetzee stages the aporia of writing that
Blanchot allusively adumbrates in "Orpheus' Gaze." On the one hand, the
scene in which Dostoevsky finally starts writing quite clearly suggests
that the "*other* dark," in inspiring him, will exorcize the demons of history
that possess him. As such, this scene raises the possibility that his writing
may transcend history and thus occupy an "autonomous place."[23] Indeed,
just before he takes up his pen, we are again reminded that Dostoevsky is
sick: "He is sick and he knows the name of his sickness. Nechaev, voice
of the age, calls it vengefulness, but a truer name, less grand, would be
resentment" (234). On the other hand, even as it moots this possibility, the
writing-scene indicates quite clearly that, even though inspiration may
perform such an exorcism, may indeed place the writer in an unrelating
relation to the exteriority of the "*other* dark," the writer must nonetheless
write and therefore use language, which is of the order of history, the
same. This is partly why Dostoevsky is, throughout the novel, so reluctant
to put pen to paper. As the imagery in the following passage suggests, he
fears that his writing will only express his madness, his possession by the
spirit of vengefulness:

> At any moment he is capable of picking up the pen and forming letters
> on the paper. But the writing, he fears, would be that of a madman –
> vileness, obscenity, page after page of it, untameable. He thinks of the
> madness as running through the artery of his right arm down to the
> fingertips and the pen and so to the page. [...] What flows on to the
> paper is neither blood nor ink but an acid, black with an unpleasing
> green sheen when the light glances off it. (18)

The question that seems to be raised in this novel is therefore very similar
to that asked in *Age of Iron*: can language serve as a vehicle for love?

In fact, though, there is much evidence in *The Master of Petersburg* to
suggest that I have framed this question far too reductively. What is at

---

[23] Coetzee, "The Novel Today," 3.

issue is not only that language may not be able to convey love but also that it may not be able *not* to convey love. Very significantly, in this regard, the novel's depiction of the tension between language and love is throughout indeterminate. For instance, when Dostoevsky, in his dream, assumes the form of a turtle and descends into the "deep dark" of the watery underworld where he encounters Pavel, he is not sure if he kisses or bites him. The point of this ambivalence is that language is unable to control the other, that the other is indifferent to names. Not being able to control the other in writing does not simply mean not being able to present it in the text, but (and I have argued this point throughout this study) not being able to render it absent from the text either.

What of the ending of this novel, though? Does it sustain or resolve this tension between language and alterity? What does it say of the outcome of Dostoevsky's literary endeavour? I ask these questions because they are raised by Dostoevsky's sexual relationship with Anna Sergeyevna. For much of the novel, Dostoevsky's lovemaking with Anna Sergeyevna is depicted as a form of *ek-stasis* that enables him, through losing himself, to establish some form of contact with Pavel:

> At the moment of climax he plunges back into sleep as into a lake. As he sinks Pavel rises to meet him. His son's face is contorted in despair: his lungs are bursting, he knows he is dying, he knows he is past hope, he calls to his father because that is the last thing left he can do, the last thing in the world. He calls out in a strangled rush of words. This is the vision in its ugly extremity that rushes at him out of the vortex of darkness into which he is descending inside the woman's body. It bursts upon him, possesses him, speeds on. (56)

Anna Sergeyevna is the medium through which Dostoevsky loses himself and, in so doing, approaches Pavel. "Through her," we read, he passes into darkness and into the waters where his son floats among the other drowned" (58). In other words, she assists him in his "labour" to open the "gate" that separates him from his son. When she temporarily suspends their sexual relationship, the metaphor of the gate recurs: "They have one more night together, after which the gate closes" (58).

As in Coetzee's earlier novels, sexual intercourse here serves as a figure for inspiration. Shortly before Dostoevsky starts writing, he tells Anna Sergeyevna that he would like to have a child with her (224). After engaging in sexual intercourse with him, she asks him whether the act "was meant to bring about the birth of the saviour" (225). Dostoevsky then reflects that, for Pavel, the child would be "no saviour but a pretender, a usurper, a sly little devil clothed in chubby baby-flesh" (226). When they again make love, Anna Sergeyevna whispers the word "*devil*" as she nears her climax (230). If Dostoevsky has been inspired by what is beyond history, the suggestion is, the narrative that he proceeds to write may be autonomous; it may transcend history. Like Mrs Curren's letter in *Age of Iron*, it would be the effect of his generous effacement and substitution of self before and for the other. Under the inspiration of the invisible, his writing will have exorcized the demons of history that possess him. This is, perhaps, what is connoted by Anna Sergeyevna's utterance of the word "*devil*" while they make love.

Even as they raise this possibility, these metaphors suggest the converse: that it is just as possible that the outcome of Dostoevsky's inspiration by the "*other* dark" will be a devil. And Coetzee here, of course, again plays on the title of the historical Dostoevsky's novel about political nihilism. But these dichotomous possibilities do not cancel each other out. Since the results of inspiration by the other are wholly unpredictable, either is possible. Quite simply, the other cannot be controlled. If anything, the disabling relation to alterity that the writer establishes in the moment of writing must render literature radically ambiguous. Blanchot has this in mind when he argues that the writer who attempts "to express things in a language that designates things according to what they mean": i.e. to bring "things" into the "light of the world," may find that his or her prose treacherously evokes the insubstantiality of the "night." Conversely, the writer who is concerned with "what things and beings would be if there were no world" – with things "prior to the day" – may find that his or her writing betrays that concern.[24] It is just such an ambiguity – one concomitant with the writer's loss of control – that is enacted in Dostoevsky and Anna Sergeyevna's uncertainty about the outcome of their sexual commerce. Will the product of their sexual activity be a devil or a saviour? Will the text that is "born," by implication, supplement history by becoming one of the devils that possesses the "sick man" of Russia, or will it transcend this context and thereby gain the ability to "save" it?

---

[24] "Literature and the Right to Death," in *The Work of Fire*, tr. Charlotte Mandell (*La Part du feu*, 1949; Stanford CA: Stanford UP, 1995): 329–33.

In raising and answering these questions, the narrative that Dostoevsky writes merely suggests one possible outcome to the treacherous literary endeavour, a possibility that in no way forecloses on other possibilities. My use of the phrase "Dostoevsky writes" is rather questionable, however. When "the hand that holds the pen begins to move" (241), "to follow the dance of the pen" (236), "the words it forms are not words of salvation. Instead they tell of flies, or of a single black fly, buzzing against a closed windowpane" (241). These sentences quite clearly indicate that Dostoevsky's story is not a saviour but the spirit of vengefulness which Dostoevsky, in his conversation with Maximov, identifies as Baal, the fly-god (44). The story that the hand forms is, in fact, a loose reconstruction of Stavrogin's confession: an episode from *The Devils* that concerns the corruption of a child and which, although originally suppressed, is now usually included as an appendix to the historical Dostoevsky's novel.[25]

Moreover, this embedded narrative is intratextually related to the story that Dostoevsky tells Matryona about Pavel's self-substituting generosity toward Maria Lebyatkin (72–74),[26] and his later idea for a chapter of a novel in which the protagonist uses a story to seduce the young daughter of his mistress (134). These intratextual parallels not only expose the Dostoevsky character's transformation of a story about generosity into, in Stephen Watson's words, "an episode of gratuitous cruelty,"[27] but also point to the effect of this revised narrative on its reader in the novel: namely, Matryona. Since Dostoevsky leaves the pages containing the story "open on the table" where Matryona is likely to find and read them, his reference to the narrative as "an assault on the innocence of a child" equates the betrayal of Pavel with the anticipated effect of the story on Matryona (249).

Before this, however, the novel's imagery of illness and disease indicates that Matryona has already been corrupted by history's economy of vengeance. In a conversation with him, Anna Sergeyevna, after referring to his "battle" with Nechaev, berates Dostoevsky as follows: "I don't want strife and hatred brought into my home! Matryona is excited enough as it

---

[25] Dostoevsky, *The Devils*, 671–704; see also Marianne de Jong, "An Incomplete Repression: *The Master of Petersburg* and *Stavrogin's Confession*," *Slavic Almanach* 3.3–4 (1995): 48–75.

[26] See Kossew, *Pen and Power*, 221.

[27] Stephen Watson, "The Writer and the Devil: J.M. Coetzee's *The Master of Petersburg*," *New Contrast* 22.4 (1994): 47–61.

is; I don't want her further infected" (113). This, together with Matryona's subsequent illness (132, 135, 138), clearly connotes her corruption by the conflict between Dostoevsky and Nechaev. By implication, the former, who has accused the latter of putting Matryona to "abominable uses" (220), is guilty on exactly the same charge. The further implication is that Dostoevsky's narrative collaborates in the corruption of a child by supplementing history. Instead of finding the "true son," his writing abandons the child.

Through his use of the biblical analogue of the Gadarene swine, Coetzee develops this argument on the impact on the reader of a literature which supplements the conflictual relations in history. As I have already indicated, Anna Sergeyevna's uttering of the word "*devil*" during sexual intercourse with Dostoevsky alludes to *The Devils*, a novel which condemns political nihilism and thus, in Coetzee's terms, supplements history's economy of vengeance. In this scene, the sexual act is pointedly depicted as an inspiration that performs an exorcism. Anna Sergeyevna occupies the role of muse, while also being aligned with Jesus Christ, who, in the tale of the Gadarene swine, is an exorcist. Since it ends shortly afterwards with the Dostoevsky character starting work on a narrative that is recognizably related to *The Devils*, Coetzee's novel identifies the historical Dostoevsky's novel with the exorcized spirits in the story of the Gadarene swine. The irony is acute: while the fictional Dostoevsky's inspiration by what is beyond history does indeed exorcize the demons of history that possess him, the expelled devils are the narrative that he writes. His narrative, by extension, will possess its readers; take up residence in them. In fact, the readers of this narrative are implicitly equated with the swine which, in the biblical story, are possessed by the devils that have been exorcized from the sick man.

It will be remembered that the Gadarene swine, once possessed by the devils, hurl themselves down a steep bank. Since Matryona, the projected reader of Dostoevsky's story, is throughout the novel identified with Pavel, who was either pushed or fell from the shot tower in Petersburg, the concluding irony of the novel is clear: Dostoevsky, who tries to establish whether Pavel was executed by the police or revolutionaries, is himself responsible for his stepson's demise. His betrayal of the reader is a betrayal of the filial bond.

Coetzee's argument here does not simply rehearse the thesis, in *Age of Iron*, that literature that supplements history brutalizes its readers. What he ruefully suggests, in addition, is that literature that sets out to occupy an "autonomous place," to engage with history on its own terms, may, ironically, end up supplementing history. This argument, of course, qualifies this writer's distinction between literature that supplements history and a form of writing that, through its autonomy, rivals history.[28] What one ultimately finds staged in *The Master of Petersburg* is not a choice but an irreducible tension between supplementarity and a rivalry premissed on autonomy. In seeking to find his "own words," to assert some form of autonomy from history, Dostoevsky eventually merely supplements history. Coetzee's point is that, owing to the uncontrollability of the other, there can be no *choice* between supplementing and rivalling history: autonomy in literary writing is never simply the achievement of a subject in a world of possibility. If a text is to be autonomous, it will be so despite the writer's intentions and despite the work's medium.

✺ ৡ

I must emphasize that the ending of *The Master of Petersburg* does not simply assert that all writing cannot help supplementing history. Instead, it foregrounds the ironic nature of writing, the fact that the literary work's radical ambiguity concomitant with its "twofold essence" as a social fact and an autonomous entity may mean that the outcome of a literary endeavour is wholly different from what was intended.[29] Moreover, Coetzee's novel, in representing Dostoevsky's failure to find the words that would render his story autonomous, *inevitably* asks whether or not it itself: i.e. the narrative that provides this representation, also simply supplements history. Does *The Master of Petersburg*, in the moment of being read, enact, and thereby ironically repeat, what it describes? In posing this question, the novel asks another of the reader: how would one know how to answer such a question? How could one *know*, that is, whether the work in hand were a saviour rather than a devil? Indeed, how could *Coetzee* know?

In asking these questions, *The Master of Petersburg* enacts the very dilemma that it stages in its description of Dostoevsky's response to the dog in distress. I have argued that this character's lack of certainty about

---

[28] Coetzee, "The Novel Today," 2–3.
[29] Adorno, *Aesthetic Theory*, 8.

whether or not he will be able to recognize Pavel, were he to arrive, means that he comes to realize that he must assume responsibility for all: the "least thing" must be treated as though it were Pavel, the "true son." By the same logic, Coetzee, like his character, can have no way of knowing that his novel, *The Master of Petersburg*, is a devil or a saviour. Given the uncontrollability of the other, and the resultant treacherousness of the literary work, all that he can know is that he cannot know, that the novel may well be what he had not intended.

In fact, this writer is acutely aware of the added irony here: that the slightest intention on his part places the novel, his gift to the reader, within an economy of exchange and thereby destroys it. Accordingly, he can only trust that his work may have the effect he desires but which he cannot expect. He must hope that the inability of language either to possess or to exorcize the other will mean that the other will haunt the text despite the latter's location in the hostile order of the same. In effect, this means that Coetzee, while aware that *The Master of Petersburg* will probably be an "imposter" or "pretender" rather than the "saviour," and therefore that he must continue to write, to search for the "true son," cannot but treat it as anything other than the "saviour," even though he knows that to treat it as such is to destroy his gift to the reader. By implication, he must love the unlovable, even as he betrays and abandons it. The radical ambivalence of literature exacts from him this deeply ironic, aporetic responsibility.

The responsibility with which the novel confronts the reader is equally aporetic. By requiring him or her to distinguish between a saviour and a devil, the text passes the burden of recognizing the "true son" to the reader. In the process, this work acknowledges that aesthetic autonomy is not merely a static feature of the individual text but, rather, something that may happen in the moment of reading, should the text affect the reader in such a way that s/he receives it pre-reflectively and thus with unconditional hospitality. Indeed, as I argued in my reading of *Foe*, autonomy is constituted in the individual text's effect on the individual reader in the event of reading. It follows, then, that the reader is simply not in a position to know whether or not s/he has been, or will be, affected in this way by a particular work. Quite simply, s/he can have neither advance knowledge nor retrospective knowledge of this pre-reflective event and thus cannot say whether or not the work will be, or has been, a saviour or a devil. In the absence of certitude, it seems, the reader must respond to the work as though it were or may become the "true son."

There is a further irony here: the only way in which the reader can respond to the novel as though it were the "true son" is by overcoming the distinction between devil and saviour. In requiring the reader to decide whether it is a devil or a saviour, *The Master of Petersburg* requires him or her to sublate this opposition. S/he must not read within the economy of exchange of which it is a part; s/he must not expect of the novel any of the expectations that this economy inscribes.[30] Most of all, the reader must not expect salvation in return for his or her reading. If s/he is to be saved, s/he must give him-/herself to the text without any form of calculation, knowledge, and thus expectation of recompense. Only then will the work, again ironically, become a saviour.

By implication, *The Master of Petersburg* attempts to teach the reader how to read, which is to say love, despite him-/herself. Tellingly, in this regard, Councillor Maximov, during his interrogation of Dostoevsky, gives him one of Pavel's stories to read. The narrative concerned, which draws heavily on stereotypes derived from the political struggle between the revolutionaries and the Czarist state, builds to a climax in which the hero, a revolutionary named Sergei, takes a hatchet and cleaves open the head of a landowner, Karamzin, who has tried to rape a peasant girl (40–41). The story is obviously informed by the logic of vengeance that Dostoevsky strives to transcend in his own writing. In fact, the axe, as becomes apparent in his later reflection, serves as an image of vengeance in this novel:

> The axe, instrument of the people's vengeance, weapon of the people, crude, heavy, unanswerable, swung with the full weight of the body behind it, the body and the life's-weight of hatred and resentment stored up in that body, swung with dark joy. (114)

Pavel, it would seem, has written precisely the kind of story that Dostoevsky, despite Sergei Nechaev's urging, later refuses to write.

For this reason, Dostoevsky's reaction to Pavel's manuscript is all the more remarkable. Although the story seems to be "a sly little devil" rather than a saviour, Dostoevsky responds protectively to it:

---

[30] See Attridge, *J.M. Coetzee and the Ethics of Reading*, 135.

> It is a child's exercise book with ruled pages. He recognizes at once
> the slanted script with its trailing loops and dashes. Orphan writing, he
> thinks: I will have to learn to love it. He places a protective hand over
> the page. (40)

Dostoevsky responds not to what the story says but to what is rendered
unsaid by what it says. That is, he responds to what lies beyond the economy of vengeance that informs the narrative and which it therefore supplements. More accurately, this character responds to the "impostor,"
"pretender," "usurper" by responding to what it has usurped, what it has
displaced, disfigured, and betrayed. By means of this excessive relationship, he is able to love what *he* finds unlovable – he is able to love the
narrative despite himself. In fact, precisely such a negotiation of both the
worldliness of the text and the reader is articulated when Dostoevsky berates Maximov for "not know[ing] how to read":

> All the time you were reading my son's story – let me say this – I
> noticed how you were holding yourself at a distance, erecting a barrier
> of ridicule, as though the words might leap out from the page and
> strangle you.
> [...]
> What is it that frightens you, Councillor Maximov? When you read
> about Karamzin or Karamzov or whatever his name is, when
> Karamzin's skull is cracked open like an egg, what is the truth: do you
> suffer with him, or do you secretly exult behind the arm that swings
> the axe? You don't answer? Let me tell you then: reading is being the
> arm and being the axe *and* being the skull; reading is giving yourself
> up, not holding yourself at a distance and jeering. (46–47)

To read in this way is to respond to what the text says despite itself and
despite oneself. In fact, to read thus is to exorcize the text, an idea that is
implicit in Dostoevsky's charge that Maximov fears the story may strangle
him, and which becomes explicit in the latter's reference to "the spirit of
Nechaev" leaping "from the page" (48). To read in the manner described
by Dostoevsky is to read *beyond* the exchange economy that the narrative
inscribes through sacrificing oneself, through giving oneself up to the text,
and thereby ecstatically transcending one's location in history. In responding to the text in a way that exorcizes from it the spirit of history, the
reader enables it to exorcize this spirit from him or her. The "mutual elec-

tion" described in *Age of Iron* is, in this novel, figured as a mutual exorcism.

   This, then, is the lesson that *The Master of Petersburg* attempts to teach the reader. If it is learnt, the reader will have discovered that there is, finally, no opposition between saviour and devil. The saviour lies within the devil, hence the devil cannot be a devil; the saviour cannot be a saviour. If the reader does not learn the lesson, s/he stands accused by this novel, this "orphan writing," of having abandoned it. The problem is again, of course, that this lesson can only be learnt through losing the will to learn. After having been castigated by him for his poor reading-habits, Maximov asks Dostoevsky to read the Nechaev papers for him. The ensuing conversation proceeds as follows:

> 'Read them for you?'
> 'Yes. Give me a reading of them.'
> 'Why?'
> 'Because you say I cannot read. Give me a demonstration of how to read. Teach me. Explain to me these ideas that are not ideas.' (48)

Dostoevsky reacts to this request by laughing for the first time since he has received the "news" of his son's death and then says: "No, I will not do your reading for you" (48). His response is brutally honest: there can be no programme or manual for the kind of reading of which he speaks. Reading is a singular experience: nobody can do it for anybody else. In this respect, it is like dying, a point already implicit in this work's depiction of this activity as a forfeiture of self. Heidegger's famous argument that "*No one can take the Other's dying away from him*" (284),[31] that nobody else can die for him or her, is apposite here. Nobody can die for *me*. I cannot be replaced. Like dying, reading is a singular 'experience' that singularizes the individual. Dostoevsky cannot read for Maximov; he cannot take his place.

   Coetzee, however, would probably disagree with Heidegger's conception of death as that "*possibility which is one's ownmost*" (294), and choose to argue instead that one cannot grasp, apprehend or appropriate death; that death is not something that can be *done*. His novels certainly suggest, repeatedly so, that this is true of the sort of reading here in ques-

---

[31] Martin Heidegger, *Being and Time*, tr. John Macquarrie & Edward Robinson (*Sein und Zeit*, 1927; London: SCM, 1962): 284.

tion: i.e. a form of reading conceived of as more of an event than an action
that can be undertaken by a subject in a world of possibility. Reading of
this kind happens or, to use a word frequently used in *The Master of
Petersburg*, "comes," and does so without the reader's prior knowledge,
intention, and expectation. Dostoevsky may well laugh at Maximov's request for tuition in reading. In the novel's conception, reading is a difficult
experience both to teach and to learn. In phenomenological terms, it is not
even an experience. It is certainly not a possibility open to an intending
subject.

✄ ❧

"One of the ways of reading" *The Master of Petersburg*, according to
Gerald Gaylard, "is to read it back into the specific moment of the
elections and the birth of the 'new South Africa'." He goes on to suggest
that this novel is about the marginality of its white writer's position in this
changed social and political context. Dostoevsky, the allegorical writer,
"cannot tell Pavel's story, the story of the new, for he has not lived it." [32]
By contrast, my contention in this chapter has been that *The Master of
Petersburg* marks no major shift in Coetzee's writing. Despite being set in
nineteenth-century Russia and having been written during South Africa's
transition from apartheid rule to a democratic dispensation, this work repeats most of Coetzee's concerns in his earlier writing. What one finds in
it, for instance, is a refinement and clarification, rather than abandonment,
of the notion of an affective engagement with history. The emphasis now
falls squarely on the numerous paradoxes and ironies that beset such a
project. As we have seen, Coetzee foregrounds the irony of intentionality,
the knowledge that the intention to *give*, on which his entire ethical and
aesthetic project hinges, destroys the gift. More so than in the earlier fiction – and this includes *Age of Iron*, in which the metaphors that connote
an affective engagement with history ultimately prove ambivalent – one
finds in this novel an acute awareness that the writer who seeks to be autonomous from history may well supplement it in his or her writing.

I hasten to add that I am certainly not arguing that Coetzee, in *The
Master of Petersburg*, exposes the failure of his attempt to engage affec-

---

[32] "Mastering Arachnophobia: The Limits of Self-Reflexivity in African Fiction,"
Journal of Commonwealth Literature 37.1 (2002): 85–99.

tively with history. After all, my discussion of its thematization of reading demonstrates that this novel intends, even as it renders this intention ironic, to affect the reader in such a way that his or her reading will exorcize from it the spirit of vengefulness and thereby enable it to exorcize this spirit from him or her. Reader and novel must each follow where the other leads. Each must affect the other; each must exorcize the other in order to enable the other to exorcize it.

From this notion of a mutual exorcism, it is again made clear that this novel is self-reflexively aware of its implication in history. Indeed, *The Master of Petersburg* presents itself as what has disfigured the unborn in its attempt to figure it. Ultimately, then, the work betrays itself by portraying itself as the unlovable. In the process, Coetzee sets its reader the same task that he sets Dostoevsky – to learn to love the unlovable. In order to fulfil this task, the reader will have to learn to read despite him-/herself and despite what the novel may be and whatever its author may have intended. The fact that this kind of reading cannot be learnt, that the reader must *make* happen what can only happen, does not nullify his or her task. It simply renders the reader unequal to his or her responsibility.

✄ ৯

6 The Task of the Imagination
ø Disgrace

ALREADY IN *THE MASTER OF PETERSBURG*, it was clear
from Coetzee's depiction of history as an order determined by a
logic of reprisal and vengeance that his next novel would not be
a praise song for the new political dispensation in South Africa. At the
very least, *Disgrace* sustains the understanding of history presented in the
earlier novel. In the previous chapter, I noted that the ethical imperative
staged in Dostoevsky's conversation with Maximov in *The Master of
Petersburg* is for the individual to identify with both oppressor and oppressed, both assailant and victim. Only in this way may the exchange
economy that informs the course of history be suspended. *Disgrace* continues this argument by considering whether or not the faculty of imagination could enable the self-effacing form of identification that is required
for such a suspension.

In an early review of this novel, Jane Taylor first relates its treatment of
violence in post-apartheid South Africa to the European Enlightenment's
legacy of the autonomy of the human subject, in terms of which each individual is conceived of as a living consciousness separated totally from
every other consciousness, and then discusses Coetzee's postulation of the
sympathetic imagination as a potential corrective to the violence attendant
on monadic individuality.[1] Taylor makes the telling point that, in the eighteenth century, the notions of sensibility, sympathy, and compassion, which
the novel repeatedly invokes, were self-consciously developed as an ethical response to the instrumentalist logic of autonomous individuality and,
in this regard, cites the following observation by Adam Smith in *The*

---

[1] Jane Taylor, "The Impossibility of Ethical Action," review of J.M. Coetzee's *Disgrace*, *Mail & Guardian* (23–29 July 1999): 25.

Theory of Moral Sentiments: "By the imagination we place ourselves in his situation, we conceive ourselves enduring all the same torments, we enter as it were into his body, and become in some measure the same person with him, and thence form some idea of his sensation."[2]

Relatively few of the many subsequent readings of *Disgrace* have elaborated on Taylor's necessarily cursory examination of the theme of imagination in *Disgrace*.[3] For the most part, this aspect of the novel seems to be regarded as self-evident and therefore not in need of elaboration. When critical discussions of the text do touch on the imagination, they tend automatically to assume that Coetzee deems this faculty capable of countering the individual's solipsistic concern with itself. By extension, they assume that the *Bildung* that Coetzee's protagonist, David Lurie, undergoes in the course of *Disgrace* involves the successful development of a sympathetic imagination and hence the capacity to empathize with the other existent.[4]

---

[2] Quoted in Taylor, "The Impossibility of Ethical Action," 25.

[3] Among the exceptions are James Meffan & Kim L. Worthington, "Ethics before Politics: J.M. Coetzee's *Disgrace*," in *Mapping the Ethical Turn: A Reader in Ethics, Culture, and Literary Theory*, ed. Todd F. Davis & Kenneth Womack (Charlottesville & London: UP of Virginia, 2001): 131–50, Margot Beard, "Lessons from the Dead Masters: Wordsworth and Byron in J.M. Coetzee's *Disgrace*," *English in Africa* 34.1 (2007): 59–77, and Laura Wright (*Writing "Out of All the Camps"*). I should note that Wright's monograph on Coetzee and the article on which my chapter is based were published in the same year, and that our respective arguments on the role of the imagination in *Disgrace* arrive at related conclusions. In addition, there is some overlap in interpretative detail in our discussions of Lurie's relationships with Melanie, Lucy, and the animals in the novel. Fortunately, the points of intersection in our analyses also inscribe considerable difference. For a discussion of the role of the imagination in the Costello narratives, see Sam Durrant, "J.M. Coetzee, Elizabeth Costello, and the Limits of the Sympathetic Imagination," in *J.M. Coetzee and the Idea of the Public Intellectual*, ed. Jane Poyner (Athens: Ohio UP, 2006): 118–34. Durrant comments on *Disgrace* in passing. See also Geoffrey Baker's argument in "The Limits of Sympathy: J.M. Coetzee's Evolving Ethics of Engagement," *ARIEL: A Review of International English Literature* 36.1–2 (2005): 27–49, and Ortwin de Graef's reflections on this novel's concern with "the crisis of the imagination in the exercise of sympathy" caused by theory's decentering of the subject "as intentional agent and as emotionally charged psyche" ("Suffering, Sympathy, Circulation: Smith, Wordsworth, Coetzee (But there's a dog)," *European Journal of English Studies* 7.3 [2003]: 312, 317).

[4] See, for instance, Elleke Boehmer, "Not Saying Sorry, Not Speaking Pain: Gender Implications in *Disgrace*," *Interventions* 4.3 (2002): 346, and J.U. Jacobs, "Writing a New Nation: South African Fiction After Apartheid," in *Latitude 63° North: Proceedings of the 8th International Region and Nation Conference*, ed. David Bell

Such interpretations of this text are quite understandable, since, as I argue in this chapter, Coetzee gives his protagonist the ethical task of developing a sympathetic imagination and, as my close reading of the textual patterning of the novel shows, places his protagonist in positions which seemingly enable precisely such a growth. I also demonstrate, however, that *Disgrace* undermines, even as it installs, the possibility of this development, thereby questioning the ability of the imagination to achieve what it is supposed to achieve. In this regard, I trace at some length the nexus between the theme of imagination and the motif of the lost child. Throughout this study, I have shown that the lost child is a complex symbol, in Coetzee's writing, for what lies beyond the order of the same. The quest for the lost child is the subject's attempt to relate to the other being outside the terms of history from its position inside history. If the faculty of the imagination can enable Lurie to transcend history's economy of exchange, it follows that he will recover the lost child.

℘ ঽ

Lurie is initially depicted as being wholly self-absorbed in his dealings with others, as is evident from the novel's opening descriptions of his relationship with Soraya. Notwithstanding the fact that she is a sex worker who, in exchange for payment, allows him to use her as an instrument with which to satisfy his sexual desires, Lurie self-indulgently deludes himself into believing that she reciprocates his feelings for her.[5] So, for instance, he decides that "they have been lucky, the two of them: he to have found her, she to have found him,"[6] and that "at the level of temperament her affinity with him can surely not be feigned" (3). As his ex-wife, Rosalind, subsequently puts it, he is "a great self-deceiver" (188). Despite his chance sighting of Soraya with her two sons, a clear indication that her emotional life and commitments extend well beyond her profes-

---

(Östersund, Sweden, 2002): 40. In fairness to both these readers, I must emphasize that their discussions of *Disgrace* deal only peripherally with the theme of imagination.

[5] See Gareth Cornwell, "Realism, Rape, and J.M. Coetzee's *Disgrace*," *Critique: Studies in Contemporary Fiction* 43.4 (2002): 314.

[6] Coetzee, *Disgrace* (London: Secker & Warburg, 1999): 2. Unless otherwise indicated, further page references are in the main text.

sional service to him,[7] Lurie does not relinquish this fantasy. In fact, he insists on sustaining it and, after she suspends her sexual arrangement with him, even hires "a detective agency to track her down" (9). Her response to his telephone call marks the introduction, in this novel, of the trope of the uninvited visitor: "You are harassing me into my own house. I demand you will never phone me here again, never" (10). In his own description, Lurie is, in this scene, an intruder, an unwanted guest: "what should a predator expect when he intrudes into the vixen's nest, into the home of her cubs?" (10).

The motif of the undesired guest, which forms an ironic counterpoint to the invasion of the self by the uninvited visitor in unconditional hospitality, recurs in the novel's depiction of Lurie's later violation of Melanie Isaacs: "He has given her no warning; she is too surprised to resist the intruder who thrusts himself upon her" (24). If not immediately evident, the parallel between these two scenes becomes so when Lurie is charged by the university with "harassment" (39, 41).

As this parallel indicates, Lurie evinces a singular lack of concern for Melanie's views and feelings: she is simply an adjunct of his ego, a means by which he is able to gratify his desires. Hence, he self-servingly chooses to believe that she has been forced by her father and cousin to lodge a complaint against him (39). And, when Rosalind tells him that she has learnt that Melanie was driven to attempt suicide by her involvement with him, he dismisses this intelligence as a "fabrication" and quite simply does not give it another thought (45). At the university inquiry into his conduct, one of the committee members, Farodia Rassool, observes that Lurie's explanation for his actions: namely, that he was acted upon by desire, makes "no mention of the pain he has caused" (53).

Toward the end of the novel, Lurie's daughter, Lucy, accounts for his pathological disregard for others in the following literary terms:

> "You behave as if everything I do is part of the story of your life. You are the main character, I am a minor character who doesn't make an appearance until halfway through. Well, contrary to what you think, people are not divided into major and minor." (198)

---

[7] See Sue Kossew, "The Politics of Shame and Redemption in J.M. Coetzee's *Disgrace*," *Research in African Literatures* 34.2 (2003): 156–57.

Given his solipsism, and the propensity for self-delusion that it engenders, the reader cannot but question Lurie's interpretations of both his actions and those of others. Indeed, one of the few things that the reader learns about Melanie Isaacs from this unreliable focalizer[8] is that he has been grossly mistaken in his self-satisfied and self-serving assumptions about her. Although he believes that he knows her, she has, throughout their relationship, remained a stranger to him.

When Lurie invades Melanie Isaacs' flat and "thrusts himself upon her," he is reluctant to interpret this violation of her as a violation: "Not rape, not quite that, but undesired nevertheless, undesired to the core. As though she had decided to go slack, die within herself for the duration,

---

[8] Curiously, some critics seem to *want* to elide the distance between Coetzee and Lurie. Shane Moran feels that such an identification is "positively invited" by the novel ("To Criticise the Critic: *Disgrace,*" *Alternation* 8.2 [2001]: 216–28). See also Florence Stratton, "Imperial Fictions: J.M. Coetzee's *Disgrace,*" *ARIEL: A Review of International English Literature* 33.3–4 (2002): 93. Almost inevitably, such inattention to basic narratology results in the charge of racism being levelled at Coetzee. Since his character evinces a racist sensibility, he must be racist. Or so the logic seems to go. For a valuable corrective to such arguments, see John Douthwaite's careful narratological analysis of the opening chapters of the novel ("Melanie: Voice and its Suppression in J.M. Coetzee's *Disgrace,*" *Current Writing: Text and Reception in Southern Africa* 13.1 [2001]: 130–60). For an especially perceptive discussion of the difficulty in distinguishing between the narrator's voice and Lurie's, and the effect of such indeterminacy on the reader, see Meffan & Worthington, "Ethics before Politics," 140. See also Gilbert Yeoh, "Negotiating Foundations: Nation, Homeland and Land in J.M. Coetzee's *Disgrace,*" *ARIEL: A Review of International English Literature* 35.3–4 (2004): 21–23, Kossew, "The Politics of Shame and Redemption," 161, and Neville Smith, "Difference and J.M. Coetzee's *Disgrace,*" *Journal of Literary Studies* 23.2 (2007): 206–10. Finally, see Louise Bethlehem's concern that the third-person narrative voice in this novel, in asserting the compliancy and pliancy of 'Soraya', lacks an ironic awareness of its masculinist authority ("Pliant/Compliant; Grace/Disgrace; Plaint/Complaint," *Scrutiny2* 7.1 [2002]: 20). In his response to this charge, Sikhumbuzo Mngadi points out that Bethlehem's argument proceeds from the assumption that the name Soraya signifies a woman: "But Soraya, as the same narrator informs, is 'a popular *nom de commerce*'; indeed, after the first 'Soraya' exits the narrative, another 'Soraya' takes her place. [...] 'Soraya' is a 'function' of the escort agency and not the woman who is traded by that name, who leaves the narrative unknown and, indeed, who shuts the door to that possibility by disclaiming 'Soraya' and Lurie: 'I don't know who you are [...]. You are harassing me into my own house'" ("Reconsidering the Copula, 'and,' in 'Literature *and* Politics,' and Some Thoughts on 'Progressive Formalism'," *Alternation* 11.1 [2004]: 36).

like a rabbit when the jaws of the fox close on its neck" (25). The image of predation here tells a different story, though.[9] Not only is this image used in Lurie's previously cited reflection on Soraya's reaction to his telephone call, but it also appears in Lucy's later equation of sexual possession with murder:

> When it comes to men and sex, David, nothing surprises me any more. Maybe, for men, hating the woman makes sex more exciting. You are a man, you ought to know. When you have sex with someone strange – when you trap her, hold her down, get her under you, put all your weight on her – isn't it a bit like killing? Pushing the knife in; exiting afterwards, leaving the body covered in blood – doesn't it feel like murder, like getting away with murder? (158).

In repeating and amplifying images used in Lurie's description of his sexual intercourse with Melanie Isaacs, this passage comments on, indeed interprets, the earlier scene. Lucy's words, "you ought to know," together with her ensuing questions, frame her description as an interrogation, even an accusation. On a metaphoric level, Lurie, in violating her, kills Melanie Isaacs. Significantly, the trope of death in his depiction of her response to his sexual attack is pointedly repeated in his subsequent recollection of the act: "He sees himself in the girl's flat, in her bedroom [...] kneeling over her, peeling off her clothes, while her arms flop like the arms of a dead person" (89).

The further inference is that, in killing Melanie Isaacs, Lurie kills a child. In this regard, the reference to her as a "girl" in the above passage is hardly incidental: despite her age, she is, throughout the novel, described as a child. While engaged in his elaborate seduction of her, Lurie thinks to himself: "*A child! [...] No more than a child! What am I doing?*" (20). What is more, Melanie Isaacs is implicitly identified with Lucy. In comforting the former, even as he desires her sexually, Lurie assumes the role of father: "He sits down on the bed, draws her to him. In his arms she begins to sob miserably. Despite all, he feels a tingling of desire. 'There, there,' he whispers, trying to comfort her. 'Tell me what is wrong.' Almost he says, 'Tell Daddy what is wrong'" (26). If anything, the slippage in the

---

[9] Cf. Gareth Cornwell, who argues that "[t]here is no evidence that Lurie's dalliance with Melanie Isaacs has permanently damaged her and re-directed her life" ("Realism, Rape, and J.M. Coetzee's *Disgrace*," 319).

roles of lover and father, mistress and daughter in these early scenes is even more apparent in Lurie's following questions: "He strokes her hair, kisses her forehead. Mistress? Daughter?" (27). In the context of such ambivalence (and here we recall Dostoevsky's contradictory urges to both protect and pervert Matryona in *The Master of Petersburg*), it is noteworthy that Lurie and Melanie Isaacs make love in the bed in Lucy's room (29). As is suggested by the roots of their names, light and dark, Lucy and Melanie are dialectically related. The one implies the other.

Coetzee's point is obviously not that Melanie Isaacs is literally a child rather than a young woman, but that it is Lurie's ethical obligation to father and protect her. What is at issue is the ethic of responsibility that is always figured by the trope of the lost child in Coetzee's writing. Like Dostoevsky in *The Master of Petersburg*, Lurie must respond responsibly to the child that is not phenomenally apparent in the other being. To respond in terms of self-interest is to abnegate this responsibility and thus to stand accused of abandoning the child. Just this emerges in Lurie's use of the words "*J'accuse*" (40), on learning of the charge that Melanie Isaacs has laid against him. From my readings of *Foe*, *Age of Iron*, and *The Master of Petersburg*, it should by now be clear that these words, or cognate ones, always appear in the context of parental or filial impiety in Coetzee's writing. On a symbolic level, it follows that the charge to which Lurie must respond at the university hearing is of having corrupted and abandoned a child.

The sentences that precede the hearing, "Blest be the infant babe. No outcast he. Blest be the babe" (46), suggest just this. In her discussion of the allusions to Wordsworth and Byron in *Disgrace*, Margot Beard points out that these sentences allude to the second book of the *Prelude*, in which Wordsworth

> apostrophises the "infant babe" who, blessed by being nursed and rocked in his loving mother's arms, acquires "[a] virtue which irradiates and exalts / objects." He is thus "[n]o outcast" for "[a]long his infant veins are interfused / The gravitation and the filial bond / Of nature that connect him with the world."[10]

---

[10] Beard, "Lessons from the Dead Masters," 64–65.

With huge irony, Lurie, a disciple of Wordsworth, perverts rather than preserves the "filial bond" in his dealings with others. *Disgrace* opens where *The Master of Petersburg* closes – with the corruption of a child.[11]

The purport of the allusion to Wordsworth's "infant babe" seems fairly clear: Lurie's selfish relations with others exemplify his disrespect for the "infant" and the "filial bond." At this stage in the novel, he is incapable of relating with cathartic altruism to the otherness of the other being or, in terms of Coetzee's metaphor, the child within the other being. Due to his failure to respect the child, he stands accused of abandonment. It is for this reason that the allusion to the *Prelude* portrays Lurie as an "outcast": his self-absorption, indeed entrapment in himself, detaches him from others.

In this novel, as in the earlier fiction, this separation is figured by the prison-metaphor. Lurie, quite unwittingly, equates his self with a prison when he says that it is necessary to "serve one's time" (67), and thereafter describes himself as "an old lag serving out my sentence" (216). He is his own prison, the host of prejudices that have "settled in his mind, settled down" (72). In his very own estimation, his mind has been taken over, is inhabited, even colonized, by patterns of thought that preclude him from respecting other beings. It "has become a refuge for old thoughts, idle, indigent, with nowhere else to go" (72). While he knows that "He ought to chase them out, sweep the premises clean," Lurie "does not care to do so, or does not care enough" (72).

Importantly, Lurie is not alone in his failure to care enough. To be sure, his condition is fairly symptomatic of relations in general in the post-apartheid society represented in *Disgrace*. One of the major structural features of this novel is the clear parallel between Lurie's violation of Melanie Isaacs and the more overtly violent gang rape of Lucy, on her smallholding in the Eastern Cape town of Salem. In the later scene, the trope of the undesired guest recurs: Lucy is surprised by intruders who proceed to rape her. It is noteworthy that Lurie repeatedly refers to the

---

[11] The fact that Melanie Isaacs may have attempted suicide after Lurie's seduction of her suggests a further parallel between these two novels. Dostoevsky's corruption of Matryona at the end of *The Master of Petersburg*, I have noted, alludes to Stavrogin's violation of a child, Matryosha, in the historical Dostoevsky's *The Devils*. Following her violation by Stavrogin, Matryosha commits suicide. Sue Kossew notes further correspondences between Lurie and Stavrogin ("The Politics of Shame and Redemption," 158, 159).

gang rapists as "intruders" (110), "invaders" (110) and "visitors" (107, 115, 158). Equally noteworthy is Coetzee's use of death as a motif in Lucy's rape. Although she never describes her violation, Lucy does depict herself as a "dead person" (161). Finally, like Melanie (25), she tries to cleanse herself of the defilement (97–98).

These parallels indicate that relations at all levels of South African society reveal a lack of respect for the other being. The ethical: i.e. the sort of compassion or care for the other that leads to respect for others, is absent from the public domain in post-apartheid South Africa. In this respect there is very little difference between Coetzee's depiction of apartheid and post-apartheid South African society: *Disgrace*, like this writer's fiction of the apartheid era, deals with a failure of love.

The parallels between the two rape-scenes also imply that Lurie, notwithstanding his outrage at Lucy's violation, is himself implicated in the instrumentalizing logic that defines relations in this society, and that leads to violence against other beings. One of the ironies that emerge from this parallel is that he is party to what he condemns. When he rails at Lucy's rapists, he is, quite ironically, railing at himself.

℘ ঽ

Through the gang rape of Lucy, Coetzee challenges his protagonist's assumption of autonomy and the careless freedom to realize his every desire that proceeds from this assumption. Crucially, Lurie is trapped in the toilet of his daughter's homestead while she is being raped. On a symbolic level, his 'incarceration' figures his separation from the child he should protect, hence his complicity in the atrocity. Indeed, this is further intimated by his remorse at not having been able to "save" Lucy. As he later "confesses" to her, "I did nothing. I did not save you" (157). Like Dostoevsky in *The Master of Petersburg*, he cannot "save" the child, because he himself is the death of the child. On the other hand, Lurie's 'imprisonment' means that he is not able to witness Lucy's violation and is thus forced to *imagine* it. In this scene of filial separation, then, we find him struggling to relate to Lucy through the imagination: "A vision comes to him of Lucy struggling with the two in the blue overalls, struggling against them. He writhes, trying to blank it out" (97). Lurie's incarceration requires him to do what he has hitherto failed to do.

After her violation, Lucy nonetheless rejects Lurie's gestures of sympathy, because she feels that he cannot "begin to know" what has happened to her (134): "'Lucy!' he calls again, and now for the first time she turns her gaze on him. A frown appears on her face. [...] 'My dearest child!' he says. He follows her into the cage and tries to take her in his arms. Gently, decisively, she wriggles loose" (97). His daughter refuses to discuss her violation with him and asks him to keep to his "story," to what happened to him, and to let her tell her own "story" (99). The implication is that Lurie would not be able to tell Lucy's story, because he cannot imagine himself into her position.

This basic point is reiterated when Bev Shaw responds to Lurie's assertion that "I know what Lucy has been through. I was there" (140), with the words "But you weren't there David. She told me. You weren't" (140). Lurie, who knows what it is like to be a rapist, does not know what it is like to be a rape victim. This is what he has to learn in the course of the novel – notwithstanding his conviction that he is too old and set in his ways to learn anything new (2, 49, 66, 77).[12] Thus we find that Lurie, after describing Lucy as "the object of a crime," asks her whether she is "trying to remind" him "Of what women undergo at the hands of men" (111). And later, Coetzee has him reflect as follows: "he can, if he concentrates, if he loses himself, be there, be the men, inhabit them, fill them with the ghost of himself. The question is, does he have it in him to be the woman?" (160). He must answer this question and those that he asks himself once Bev Shaw has pointed out that he did not witness Lucy's violation:

> *You weren't there. You don't know what happened.* He is baffled. Where, according to Bev Shaw, according to Lucy, was he not? In the room where the intruders were committing their outrages? Do they think he does not know what rape is? Do they think he has not suffered with his daughter? What more could he have witnessed than he is capable of imagining? Or do they think that, where rape is concerned, no man can be where the woman is? (140–41)

The imaginative task that Coetzee assigns his protagonist is therefore to learn "to be the woman," to be where the woman is in being raped by a

---

[12] See Meffan and Worthington, "Ethics before Politics," 144–46.

man. Lurie must sympathize with his daughter and, as is implied by the parallel between the two rape scenes, Melanie Isaacs.

David Lurie's faltering development of a sympathetic imagination commences soon after the rape, when, in a scene that recalls the earlier one in which he makes love to Melanie Isaacs in Lucy's bedroom in his Cape Town house, he occupies the bedroom that his daughter has vacated (111). The implication is that he must try to imagine what had happened there. He must put himself in Lucy's place and "be the woman" in order to "understand" (160). Significantly, he does eventually manage to view the events that transpired in the bedroom from her perspective: "Lucy was frightened, frightened near to death. Her voice choked, she could not breathe, her limbs went numb. *This is not happening,* she said to herself as the men forced her down; *it is just a dream, a nightmare"* (160).

Immediately before this passage describing his imaginative identification with his daughter, Lurie reflects on Byron's relationship with women and the probability that "Among the legions of countesses and kitchen-maids Byron pushed himself into there were no doubt those who called it rape" (160). The opera that Lurie is composing is, of course, about Byron's liaison with one of these young women, Teresa Guiccioli. Once Lurie succeeds in "losing himself" by occupying Lucy's position, the opera changes. It is no longer about the predatory Byron and the young Teresa Guiccioli, but about Teresa Guiccioli in middle age, after the death of Byron. Lurie, it seems, has discovered the ability imaginatively to project himself into a "dumpy little widow" (181), a "plain, ordinary woman" (182). He has, in Segall's words, become "a ghostwriter for an abandoned woman."[13]

Towards the end of the novel, then, there appear to be clear indications that this character has completed the task assigned him by his author. The "lyric impulse" (214) that enables him to compose the opera himself, rather than merely "lifting" sections from the "masters" (183), has also enabled him to lose himself by imagining himself into the existence of his daughter. And, in putting himself into Lucy's place, Lurie is thinking his way into Melanie Isaacs' life or, at the very least, encountering some of the hardships with which she may have had to contend following his violation of her.

---

[13] Kimberly Wedeven Segall, "Pursuing Ghosts: The Traumatic Sublime in J.M. Coetzee's *Disgrace," Research in African Literatures* 36.4 (2005): 45.

It should be emphasized here that the "lyric impulse" that allows this character to compose the opera himself is definitely not merely an isolated, aesthetic category. When he explains his violation of Melanie to Mr Isaacs, Lurie does so in terms of the absence of the lyrical. He tells Isaacs that Melanie "struck up a fire" in him, and then says that it was "Not hot enough to burn" him "up, but real: real fire" (166). A little later, he adds to this confession with the following words: "I lack the lyrical. I manage love too well. Even when I burn I don't sing, if you understand me. For which I am sorry. I am sorry for what I took your daughter through" (171). Clearly, Lurie's discovery of the "lyric impulse" in his composition of the opera marks a qualitative change in his existential relations.

Indeed, this discovery constitutes a significant development in this character's quest for the lost child. Earlier, in commenting on Coetzee's use of the child-image in this novel, I argued that Lurie's entrapment during his daughter's violation signifies his separation from the abandoned child. In this regard, it is revealing that, while he is shut up, he is doused with methylated spirits and then set alight. "At once," we read, "he is bathed in cool blue flames" (96). While Lurie here burns, quite literally, he is, in terms of his preoccupation with the perfective, not "burnt up" (166). If he is to "save" his daughter, the child, he must be consumed entirely. Importantly, the opera helps in this respect: "It consumes him night and day" (214).

The change that Lurie undergoes in discovering the "lyric impulse" places him in a number of roles and positions that are ironic reversals of those he has previously occupied. So, for instance, in allowing him to identify with his daughter and, by extension, Melanie Isaacs, this impulse confronts him with what it would have been like to have been raped by himself. In addition, his newfound generosity exposes him to the effect of his rape of Melanie on her family, because he now finds himself in their position. Hence Lurie, after Lucy's rape, begins to find it possible to sympathize with Melanie Isaacs' father (164–74). Because he finds himself in a position similar to that of Mr Isaacs, he can now understand what the latter is going through, and that is why he asks his forgiveness. The irony is patent: David Lurie comes to sympathize with the parents of a girl whom he used in much the same way as the gang rapists used his own daughter.

Through these ironic reversals, Coetzee thus introduces his protagonist to realms of experience from which he has previously been excluded. This is not to say, however, that the sympathetic imagination, as conceived in this novel, is entirely premissed on experience, and that Lurie must therefore first experience what others have undergone before he can sympathize with them. From his depiction of this character's relationship to the dogs in the novel (142–46) and Petrus's sheep, or "slaughter-animals" (123-26), it is clear that, for Coetzee, this is not the case. Seemingly, this writer agrees with Elizabeth Costello's argument, in "The Lives of Animals" section of *Elizabeth Costello*, that "There are no bounds to the sympathetic imagination" (80), and therefore that a human "can think" its "way into the existence of a bat or a chimpanzee or an oyster, any being with whom" it "share[s] the substrate of life" (80). By the end of *Disgrace*, it would appear, Lurie has gained the ability imaginatively to identify with creatures other than human beings. Significantly, in this regard, the novel closes with a scene in which this character, who was previously averse to dogs but now "goes off to the Animal Welfare clinic as often as he can, offering himself for whatever jobs call for no skill," and who finds it curious "that a man as selfish as he should be offering himself to the service of dead dogs" (142, 146) selflessly sacrifices the lame dog that he has come to love.[14]

---

[14] Zoë Wicomb argues that if Lurie's "professed humility in the company of dogs is not simply a matter of hyperbolic posturing, it certainly escapes ethical engagement with the human condition" ("Translations in the Yard of Africa," *Journal of Literary Studies* 18.3–4 [2002]: 219). See also Benaouda Lebdai's related contention ("Identity: Bodies and Voices in Coetzee's *Disgrace* and Bouraoui's *Garçon manqué*," in *Bodies and Voices: The Force-Field of Representation and Discourse in Colonial and Postcolonial Studies*, ed. Merete Falck Borch et al. [Cross/Cultures 94; Amsterdam & New York: Rodopi, 2008]: 36). As I have shown, Lurie's development of a sympathetic imagination is certainly not limited to his relations with dogs and, for that matter, sheep. Also, I am not at all sure how one begins to separate the human condition from the condition of other animals without relying on a series of dubious metaphysical and/or rational assumptions, most of which are deeply embedded in colonial discourse. Derrida's sentiment that "There is no animal in the general singular, separated from man by a single indivisible limit" ("The Animal that therefore I Am (More to Follow)," tr. David Wills, *Critical Inquiry* 28 [2002]: 415) is clearly one that Coetzee shares. In this regard, see my discussion of the Magistrate's sense of infinite responsibility in *Waiting for the Barbarians*. Finally, for nuanced discussions of the role of animals in *Disgrace* (and Coetzee's other fiction), see Josephine Donovan, "'Miracles of Creation'," 78–93, Wendy Woodward, "Dog Stars and Dog Souls: The Lives of Dogs in *Triomf* by Marlene van Niekerk and *Disgrace* by J.M. Coetzee," *Journal of*

Apart from suggesting that the imagination is not limited by experience, this ending provides the reader with some insight into the logic of *ek-stasis* and self-sacrifice that informs Coetzee's conception of the imagination. Irrespective of his love for it, Lurie must sacrifice the dog. This is the implication of the question that Bev Shaw asks him, "Are you giving him up?" (220), and to which he responds with the words "Yes, I am giving him up" (220). Lurie must give up the dog because it is in the dog's interests that he does so. His own needs, desires, feelings, predilections, and predispositions are wholly immaterial. To sympathize, Lurie must lose – indeed, sacrifice or offer – himself. The basic principle here is the same as the one that applies in Mrs Curren's relationship with John in *Age of Iron* and Dostoevsky's relationship with Nechaev in *The Master of Petersburg*: contrary to the Levitical injunction, Lurie must love his neighbour, the dog, generously – not as himself, but despite himself.

Through the agency of the imagination, Coetzee seems to be saying, the self may achieve *ek-stasis* and so identify with the other being. It is precisely its apparent ability to precipitate a forfeiture or transcendence of self that invests the imagination with ethical efficacy. In losing itself, the self renders itself incapable of violating other existents. Violence, as Costello explains in *Elizabeth Costello*, is precisely a failure of imaginative ecstasy:

> The particular horror of the [Nazi death] camps, the horror that convinces us that what went on there was a crime against humanity, is not that despite a humanity shared with their victims, the killers treated them like lice. That is too abstract. The horror is that the killers refused to think themselves into the place of their victims, as did everyone else. They said, "It is *they* in those cattle-cars rattling past." They did not say, "How would it be if it were I in that cattle-car?" They did not say, "It is I who am in that cattle-car." They said, "It must be the dead who are being burnt today, making the air stink and falling in ash on my cabbages." They did not say, "How would it be if I were burning?" They did not say, "I am burning, I am falling in ash." (79)

One is therefore tempted to agree with Elleke Boehmer that "The surrender of self through empathy is a state which Lurie in time comes to

---

Literary Studies 17.3–4 (2001): 90–119, and Laura Wright, *Writing "Out of All the Camps"*.

achieve."[15] As I have indicated, there is much evidence in *Disgrace* to support the claim that Coetzee has furnished this work with the structure of an anti-*Bildungsroman*, a novel which involves the forfeiture rather than consolidation of the protagonist's sense of self. On the strength of the evidence I have adduced, one could even argue that this ethical trajectory, which stretches from Lurie's initial assertion of the "rights of desire" (52), and description of himself as a "servant of Eros" (89) to his eventual placement of himself in the service of other beings, is laid bare in the text when this character finds himself taking care of Lucy and taking over her chores on the smallholding:

> This is not what he came for – to be stuck in the back of beyond, ward-
> ing off demons, nursing his daughter, attending to a dying enterprise.
> If he came for anything, it was to *gather himself*, gather his forces.
> Here he is *losing himself* day by day. (121; my emphasis)

Thus construed, the ethical trajectory of *Disgrace* is not dissimilar to the movement from selfish egotism to cathartic altruism that one finds in a poem like Coleridge's "This Lime-Tree Bower My Prison."[16] All in all, this novel's apparent confidence in the imagination could be read as an endorsement of the central, self-reflexive contention of Coleridge's poem: namely, that this faculty cannot be incarcerated, that it is a means by which the self may transcend its incarceration in itself. In losing himself, Lurie frees himself from his entrapment in himself.

℘ ৯

I have already suggested, though, that the ethical trajectory of *Disgrace* is by no means this clear-cut. If anything, its movement is chiastic and involves a doubling back on itself that disputes what it seems to assert even as it is asserted.[17] In tracing this double movement, I show that,

---

[15] Boehmer, "Not Saying Sorry, Not Speaking Pain," 346.

[16] Samuel Taylor Coleridge, "This Lime-Tree Bower My Prison," in *The Complete Poetical and Dramatic Works of Samuel Taylor Coleridge*, ed. James Dykes Campbell (London: Macmillan, 1893).

[17] For insightful discussions of Coetzee's "predilection for chiastic formulations," see J.U. Jacobs, "Writing a New Nation," 35, and Graham Pechey, "Coetzee's Purgatorial Africa: The Case of *Disgrace*," *Interventions* 4.3 (2002): 382–83.

while this novel certainly does thematize the power of the imagination, it at the same time questions its ability to serve as a vehicle for *ek-stasis*. Nevertheless, this interrogation does not simply culminate in a dismissal of the imagination. In keeping with the logic of the cross-over, the text's questioning of the imagination and articulation of its aporetic nature paradoxically establishes its ethical necessity.[18]

The penultimate chapter of Coetzee's novel, in which David Lurie strikes Pollux (206–209), one of his daughter's assailants, suggests that, although the imagination may not be limited by experience, it does have limits and consequently may be imprisoned. After all, in assaulting Pollux, Lurie shows a failure of imagination, and this, of course, is emphasized in the novel by the comparatively more sympathetic treatment he, the violator of Melanie Isaacs, receives from Mr Isaacs. Lurie's failure of sympathy is further evident in Coetzee's portrayal of Pollux as a child not so much in age as in mental capability, a portrayal of which the reader is reminded when, after Lurie strikes him, Lucy defends Pollux with the words "He is disturbed. A disturbed child" (208). The implication is fairly obvious: Coetzee's use of the child-metaphor in this scene creates a parallel between Lurie's relationship with Pollux and Lurie's violation of Melanie Isaacs, who, as we have seen, is also depicted as a child (20), a parallel which reminds one that the protagonist is himself guilty of the violence for which he berates Pollux and that, in striking him, he repeats this original violence.

In the novel, the juxtaposition of the scene in which Lurie assaults Pollux with the one in which he selflessly sacrifices the dog indicates what, in terms of the logic of *ek-stasis*, should happen in Lurie's relationship with Pollux. Lurie should sympathize with Pollux despite his hatred of him and desire for vengeance. Again to use Mrs Curren's words, in her description of her relationship with John in *Age of Iron*, Lurie must "love" Pollux even though he finds him "unlovable" (125). He must love him because he finds him unlovable. If he is to achieve *ek-stasis*, his hatred of Pollux and his desire for vengeance are quite simply beside the point, or merely what will be transcended when he loses himself.

---

[18] This part of my discussion intersects with Meffan and Worthington's contention that it is precisely the failure of the "imaginative attempt" that renders it "ethically productive" ("Ethics before Politics," 145).

Clearly, the juxtaposition of these contrasting scenes complicates and qualifies the ethical trajectory of the novel by requiring the reader to reflect on the reasons for Lurie's inability to respond to Pollux despite himself. The juxtaposition seems to suggest that, although the imagination does enable a degree of sympathy and even identification with other beings, it is located in the self and will thus always, to a greater or lesser extent, be limited by the desires and antipathies of the self of which it is ultimately an emanation or expression. To complicate matters further, the juxtaposition also suggests that, together with its values and attitudes, the self's desires and antipathies are not pure, but situated by the self's location in a particular cultural and historical context. In this regard, Lurie's violation of Pollux is directly related to his perception that the gang rape of his daughter was motivated by "vengeance" (112), by the rapists' apparent need to avenge themselves on white South Africans for the crime of apartheid. For Lurie, the rape is an expression not of individual agents, but of history working through the individuals involved – hence his assertion that "It was history speaking through them. [...] A history of wrong" (156). The rapists' action has been *inspired* by the intertext of racial discourse that has shaped the history of South African society. They rape Lucy because she is a white woman and accordingly complicit in the colonial oppression of black people. Their response to her is determined by their location in a culture in which difference among people has been inscribed by the discourse of race. In fact, their embeddedness as subjects in this generic discourse prevents the rapists from responding to Lucy other than as a white woman – other than what has always already been said and which is therefore what they expect in their encounter with her. Being general, the category of race is repeatable and its iterative movement routinely qualifies the very singularity of the individual. In doing so, the trope of race enables physical violence.

Ironically, Lurie's explanation of the gang rape also explains his violation of Pollux. In wishing them "harm" (107), and in finally striking Pollux, he retaliates for the rapists' sexual attack on Lucy and does so on their terms or, rather, to use his argument, the terms of history. By vengefully opposing the black men, he places himself in a position that has been defined against the one they occupy. That is, he occupies an already given position, one that has been inscribed in the political dynamic of South African culture by the discourse of race which, in his reading, informed the rape of Lucy. In seeking to avenge Lucy, Lurie is located by the rapists' location in this discourse. His relationship with them is deter-mined by the discursively constructed opposition of race and, when he strikes Pollux, history thus speaks through him, too. Lurie's desire for vengeance and his expression of this desire have their origin in the dis-courses of the context in which he is situated.

In its emphasis on the extent to which the individual's constitution in culture contributes to his or her perception of the world, the scene in which Lurie assaults Pollux raises the question of whether the imagination can, in fact, engender *ek-stasis*. While Coetzee would agree with Coler-idge that perception is *poietic* rather than passive,[19] that "We half perceive but we also half create," to borrow once more Mrs Curren's Words-worthian sentiment,[20] he would probably wish to add that the Primary Imagination is located in the self who is in the world and, accordingly, that the imaginative expression of this self is worldly, rather than a repeti-tion of the transcendent "eternal act of creation in the infinite I AM."[21] If this is so, how can *ek-stasis* possibly be achieved through the agency of the imagination? For this to happen, what is required of the imagination is not simply a relocation of the self from one subject position to another position that is presupposed and defined in opposition to the position the self has vacated. Instead, the imagination must ecstatically divest the self of *all* subject positions in language and culture. To extrapolate from Coet-zee's description of *ek-stasis* in his essay on Desiderius Erasmus's *Praise of Folly*, the imagination must enable the self to occupy an uncommitted non-position: i.e. "a position not already given, defined, limited and sanc-tioned" by the political dynamic.[22] That is, the imagination must achieve what appears to be impossible: it must enable the self to abandon its point of view in culture and, in so doing, construct for it a position that is pre-cisely not a position, which would therefore allow the self to be within the world while viewing it from nowhere within it. Only then would the self, as a singular entity, be able to relate to other entities as singular entities.

---

[19] Coleridge, *Biographia Literaria* (London: Dent, 1956): 167.

[20] Coetzee, *Age of Iron*, 153.

[21] Coleridge, *Biographia Literaria*, 167.

[22] Coetzee, "Erasmus' *Praise of Folly*," 2. The focus of this essay is Erasmus's argu-ment for a type of madness that is "a kind of *ek-stasis*, a being outside oneself, a being beside oneself, a state in which truth is known (and spoken) from a position that does not know itself to be the position of truth" (10).

Only then would history stop speaking through the self in its predetermined relations with other beings.[23]

What is at issue in *Disgrace*, then, is not so much a case of speaking with "the tongue of a god,"[24] of speaking "from the standpoint of redemption,"[25] as locating an interstitial non-position within culture. In this regard, Lurie's task is similar to that of Dostoevsky, who, it will be recalled, explains his reluctance to take sides in the conflict between the Czarist state and the nihilists in terms of his desire to find the "true words," to "speak in a voice from under the waters."[26] It will also be remembered that Dostoevsky, in his dream encounter with Pavel in the watery underworld, finds that each syllable he tries to articulate is replaced by a syllable of water.[27] If Lurie is to complete the task of the imagination that

---

[23] See David Attwell's insightful observation on the role of the imagination in *Disgrace*: "There are two features of the ethical turn in *Disgrace* which deserve comment, for they repeat patterns discernible in the other novels. The first is that an ethical consciousness – which is well this side of being turned into a system – arises from an imaginative act of circumvention, a circumventing of a corrupt history. This pattern is linked in *Disgrace*, as it is in *Age of Iron*, with the presence and consciousness of death; only an alterity so complete as death is capable of eliciting from the subject a transcendent act of consciousness which overcomes the failure of history" ("Race in *Disgrace*," *Interventions* 4.3 [2002]: 339).

[24] Coetzee, *Age of Iron*, 91.

[25] Adorno, *Minima Moralia*, 247.

[26] Coetzee, *The Master of Petersburg*, 110–11.

[27] Coetzee, *The Master of Petersburg*, 17. See Michael Holland's cogent argument on the range of non-verbal sounds in *Disgrace*, which suggests a linguistic progression toward "a single animal voice," on the one hand, and "a single mechanical sound on the other: the *plink-plunk* of a banjo" ("'*Plink-Plunk*': Unforgetting the Present in Coetzee's *Disgrace*," *Interventions* 4.3 [2002]: 403; see also Tom Herron, "The Dog Man: Becoming Animal in Coetzee's *Disgrace*," *Twentieth-Century Literature* 51.4 [2005]: 485–86). In the novel, the pivotal scene in this progression is that in which Lurie, together with the dog who "seems on the point of singing too, or howling" (215), strums on his banjo "in the desolate yard in Africa" (214), hoping for "a single authentic note of immortal longing" (214). To this argument, it may be added that the note for which Lurie strives, and which he thinks may be recognised by "the scholars of the future" (214), stands in ironic contrast to his inauthentic testimony to the university's commission of inquiry. Farodia Rassool feels that his statement "should come from him, in his own words." It should come "from his heart" (54). Lurie responds somewhat cynically to this sentiment: "And you trust yourself to divine that, from the words I use – to divine whether it comes from my heart?" (54). Once again, the issue

Coetzee assigns him in *Disgrace*, he must do what Dostoevsky tries, yet fails, to do in *The Master of Petersburg*: i.e. attain an uncommitted non-position. It follows that he must sympathize not only with Lucy, as I initially suggested, but also with Pollux and his fellow rapists. In fact, the logic of *ek-stasis* is rather more uncompromising than this statement would allow: Lurie's failure to transcend the discursively inscribed relations of contestation within his culture, and consequent inability to sympathize with Pollux, implies that he is also unable properly to sympathize with Lucy. In order to sympathize with her, Lurie must sympathize with Pollux. Like Mrs Curren, in *Age of Iron*, who realizes that, to love her daughter, she must love John (124–25), and Dostoevsky, in *The Master of Petersburg*, who realizes that, to love Pavel, he must first love Nechaev (238), the possible murderer of his son, Lurie must love Pollux. He must sympathize with Pollux precisely because he cannot find it in himself to do so.

The further suggestion here is that, in locating himself and Lucy's assailants within a discursively installed opposition, Lurie inevitably reduces Lucy herself to a term in the same opposition and that this precludes him from effectively sympathizing with her. As much emerges in his interpretation of her response to her violation and in her response to his interpretation. After the sexual attack on his daughter, Lurie feels that Lucy should fortify her home against future attacks:

> They ought to instal bars, security gates, a perimeter fence, as Ettinger
> has done. They ought to turn the farmhouse into a fortress. Lucy ought
> to buy a pistol and a two-way radio, and take shooting lessons. (113)

As in *Foe* and *Age of Iron*, the house-image at this point in *Disgrace* serves as a metaphor for the way in which the self's position within culture's differential relations secures him or her against the danger of otherness, of what exceeds this system of differences.

Just as revealing, in this regard, is Lurie's attempt to persuade Lucy to lay a charge with the police against her violators, and hunt them down (113). He eventually reads her refusal to seek retribution for the violence perpetrated against her as a product of her white liberal guilt, as becomes

---

here at stake is how to recognise the lost child, how to tell the difference between the "true words," the saviour, and the impostor or usurper.

apparent when he challenges her with the following questions: "Is it some form of private salvation you are trying to work out? Do you hope you can expiate the crimes of the past by suffering in the present?" (112). Lucy's response to these questions, "No. You keep *misreading* me. Guilt and salvation are abstractions. Until you make an effort to see that, I can't help you" (my emphasis, 112), lays bare a disjunction between Lurie's interpretation of Lucy and Lucy herself, and raises a question about the origin of Lurie's reading.[28] If the latter does not bear an *a priori* relation to what it purports to comprehend, where does it come from? The answer is fairly self-evident. Apart from its lack of foundation in material reality, the racial overtones of Lurie's interpretation (or interpretative construct) indicate that, far from proceeding *ex nihilo*, it is grounded in the discourse of race in South African society. In averring that Lucy wishes to "humble" herself "before history" (160) – that her passivity is prompted by a desire, born of guilt, to atone for the history of white oppression in South Africa – Lurie offers an historical reading of Lucy's passivity, a reading which is itself determined by the discourse that has shaped the history in question.

In inscribing this dissonance between Lurie's interpretative activity and the object of that activity, and thereby indicating that Lurie's hermeneutic operation is inspired and determined by racial discourse, Coetzee insinuates that, rather than sympathizing with her, Lurie, in using the trope of race to read his daughter and her behaviour, repeats her rapists' "misreading" of her. In Lurie's understanding, as I have indicated, the men rape Lucy because she is a white woman. Tellingly, in this respect, the only information about her experience of the violation that Lucy divulges to her father is the curious, yet crucial, detail that those who raped her did so in a horrifyingly familiar and personal manner:

> "It was so personal. [...] it was done with such personal hatred. That was what stunned me more than anything. The rest was [...] expected. But why did they hate me so? I had never set eyes on them."
> (156)

What Lucy had not expected was that her rapists had expected her. In other words, despite being a stranger to these strangers, they knew her or, at least, behaved as though they did. The implication here is that the men

---

[28] See Pechey, "Coetzee's Purgatorial Africa," 381.

know her through the generic categories of race in South African society. They approach her from within the sets of expectations of people that have been produced by these categories. Indeed, they rape her because they believe they know her.

Lucy's horror at the personal nature of the rapists' violence exposes a dissonance between her attackers' systems of knowledge and the object of their knowledge. That is, the surprise that she expresses at the familiarity with which they treat her points to the fact that their epistemic structures have constructed the object of their knowledge. In recording this dissonance, and thereby establishing a parallel between it and the dissonance between Lucy and Lurie's interpretation of her, the novel suggests that Lucy's response to her father: namely, "I am not the person you know" (161), applies equally to the rapists. History speaks through both Lurie and the rapists when they presume to know Lucy.

What this set of parallels reveals, then, is that Lurie and the rapists are guilty of a similar failure of imagination in their respective interactions with Lucy. While they certainly do imagine Lucy, their attempts in this regard are inspired by the position they occupy in history's economy of exchange.[29] They construct for her an identity by recuperating her within a set of pre-existing paradigms. It is probably for this reason that Coetzee has Lucy use the activity of reading as a metaphor when she tells Lurie that he has misunderstood her. As it is here conceived, reading is a culturally determined operation in making known the unknown, familiar the

---

[29] Louise Bethlehem contends that Lucy's pregnant body is aneconomic, heterogeneous to the logic of the masculinist economy of significatory exchange in which it is nonetheless located. Its meaning within this economy is delayed, deferred ("Aneconomy in an Economy of Melancholy: Embodiment and Gendered Identity in J.M. Coetzee's *Disgrace*," *African Identities* 1.2 [2003]: 167–85). For a different, though equally insightful, reading, see Georgina Horrell's argument that Lucy's body is depicted as a "site for the inscription of guilt, as well as an apt place for the exacting of penalty"; that it is a "notepad on which the debt of colonists is written and payment exacted" ("Postcolonial *Disgrace*: (White) Women and (White) Guilt in the 'New' South Africa," in *Bodies and Voices*, ed. Merete Falck Borch et al., 19, 25). Horrel's essay, despite her concluding caveat, foregrounds the complexity of Coetzee's engagement with the racialization and sexualization of the body in *Disgrace* and therefore serves as a valuable response to Grant Farred's ascription to Coetzee of a strangely naive position on the issue of whiteness ("Bulletproof Settlers: The Politics of Offense in the New South Africa," in *Whiteness: A Critical Reader*, ed. Mike Hill [New York: New York UP, 1997]: 65–77).

unfamiliar, general the singular, by integrating it into those signifying codes that culture makes available. If Lurie is to "find" his "own words,"[30] and thereby locate the lost child, he must read differently. The kind of reading that is called for is one in which he responds to Lucy as a stranger, and so acknowledges her singularity, by forfeiting his subject positions in language and culture. In order to do this, he must overcome the positions inscribed by his culture's economy of vengeance and retribution. He must learn, in other words, to read in the manner described by Dostoevsky in *The Master of Petersburg* – he must give himself up and be both the assailant and the victim.

This understanding of reading as a form of *ek-stasis* is not developed on the presentational surface of *Disgrace.* The reader is provided with no firm indication of whether or not Lurie ever develops the capacity to read Lucy in terms other than those provided by history, of whether or not, that is to say, he develops the capacity to use the imagination as a means not of knowing other beings, but of encountering those beings as strangers.

✍ ঽ

Disgrace does, however, attempt to secure a performative elaboration of this notion of reading as *ek-stasis.* This is evident in Coetzee's alignment of the reader of the text with Lurie, the reader-figure in the text, through his management of point of view. In using Lurie as a focalizer, the novel denies the reader direct access to Lucy. And, in emphasizing Lurie's unreliability, and thereby self-consciously presenting his reading of Lucy as discursively mediated, the novel requires the reader to find the true Lucy, the lost child. In fact, the irony which proceeds from Lurie's "misreading" of his daughter places the reader in the position of having to determine what is *not* said about Lucy from what is said about her.[31] In other words, as is always the case in the literary use of irony, the reader is required to determine the unsaid from the said. If s/he succeeds in doing so, s/he will have managed to "find" the "true words" for Lucy's singularity,[32] for

---

[30] Coetzee, *Age of Iron,* 91.

[31] In what follows, I am again indebted to Geertsema's discussion of the relation between irony and otherness ("Irony and Otherness").

[32] Coetzee, *The Master of Petersburg,* 111.

what has been negated, but is nevertheless invoked, by the generic and
generalizing discourses through which Lurie fails to know her.

In attempting to complete the task that is assigned him or her by Lurie's
ironic misreadings, the reader, however, finds that it is impossible to
engage in a simple antiphrastic substitution of the unsaid for the said.
Crucially, in this respect, his or her awareness that Lurie does not know
his daughter derives not from superior knowledge of Lucy that s/he possesses and that has been enabled by the text's provision of a more reliable
perspective on this character. The reader only ever knows that Lurie does
not know Lucy, because s/he has been made aware that the latter exceeds
the former's cognitive grasp. Accordingly, the novel prevents the reader
from comfortably distancing him-/herself from Lurie by establishing an
ironic contract with the author that is premissed on knowledge that they
share but that has been withheld from Lurie. Not being able to rely on the
author as guarantor of meaning in his or her attempt to determine the unsaid from the said, the reader finds that the relationship between these
terms is not simply differential. In fact, the difference between them is
constantly deferred and, in consequence, the unsaid is never simply presupposed and already defined by the said. It is always more than the said.

My argument is not that the relationship between said and unsaid that is
installed by the novel's presentation of Lucy is rendered indeterminate by
Coetzee's withholding of information from the reader. It is, rather, that
this relationship's indeterminacy is the direct and inevitable consequence
of Coetzee's disavowal of authority, his deconstruction of both his and his
novel's claims in this regard. Indeed, the non-dialectical nature of the relationship between said and unsaid is asserted by Coetzee's intertextual affiliation of his Lucy with William Wordsworth's Lucy – an affiliation
that, apart from the shared name, is evident in Lurie's scholarly interest in
Wordsworth, the presentation of both Lucys as lost daughters from an uncomprehending male perspective, and their association with nature, rural
existence, and the alterity of death.

While the Romantic project celebrates the power of the imagination, its
ability to grasp "The spiritual presences of absent things"[33] and to "arouse

---

[33] Wordsworth, *The Excursion* IV, l. 1234, in *Wordsworth: Poetical Works*, ed.
Thomas Hutchinson (Oxford: Oxford UP, 1936).

the sensual from their sleep / Of Death,"[34] the Lucy poems evince a fine sense of the possible failure of this faculty's "synthetic and magical power."[35] They signal the ambiguity at the heart of Romanticism, the fact that its aesthetic confidence is accompanied by a sense of inevitable failure. As Tillotama Rajan observes,

> Revenants and surrogates – whether they come back literally, or metaphorically like Lucy and the Boy of Winander, whom the poet summons back through an act of orphic commemoration – speak for the power of imaginary representation, *but also for the duplicity of its substitutions.*[36]

Rajan makes this point in the course of his argument that, despite its claims for the power of imaginary representation, its tendency "to range life-oriented terms such as 'genius,' 'organic,' and 'vital' against their mechanistic opposites, and to accord poetry a privileged position in this secular debate between body and soul," Romantic poetry evinces unease "on whether poetic reproduction is an 'imitation' which masters the very 'essence' of the object of desire, or a 'copy' which merely represents it and therefore reveals 'an emptiness [...] an unreality' within the fabrications of language."[37]

It is precisely this representational tension between presence and absence that the allusions to the Lucy poems in *Disgrace* invoke, thereby suggesting that Lucy exceeds not only Lurie's representational endeavours but also those of Coetzee. In this respect, the nexus formed by death between Coetzee's Lucy and her thematic ancestor is of central importance. While his daughter is being raped, David Lurie wonders whether or not she is dead (96), thus echoing the male speaker of "Strange Fits of Passion," who, upon approaching Lucy's house, exclaims: "'O mercy!' to myself I cried, / 'If Lucy should be dead'."[38] Later, Lucy Lurie's affinity

---

[34] Wordsworth, *The Excursion* ["Prospectus"], ll. 60–61, in *Wordsworth: Poetical Works.*

[35] Coleridge, *Biographia Literaria,* 174.

[36] Tilottama Rajan, *Dark Interpreter: The Discourse of Romanticism* (Ithaca NY: Cornell UP, 1980): 211. My emphasis.

[37] Rajan, *Dark Interpreter,* 210.

[38] Wordsworth, "Strange Fits of Passion," ll. 27–28, in *Wordsworth: Poetical Works.*

with death is directly articulated in her aforementioned words to her father: "I am a dead person and I do not know yet what will bring me back to life" (161).

In the novel, the affinity with death that Coetzee's Lucy shares with Wordsworth's Lucy establishes a highly ironic relation between the signifier Lucy and what it purports to signify. By relating their characters to death, Coetzee and Wordsworth associate them with precisely what cannot be named, or what words cannot show or elucidate. The very word 'death' is in itself an attempt at naming the unnameable – of establishing, in language, a relation of correlation with what is irrevocably beyond language. By extension, the name Lucy is prosopopeial: the ascription, yet again to recall J. Hillis Miller's description, of a name to "the absent, the inanimate, or the dead,"[39] a representation that indicates the failure of presence. In fact, the name Lucy is self-consciously prosopopeial. By linking their respective figures of alterity to death, both Wordsworth and Coetzee foreground the irony implicit in the name Lucy, a name that, despite its etymological associations with illumination and epiphany, only ever reveals its inadequate, and thus ironic, relation to what it promises to reveal. What the signifier Lucy reveals, namely, is that what it must reveal cannot be revealed because it is not of the lucid order of the phenomenon and its logic of manifestation.

Through these allusions to Wordsworth, Coetzee announces his inability to know Lucy by finding "true words" for her singularity, and suggests that the absence of this singularity from its economy renders the text incomplete. It follows that, in requiring the reader to know Lucy's singularity, to "find" for it "true words" outside discourse, the ironic relation the text establishes between said and unsaid obliges the reader to engage in the imaginative task of completing the novel. The reader must do what the novel itself admits the writer cannot do and, indeed, what cannot be done.

Premissed as it ultimately is on the sublime unsayability of the unsaid, the text's use of irony does not therefore inscribe distance that is predicated on a disparity in knowledge between, on the one hand, the author and reader and, on the other, the character David Lurie but, rather, aligns their respective attempts at determining Lucy's singularity. In this regard, it is noteworthy that the question David Lurie asks of himself when Lucy

---

[39] Miller, "Prosopopeia in Hardy and Stevens," 245.

refuses to discuss with him her response to having been raped, "How [...] can a man in his state find words that will bring back the dead?" (156), and that he constantly ponders in composing his chamber opera, is the very question that Coetzee asks himself, and scripts in the novel, by relating the name Lucy to death. By extension, this question is also the one the text requires the reader to ask him-/herself by placing him or her in relation to what remains unsaid about Lucy in the novel.

In staging this question (in effect, 'how can I express, in form, that which is other than form and, accordingly, which form can only deform?'), *Disgrace* thus enters a conversation on aesthetics that was initiated by the Romantic project's awareness of the ambiguous nature of *poiesis*, that the synthesis to which it aspires goes together with *diaeresis* – an awareness that is, arguably, most pronounced in the Jena Romantics' preoccupation with the way in which the fragment, through its incompletion, announces its finiteness, hence the inadequacy of its medium to the infiniteness of what it does not contain.[40] By the time Maurice Blanchot entered this conversation, the question about stating what is *ex hypothesi* had been taken up by Hegel,[41] for whom Romantic art's very inability to convey the absolute, the Idea, in fact intimates it and, in so doing, directs the reader to the ultimate goal of consciousness. Blanchot divests the

---

[40] See Critchley, *Very Little ... Almost Nothing*, 107–15, Rajan, *Dark Interpreter*, 178–81, and Friedrich Schlegel, "Athenäum Fragments," in *Philosophical Fragments*, tr. P. Firchow (Minneapolis: U of Minnesota P, 1991): 18–93; see also Isaiah Berlin's description of the intensely ironic and paradoxical nature of this *Streben nach dem Uneindlichen* in *The Roots of Romanticism*, ed. H. Hardy (London: Chatto & Windus, 1999):

> Your relation to the universe is inexpressible, but you must nevertheless express it. This is the agony, this is the problem. This is the unending *Sehnsucht*, this is the yearning [...]. This is the typical romantic nostalgia. If the home for which they are seeking, if the harmony, the perfection about which they talk could be granted to them, they would reject it. It is in principle, by definition, something to which an approach can be made but which cannot be seized, because that is the nature of reality. (105–106)

Finally, Laurence Wright perceptively examines exactly this ironic tension between the differentiated, experiential, phenomenal realm and the undifferentiated, noumenal 'realm' in "David Lurie's Learning and the Meaning of J.M. Coetzee's *Disgrace*," in *Austerities: Essays on J.M. Coetzee*, ed. Michael Neill & Graham Bradshaw (London: Ashgate [forthcoming]).

[41] Georg Wilhelm Friedrich Hegel, *Aesthetics: Lectures on Fine Art*, tr. T.M. Knox (*Vorlesungen über die Ästhetik*, 1843; Oxford: Clarendon, 1975), vol. 1: 77–81.

question of such idealism, detaches it from the *telos* of history as progress, by shifting its emphasis to what transpires in the very event of writing and reading, to the moment in which the writer or reader encounters and attempts to name the unnameable.

This shift in emphasis is, of course, most apparent in Blanchot's reading of the Orpheus myth as an allegory of the aporetic nature of writing (and, indeed, interpretation). As we have seen, Orpheus's impossible task in the space of death, which is beyond history and language, is to possess Eurydice, the "*other* dark," to return to the world, "the light," with this absolute exteriority and, in the light, to invest it with form and substance.[42] It will also be recalled that the problem with this enterprise is that Orpheus's actual desire is not to render visible (and so destroy) the invisible but to see the invisible *as* invisible in the "*other* dark." Elsewhere, Blanchot frames this aporia as follows: "How can I recover it, how can I turn around and look at what exists *before*, if all my power consists of making it into what exists *after*?"[43]

In establishing the homologous nature of the author's, reader's, and character's respective relations to Lucy, *Disgrace*'s irony foregrounds this version of the question of stating the unstatable and, in so doing, the aporetic nature of the endeavour that poses it. That is to say, even as it indicates the commonality of the author's, protagonist's, and reader's enterprise, the irony one finds in *Disgrace* ironizes this endeavour by intimating that it is precisely the act of naming that renders what is named unnameable. For Hillis Miller, as we have seen, the irreducible irony of prosopopeia is that the ascription of a name to the absent or the dead, the attempt at raising the dead, "always buries what it invokes."[44] *Disgrace* is ironically aware that this is precisely what it does. It mourns what it buries in trying to bear.

It follows from its use of irony that this novel depicts reading as an act in which the reader must achieve what cannot be achieved. At the same time as it assigns the reader the task of completing it, the novel indicates that this cannot be done, and consequently that the task that it requires the reader to perform is not properly a task: i.e. a work that the subject is able

---

[42] Blanchot, "Orpheus' Gaze," 177.
[43] Blanchot, "Literature and the Right to Death," 327.
[44] Miller, "Topography and Tropography in Thomas Hardy's *In Front of the Landscape*," 210.

to accomplish in a world of possibility and action. In stating this paradox, the novel seeks not to render futile the reader's endeavour to say the unsayable, to imagine the unimaginable, but, rather, to inscribe infinite distance between itself and its own reading, and thereby attempt to make of reading an event in which the reader encounters what exceeds the cognitive categories of his or her culture and over which s/he can thus exercise no control. What is important here is that the reader be enabled to experience exactly the aporetic nature of the activity in which s/he is engaged and therefore his or her inability to accomplish the task assigned him or her by the novel. In finding that every attempt at imagining Lucy's singularity merely renders it unimaginable, the reader would find him-/herself in relation to what exceeds the generic categories of the culture in which s/he is located as a subject. S/he would find him-/herself in relation to what s/he cannot correlate with, and thereby subsume under, culture's epistemological paradigms.

Should this happen, the reader's encounter with the novel and its characters would enact precisely the kind of *ek-stasis* that the novel thematizes on its presentational surface. In other words, his or her loss of subjective control over what s/he reads would place him or her in an uncommitted non-position, rather than an oppositionally defined and so already given position, in his or her relation to the characters in *Disgrace.* Accordingly, in the engagement with the text, history would no longer speak through the reader. There is more at stake here, however. The point is not simply that the reader would be precluded from including the alterity of what s/he reads in his or her psyche by recuperating it within the discourses of history; it is also, as in the earlier novels, that the reader would be unable to exclude the otherness of what s/he reads from his or her psyche. In being unable to complete the novel, s/he would be invaded and possessed by what exceeds its economy and the language and discourses in which it is situated. Differently put, this exteriority would pay the reader an uninvited visit. Unlike Lurie's mind in the early sections of the novel, the reader's could therefore not remain "a refuge for old thoughts, idle, indigent, with nowhere to go" (72). In making of him or her a home for it, this uninvited visitor would inspire the reader to "chase" out "old thoughts," to "sweep the premises clean" (72).[45]

The ecstatic reading suggested in *Disgrace* is therefore a form of un-conditional hospitality in which the reader gives him-/herself up in being possessed.[46] To read despite oneself, which is to say anonymously, is to have one's reading of the text inspired (indeed, mediated) not by the dis-courses of history but by their excess. In such a depersonalized reading, one has given oneself to both Lucy and the rapists in being possessed by their strangeness. One is, to apply to *Disgrace* the terms of Dostoevsky's opposition, the skull that receives the blow and the arm that wields the axe.

Ultimately, then, the meditation on the imagination that one finds in *Disgrace* argues not for the power of the imagination but for the inspira-tion that may derive from the sense the imagination imparts of that over which it has no power, of what its attempts to reveal inevitably destroy. It is for this reason that one finds in this novel such a strong emphasis on the aporetic nature of saying the unsayable and, by extension, on the actual events of writing and reading. In this regard, the significance of the novel's preoccupation with its incompletion cannot be overstated. By sig-nalling its incompletion, the text depicts itself as the effect of the singular and irrevocably past event of the writer's encounter with the excess of his imagination in the moment of writing. Its incompletion, in other words, is a trace of what existed before, but which the power of the imagination has made into what comes after. My argument has been that, in contriving that s/he complete it, the text entertains the possibility that the reader, in read-ing, may also encounter the excess of closure. Specifically, the novel seeks to ensure that its own reading repeats the unrepeatable encounter with alterity of which it can only ever bear a trace. If this were to trans-pire, the reader would gain a sense of, and so be inspired by, what exceeds the grasp of the imagination, and which, despite his or her intentions, turns

---

[45] See Attridge's discussion of grace and inspiration with reference to Lurie's com-position of the chamber opera and his bond with the dogs (*J.M. Coetzee and the Ethics of Reading*, 162–91).

[46] See Blanchot's reference to "passivity's reading" in his description of the state to which the reader is reduced on encountering the "*other* dark" in the space of reading (*The Writing of the Disaster*, tr. Ann Smock (*Écriture du désastre*, 1980; Lincoln: U of Nebraska P, 1995): 101.

his or her reading into an "orphic commemoration," a katabatic work of mourning.

In this eventuality, the reader's reading would mirror the endless, careful endeavour staged by the novel's ending. While I have argued that the discovery of the "lyric impulse" enables Lurie to "burn," I must now stress that the outcome or "resolution," to use Geoffrey Baker's word,[47] of such self-sacrificing love is questioned in the novel's concluding scene. With regard to this qualification, the interplay between the fire-motif and the trope of the lost child is instructive. Apart from Lucy, Melanie, and Pollux, the dogs in this novel are also figured as lost children. They are, in Lurie's words, "unwanted" or "abandoned" (146, 62, 78). Read in this symbolic context, Lurie's work at the Animal Welfare Clinic is deeply suggestive. Despite having learnt to love the dogs, he is only able to "take care of them" (and this phrase is, of course, highly ambiguous) once they are dead (146). By his own admission, he is not their "saviour" (146). The novel's ending stages the irony implicit here. In "giving him up," as I have argued, Lurie sacrifices his own feelings for the young, deformed dog. Importantly, though, the outcome of this sacrifice is not the dog's salvation: even though *he* burns, Lurie, it would seem, is only able to see to it that this dog is "burnt, burnt up" (220). In other words, the only action carried through to completion in the novel's ending is the death of the dog. In itself, however, this leaves Lurie to mourn the passing of the animal, the child. The task of the imagination thus culminates in a work of inconsolable mourning which is ceaseless and therefore precisely not a culmination. To care, and I have already indicated that this is implicit in the root of this word, is to lament, to mourn the dead.

℘ ཟ

---

[47] Baker, "The Limits of Sympathy," 43.

7 A Slow Story?[1]
∅ *Slow Man*

O NE OF THE MOST STRIKING FEATURES of Coetzee's
Australian fiction is his perfunctory treatment of narrative. For
the most part, *Elizabeth Costello* consists of lecture narratives:
i.e. narratives in which narrative, in the sense of "the narration of a suc-
cession of fictional events,"[2] is rudimentary, little more than a rhetorical
device which advertises its rhetorical nature. Much of *Diary of a Bad Year*
consists of formal essays held together by a slender narrative thread that
literally takes the form of a footnote to the text of the essays. Even in *Slow
Man*, one encounters a form of narrative minimalism: although devoid of
the trappings of academic discourse, this is a novel in which nothing much
ever happens. It goes nowhere and announces that this is so.

In my discussion of *The Master of Petersburg*, I argued that Dostoevsky uses Anna Sergeyevna as a medium through which to establish
contact with Pavel. The narrative minimalism of Coetzee's Australian
novels stages narrative's attempt to serve a similar purpose – to be the
means by which this writer gains access to the invisible. At one point in
Diary of a Bad Year, JC comments as follows on the spareness of his
prose:

> I read the work of other writers, read the passages of dense description
> they have with care and labour composed with the purpose of evoking
> imaginary spectacles before the inner eye, and my heart sinks. I was
> never much good at evocation of the real, and have even less stomach

---

[1] Some of the ideas in this reading of *Slow Man* derive from discussions with two of
my students, Neil Luyt and Harry Haddon. I am also indebted to Johan Geertsema for
his deeply insightful commentary on an earlier draft of this chapter.

[2] Shlomith Rimmon–Kenan, *Narrative Fiction: Contemporary Poetics* (1983; London: Routledge, 2nd ed. 2002): 2.

for the task now. The truth is, I have never taken much pleasure in the
visible world, don't feel with much conviction the urge to recreate it in
words.[3]

Even though we have no way of telling whether or not this character's
sentiments reflect those of his author, their articulation in the novel foregrounds its impatience with narrative. While the author, writing under inspiration, wishes to evoke – indeed, follow – the invisible, narrative prose
evokes only the visible.

Although far more pronounced than in his South African novels, this
narrative minimalism does not constitute a new departure in Coetzee's
writing: in fact, it signals his continued concern with the issue of responsibility to what has not yet emerged. In this chapter, I show that Coetzee's
Australian fiction shares the dominant concerns of his apartheid and post-
apartheid South African writing. To be sure, I demonstrate that *Slow Man*,
the work on which I base my discussion, repeats these concerns: it not
only scripts the writer's responsibility to accommodate the other in the
hostile economy of the same, but also entertains the possibility that literary writing may affect the reader and so render him or her responsible for
the other. Besides, these preoccupations are articulated in a metaphoric
vocabulary with which the reader of the South African fiction is very
familiar: the imbricated tropes of hospitality, inspiration, the unborn child,
and following.

I should add that the marked similarity between Coetzee's South African and Australian fiction is in itself not at all surprising. Throughout this
study, I have argued that this writer's work steadfastly resists treating history as an *a priori* structure. Indeed, as we have seen, the political dispensation inaugurated in South Africa in 1994 can hardly be said to have
altered the focus of his writing. Whether it be the USA, apartheid South
Africa, post-apartheid South Africa, or Australia, history is, in Coetzee's
novels, cast as a realm that defines itself through its hostility to radical difference. It constructs itself through a logic of exclusion. In other words,
history is the order of the same; an order premised on the violent reduction of the other. While the degree of violence involved in this reduction
of difference may differ from one location to another, and from one period

---

[3] J.M. Coetzee, *Diary of a Bad Year* (London: Harvill Secker, 2007): 192.

to the next, the logic of exclusion and the indifference to others that it inscribes cannot not remain the same.

Given this irreducible tension between the same and the other, it would,
in fact, have been most surprising had Coetzee, following his emigration
from South Africa to Australia, written fiction celebrating the openness of
this society. Owing to the irreducibility of the relationship between the
same and the other, there can be no such thing as a utopian community. At
best, a community can attempt to reduce its violence by disavowing itself
as it avows itself: i.e. by constantly questioning the exclusions through
which it has and continues to constitute itself. Such a community would
ceaselessly render itself incomplete.[4] Since a community like this simply
does not exist, it is quite understandable that Coetzee's concern in *Elizabeth Costello*, *Slow Man*, and *Diary of a Bad Year* remains the *possibility*
of community. Accordingly, he, in these novels, is *still* preoccupied with
how *not* to supplement history or, considering his understanding that supplementarity and rivalry are not fixed opposites, how to supplement history in a way that interrupts and lessens its violence.

Does this mean that Coetzee, to use Susan Barton's reflection on Foe's
writing endeavours, turns out "the same story over and over, in version
after version, stillborn every time" (151)? The reason that I have elected to

---

[4] See Jean–Luc Nancy's *The Inoperative Community*, tr. & ed. Peter Connor et al.
(*La Communauté désœuvrée*, 1986; Minneapolis: U of Minnesota P, 1991), and Blanchot's response to it in *The Unavowable Community*, tr. Pierre Joris (*La Communauté
inavouable*, 1983; Barrytown NY: Station Hill, 1988). Especially interesting is the following observation by the latter:

> This reciprocity between communism and individualism [...] leads us to
> question the very notion of reciprocity. However, if the relation of man with
> man ceases to be that of Same with the Same, but rather introduces the Other
> as irreducible and – given the equality between them – always in a situation
> of dissymmetry in relation to the one looking at the Other, then a completely
> different relationship imposes itself and imposes another form of society
> which one would hardly call a 'community'. (3)

Later, in discussing Georges Bataille's "The Inner Experience," Blanchot elaborates on
the possibility of a community 'grounded' in alterity, the unknown, absence, death. A
community that "proposes or imposes the knowledge (the experience, *Erfahrung*) of
what cannot be known; that 'beside-ourself' (the outside) which is abyss and ecstasy
without ceasing to be a singular relationship" (17), "puts its members to the test of an
unknown inequality," and, rather than subordinating the one to the other, "makes them
accessible to what is inaccessible in this new relationship of responsibility (of sovereignty)" (17).

write on *Slow Man*, rather than on either *Elizabeth Costello* or *Diary of a Bad Year*, is that this novel's narrative minimalism, which takes the form of a parody of narrative and therefore of itself,[5] illustrates some of the ways in which Coetzee, in rearticulating the same concerns, reconfigures and so changes them. The "same story" is never quite the same.

ॠ ॠ

In *Slow Man*, the focus on the unannounced visitor and the unwilled change that s/he may precipitate in the unwilling host is more apparent than in any of the previous novels. Much of the narrative consists of the forms of hospitality that Paul Rayment extends to various guests and visitors, both invited and uninvited: e.g., Marijana Jokić, Margaret McCord, Elizabeth Costello, Marianna, Drago Jokić. In their turn, these visits are framed by the hospitality that he receives from the hospital and the Jokić family.

After the accident on Magill Road, Paul Rayment experiences the institutionalized hospitality of the hospital and various professional caregivers – what he refers to as a "regimen of care."[6] In turn, this calculated practice of care is offset by the unconditional care that *he* comes to feel for one of these caregivers, Marijana Jokić. She, we read, "come[s] into his life" (33), the implication being that she arrives uninvited or "befalls" him (21). The accidental nature of the change that Rayment undergoes following this visitation is clearly delineated in the novel. Initially, he is depicted as a man who believes that reason provides him with the ability to control himself. In terms of his reflection on the Platonic image of the self as charioteer, "gripping the reins" of "a black steed with flashing eyes and distended nostrils representing the base appetites, and a white steed of calmer mien representing the less easily identifiable nobler passions" (53), he relies on reason to invest him with agency, the ability to harness the "base appetites." In this regard, we also learn that he has "never been fond of immoderacy, immodesty, wild motions, grunts and shouts and cries" (109). "Passionate outpourings," he confesses, "are not part of his nature"

---

[5] See Laura Wright's perceptive discussion of parody in *Disgrace* and *The Lives of Animals* (*Writing "Out of All the Camps,"* 102–105). Although she examines *performative* parody, our discussions nonetheless intersect.

[6] J.M. Coetzee, *Slow Man* (London: Secker & Warburg, 2005): 32. Further page references are in the main text.

(45). His "tortoise variety of passion" (228) or, in Costello's words, "aversion to the physical" (234), stems from his fear of losing control over himself. In his own estimation, what Margaret McCord and "half a dozen other women" will "recall about him" is not passion, which to him is "foreign territory," but a "mild and gratifying sensuality" (45). He disapproves of being caught in the "grip of passion" (46), of orgasm, the 'little death' which serves as a prelude to death by ecstatically relieving the self of control of itself.

Soon after the arrival of Marijana, all of this changes. In the following passage, a clearly bewildered Paul Rayment finds himself wondering at his reckless desire to offer himself to a stranger: "Who is this woman, he thinks, to whom I yearn to give myself? A mystery, all a mystery" (127). The measure of the transformation that he has undergone is precisely his surprise at himself; the implication being that he has become strange, a stranger, to himself. What this indicates, in turn, is that he has changed despite himself.

The unconscious nature of this change is emphasized throughout the novel. After the accident, Margaret McCord comforts Rayment with the following words: "You are still yourself" (38). Later, he himself reflects that "He is trapped with the same old self as before" (54): Rayment is changing even as he, quite ironically, reflects on his apparent inability to do so. The metaphor of self-imprisonment here, of course, recalls the predicament of most of the protagonists of the earlier novels, but especially that of Dostoevsky, who, in *The Master of Petersburg*, despairingly senses that he is "manacled to [him]self till the day [he] die[s]" (82). In *Slow Man*, however, the notion of the self as a prison is directly related to Rayment's rationality. By routinely foreclosing on alterity, Coetzee implies, a controlling subjectivity grounded in reason actively resists change. The vigour, power, and control of ratiocinative consciousness protect the self from change and, in the process, enthrals it to itself. In terms of the trope of hospitality, the host is imprisoned in his or her home.

In a closely related context, Derrida muses as follows on just this point: "it's as if the master, qua master, were prisoner of his place and his power, of his ipseity, of his subjectivity."[7] Earlier still, Levinas, in referring to the self's sacrifice, or substitution, of itself for the other person, says much the same: "Substitution frees the subject from ennui, that is, from the enchain-

---

[7] Derrida, *Of Hospitality*, 123.

ment to itself, where the ego suffocates in itself."[8] This description adds
yet another metaphor to the already imbricated figure of hospitality by
suggesting that the visitor is a breath of air. If the self "suffocates in itself," the advent of the other is inspiration (and, I must here interpolate,
the trope of inspiration, of air, spirit, gas, breath is more pronounced in
Slow Man than in any of Coetzee's previous novels). Hence, Levinas
refers to the "wind of alterity," and describes "Freedom" as "animation
itself, breath, the breathing of outside air, where inwardness frees itself
from itself, and is exposed to all the winds." To open oneself to the other
is "to free oneself by breathing from closure in oneself."[9] Cumulatively,
these metaphors depict the surprising, yet unobtrusive, change wrought by
the uninvited visitor on the host in terms of liberation and animation. The
visitor is not only a "liberator" and "emancipator," as Derrida contends,[10]
but also (and this bears comparison with Coetzee's vocabulary of salvation in his novels) a saviour and life-giver.

Paradoxically, then, Paul Rayment, in sacrificing himself to Marijana
Jokić, saves himself. He saves himself by becoming other than himself.
When he visits the Jokić family in the penultimate scene of the novel, and
Costello comforts him with the words "I'm sure it will take you out of
yourself" (241), what is being suggested is a notion with which we are
familiar from the earlier novels: namely, that the enabling condition for
change, given the self's imprisonment by its subjectivity, is *ek-stasis*. One
can only save oneself through an act of unconditional hospitality: i.e. by
forfeiting oneself through sacrificing oneself to the unexpected visitor.
And, it should be recalled, such "gracious" hospitality expects nothing in
return; in Derrida's terms, it is aneconomic, "beyond debt and economy."[11]

ᚠ ᚬ

Grounded as it is in a *Bildung* that tends toward a loss, rather than consolidation, of self, the trajectory of *Slow Man* is fairly similar to that of
Age of Iron and *Disgrace*. In *Slow Man*, though, this movement is com-

---

[8] Levinas, *Otherwise Than Being*, 124.
[9] *Otherwise Than Being*, 180.
[10] Derrida, *Of Hospitality*, 123.
[11] *Of Hospitality*, 83.

plicated by the arrival of Elizabeth Costello in chapter thirteen,[12] which
extends the novel's debate on hospitality from the presentational surface
of the narrative to a self-reflexive level involving the relationship between
author and character and, ultimately, text and reader. Costello's recitation
of the opening sentences of the novel, which deal with Rayment's accident, requires the reader to re-read this passage as an allegory of the
accident of inspiration, of the writer's loss of control in the moment of
writing. That is, the repetition of the passage makes the reader aware that
when s/he reads of "something coming" to Paul Rayment, s/he is also
reading of *him* happening to Elizabeth Costello. Indeed, the presence of
the typewriter in this description indicates that Rayment's sense of his
ontogenesis is his visitation of Costello, his unannounced arrival or
"coming" to her: "Something is coming to him. A letter at a time, clack
clack clack, a message is being typed on a rose-pink screen that trembles
like water each time he blinks and is therefore quite likely his own inner
eyelid" (3).

Importantly, Costello later describes having *heard* the opening words
of the novel. Evidently, they 'come' to her; she receives them, which is to
say Paul Rayment, from an unknown source. As her reference to Marianna intimates, they are a command issued from a source that is wholly
other: "SHE CAME TO me as you came to me," says Costello. "A woman of darkness, a woman in darkness. *Take up the story of such a one*:
words in my sleeping ear, spoken by what in the old days we would have
called an angel calling me out to a wrestling match" (115).

In this novel, as in *Foe*, the trope of sleep connotes the extreme
passivity of the self in the moment of inspiration. The metaphor of the
"sleeping ear," which implies a contrast with a wakeful and masterful
eye, suggests a pre-reflective state of openness to an alterity that would
be foreclosed upon and possessed by subject-centred consciousness.
Given the nature of this contrast, it is necessary to add to what I have previously said about the self's passivity upon being exposed to otherness.
Maurice Blanchot refers to this passive and receptive state as "attentionality," as opposed to projective intentionality, a waiting without

---

[12] Cf. chapter thirteen of John Fowles's *The French Lieutenant's Woman* (1969;
London: Triad/Granada, 1977): 85–88. Obviously, the 'Fowles' that one encounters in
this chapter is, like Elizabeth Costello in *Slow Man*, an author-figure: i.e. a character.

expectation or intention for the command of the other.[13] Significantly, the
time of such waiting is beyond time or history; it is an interruption of
temporal experience, to use Levinas' word, an "instant" or *Augenblick*.
During the *Augenblick*, the eye "listens"[14] or, as John Llewelyn puts it,
"opening one's eyes is called to make way for opening one's ears."[15]

This point about the refractoriness to time of the encounter with alterity
is, of course, implicit in what I have already said about the non-intentional
nature of such encounters. In being exposed to the other, the self encounters that which cannot be reduced to an object for intentional consciousness, and so rendered *present*. Being entirely non-phenomenological, the
"instant" of this exposure is a "lapse of time,"[16] or discontinuity, that cannot form part of a retentional past or a present from which the future may
be anticipated. Hence Levinas refers to "the diachrony of the instant." The
Augenblick is "something irrecuperable, refractory to the simultaneity of
the present, something unrepresentable, immemorial, prehistorical."[17]

---

[13] Maurice Blanchot, *The Infinite Conversation*, tr. Susan Hanson (*L'Entretien
infini*, 1969; Minneapolis: U of Minnesota P, 1995): 53; see also Bauman, *Postmodern
Ethics*, 87–88.

[14] Levinas, *Otherwise Than Being*, 30, 37, 38.

[15] John Llewelyn, *Emmanuel Levinas*, 55.

[16] Levinas, *Otherwise Than Being*, 38.

[17] *Otherwise Than Being*, 49, 38. See also the following description by Blanchot of
the 'experience' of ecstasy:

> On the contrary, there is evidence [...] that ecstasy is without object, just as
> it is without a why, just as it challenges any certainty. One can write that
> word (ecstasy) only by putting it carefully between quotation marks, because
> nobody can know what it is about, and, above all, whether it ever took place:
> going beyond knowledge, implying un-knowledge, it refuses to be stated
> other than through random words that cannot guarantee it. Its decisive aspect
> is that the one who experiences it is no longer there when he experiences it, is
> thus no longer there to experience it. The same person (but he is no longer
> the same) may believe that he recaptures it in the past as one does a memory:
> I remember, I recall to mind, I talk or I write in a rapture that overflows and
> unsettles the very possibility of remembering. All mystics, the most rigorous,
> the most sober (and first of all Saint John of the Cross), have known that that
> remembrance, considered as personal, could only be doubtful, and, belonging
> to memory, took rank among that which demanded escape from it: extra-
> temporal memory or remembrance of a past which has never been lived in
> the present (and thus a stranger to all *Erlebnis*). (*The Unavowable Com-
> munity*, 18–19).

Apart from elaborating on its temporality, Elizabeth Costello's description of inspiration repeats a point with which we are by now quite familiar: namely, that inspiration is a process through which the writing subject is subordinated to an unknown authority. In the description, the reference to the "sleeping ear," to a passive form of hearing, emphasizes the obedience of the self under inspiration. Indeed, the very word 'obey' is etymologically related to *audire* 'to hear'. To be inspired is to be mastered, to respond unquestioningly to an order received from a wholly unknown and unknowable source. In the passage, the alterity of this source is stressed through its association with the face of the Judaeo-Christian God. It is Jacob who wrestles with an angel, a messenger, and thereafter, relieved at having survived seeing God "face to face," names the place where the bout occurred Peniel, which means 'face of God'.[18]

As in the earlier fiction, then, inspiration is in this novel depicted as a form of unconditional hospitality. That which inspires cannot be invited. When it arrives, it does so unannounced by infiltrating the individual's consciousness and possessing him or her. The writer becomes host to an unknown and unknowable visitor. Nevertheless, the host is not sovereign in this relationship: s/he is invaded and taken hostage by the unannounced visitor and, in the process, dispossessed of self-possession. To respond obediently to inspiration in the way described by Costello is thus to give oneself up to that inspiration. It is to write, and therefore to act, while being acted upon by an unknown authority.[19]

On a number of occasions in this study, I have commented on Coetzee's use of the metaphor of following in his portrayal of the writer as a being who is acted upon simultaneously by the forces of history and the invisible. Even as she is adjured to represent the political violence in her

---

[18] *Authorised King James Version of the Holy Bible*, Gen. 32.30.

[19] In this study, I have frequently referred and alluded to Levinas' account of the passivity to which the self is reduced in its encounter with the alterity, or face, of the human other. Interestingly, in arguing that passivity involves not inaction but responsiveness and obedience to the other, he uses the air-metaphor discussed above. The self is a "lung" opened to "invisible air" which, although "hidden from perception," "penetrate[s]" and "obsesses" him or her (*Otherwise Than Being*, 180). Such inspiration, Levinas maintains, is profoundly ambiguous: it confronts "me" with the "possibility of being the author of what had been breathed in unbeknownst to me, of having received, one knows not from where, that of which I am author" (*Otherwise Than Being*, 148–49). Despite his scepticism towards art (see "Reality and its Shadow," 1–13), Levinas' ethic is thus an aesthetic of sorts: the self acts: i.e. creates, in being acted upon.

society: i.e. to supplement and so follow history, Mrs Curren "follows the pen." Dostoevsky, in *The Master of Petersburg*, wonders whether he is to follow a shade through the gates of hell and finally observes "the hand that holds the pen begin[] to move," "to follow the dance of the pen." Clearly, too, this notion of the other's mastery of the writer through inspiration is implicit in Elizabeth Costello's description of herself as a "secretary of the invisible."[20] In the earlier novels as well, the same metaphor may be discerned in the descriptions of the medical officer following K across the Cape Flats in his imagination, and of Friday taking up Foe's pen and sitting at his writing desk.

While he uses the trope of following in *Slow Man*, Coetzee does so in a way that foregrounds the deeply ambivalent, conflicted nature of the responsibility concomitant with the writer's inspiration by the invisible. In order to follow the invisible, the writer must follow the text – i.e. s/he must respect the language, grammar and representational logic of the novel-as-genre. At the same time, though, s/he must ensure that the text *does* obey, which is to say follow, the invisible.

In terms of *Slow Man*'s self-reflexive illusion, Rayment depends on Costello's authorship for his being as a character. Oppressed by her authorial authority, he attempts to resist "her schemes," but fears that, were he to look in a mirror, he would see "grinning over his shoulder, gripping his throat, the shape of a wild-haired, bare-breasted hag brandishing a whip" (164). Notwithstanding this image, which draws on the story of the old man of the river's persecution of Sinbad (to which, it may be recalled, Susan Barton refers in *Foe*), the text makes it quite clear that Costello is as dependent on Rayment as he is on her.[21] She "follows" him throughout, a state of servitude that becomes apparent in her remarks that she "must wait upon" him (136), and that "His is the power of leading," and hers of "following" (233). Costello is mastered by Rayment because she is enthralled to the invisible by which she has been inspired to write. As she puts it when he wishes her to leave his apartment, "I am to accompany you" (84). She follows him because she has no choice in the matter. He is the "penance" that she is "sentenced to speak" (162).

---

[20] Coetzee, *Age of Iron*, 99; *The Master of Petersburg*, 241, 236; *Elizabeth Costello*, 194.

[21] See Gareth Cornwell, "'He and His Man': Allegory and Catachresis in J.M. Coetzee's Nobel Lecture," *English in Africa* 34.1 (2007): 97–114.

Costello depends on Rayment because he is the means by which she must obey the command received in her "sleeping ear." That is to say, he is quite literally the "sentence," the medium and form through which she gives herself up to the alterior source of her inspiration. The logic of transubstantiation in this novel is identical to that in *Age of Iron*. Rayment (the language and form of the novel-as-genre) must embody Costello's gift of self and thereby instantiate her unconditional love. It is for this reason that she is often depicted as being incorporeal, an insubstantial, even spectral, presence. Rayment, for instance, reflects on her "blankness" (120), and "finds her so colourless, so featureless" (160). He – the medium and form of the novel – must invest her with substance.

Costello must therefore obey both the invisible *and* the text. In order to obey the former, she must obey the latter. The problem, of course, is that the text is resistant to following the invisible. Paul Rayment, the text-figure in the novel, is an amputee, a slow man. He is words, part of the language of the same, and therefore antipathetic to otherness. As is so often the case in his writing, Coetzee's point here is that the invisible cannot be named and therefore grasped in language. Language cannot accommodate the writer's self-sacrificing generosity. For this reason, Costello complains as follows to Rayment about the text's lacklustre description of his discovery of her by the riverside, feeding ducks:

> it is not good enough. It does not bring me to life. Bringing me to life may not be important to you, but it has the drawback of not bringing you to life either. (159)

In his turn, Rayment reflects that the language he speaks "does not come from my core" (198). Instead of coming "From the heart" (231), which is earlier described as the seat, or indeed home, of love, the place where it "takes up residence" (149), his words come from the "word-box" that he carries around in place of a heart (230, 234). English, in Costello's description, is part of his "tortoiseshell armour" (230), a depiction that recalls Dostoevsky's suspicion that, while he is called upon to be "a lyre-player," to raise the dead through the lyre's music of love, he is a purveyor of words and thus unable to do so: "And the truth? Stiff shoulders humped over the writing table, and the ache of a heart slow to move. A tortoise heart."[22]

The motif of slowness, in *Slow Man*, thus signifies language's resistance to unconditional hospitality. Although a product of love, the work, as its very title announces, may be the loss of what has inspired it. To apply to it Foe's description of the story of the island, *Slow Man* is a "slow story,"[23] ill-equipped to follow the invisible. Like Dostoevsky in *The Master of Petersburg*, this novel is capable only of a "plodding chase […] after the rumour of a ghost" (53).

Given Paul Rayment's inertia, it is hardly surprising that much of *Slow Man* consists of Costello's attempts to coax, cajole, even harry and harass, him into following the invisible. If she is to obey the order she has received, she must *make* him lead her. Her following must be more than simply a following: it must become a pursuit, and thereby a form of following that is a not-following. Precisely because the medium and form of the novel are hostile to love, the inspired writer must make them accommodate it; must open them out to what they seek to exclude. Whether or not this is possible is quite simply beside the point. Under inspiration, the writer cannot but obey the ethical command to do so. Despite him-/herself, then, s/he must render language hospitable to that to which it is hostile. Despite itself, the medium of the novel must be made hospitable. It is the writer's aesthetic obligation to make the work "reduce language's reduction of love."[24]

Hence Costello repeatedly accuses Rayment of "dithering" (159), complains that "nothing is happening" (141), urges him to "hurry up" (160), and berates him with these words:

> I urge you: don't cut short these thought-trains of yours. Follow them through to their end. Your thoughts and your feelings. Follow them through and you will grow with them. (158)

In fact, her following of him progressively becomes a persecution (a word whose etymology signifies a form of following), as emerges when she herself uses the Sinbad story as an analogue for her relationship with him:

---

[22] Coetzee, *The Master of Petersburg*, 152–53.

[23] Coetzee, *Foe*, 114.

[24] Johan Geertsema uses this phrase in an e-mail letter to me (7 November 2007).

"As I keep telling myself, Have patience, Paul Rayment did not ask you to descend upon his shoulders" (160).[25] Her following is *both* an act of obedience *and* a tyranny, pursuit or persecution. The paradoxical nature of this form of following is articulated in yet another of Costello's invocations of the Sinbad story. After having promised to keep out of Rayment's way during her visit, she goes on to say: "Most of the time you won't notice I am here. Just a touch on the shoulder, now and then, left or right, to keep you on the path" (87).

Ultimately, then, what we find in *Slow Man* is an erosion of the apparent opposition between following and not-following. While the logic of this metaphor seems to suggest that the writer, to follow the invisible, must follow the text, it simultaneously indicates that s/he can only follow the text through interrupting the process of following. Not-following, it would appear, may enable following. Disobedience may enable obedience. In a discussion of the figures of the *acoluthon* ("follower," "acolyte") and *anacoluthon* ("without following"),[26] Derrida clarifies this paradox in responding to a question from Nicholas Royle:

> there is no simple opposition between the acolyte, or the 'acoluthon' and the 'anacoluthon.' That is a problem, because to accompany, or to follow in the most demanding and authentic way, implies the 'anacol,' the 'not-following,' the break in the following, in the company so to speak. So, if we agree on this, a number of consequences will follow: you cannot simply oppose the acolyte and the anacoluthon – logically they are opposed; but in fact, what appears as a necessity is that, in order to follow in a consistent way, to be true to what you follow, you have to interrupt the following.[27]

In this view, not-following is part of the process of following. By the same token, disobedience is a necessary part of obedience, and betrayal a part of fidelity.

---

[25] It may be recalled that, in my reading of Coetzee's use of the Sinbad story in *Foe*, I made the point that Susan Barton's relationship to Friday is ultimately 'grounded' in responsibility rather than a dialectic of recognition, and therefore qualitatively different to the Hegelian master–servant relationship.

[26] See also Hillis Miller's discussion of the *anacoluthon* in *Reading Narrative* (Norman: U Of Oklahoma P, 1998): 149–57.

[27] Derrida, "Following Theory: Jacques Derrida," interview, in *life. after. theory*, 7.

Costello's following, through not following, of Paul Rayment accounts
for the unresolved tension between love and betrayal in the ending of
Slow Man, which stages the outcome of her pursuit of him. In the penultimate scene, she, having finally managed to persuade Rayment to leave his
apartment–prison, accompanies him on an "UNANNOUNCED visit" to
the Jokić family (239). Once they arrive, she enthuses at the animate
nature of the text's descriptions: "So real! [...] Who would have thought
it!" (242). Crucially, Rayment notices that she "is leaning back, eyes shut,
abstracted" (247). The implication is clear: she is writing under inspiration or, as Mrs Curren in yet another invocation of the *Augenblick* puts it,
writing with eyes "shut" (159). Costello, in short, is trying to invest her
gift of self with form and substance through language. On the final page
of the novel, when Rayment "takes a good look at her," she is no longer
"blank," "colourless," and "featureless": "In the clear late-afternoon light
he can see every detail, every hair, every vein" (263). From this description, it would seem that her writing has indeed been able to accommodate
her gift of self in the instant of inspiration. Nevertheless, this conclusion is
immediately qualified by the fact that Rayment's scrutiny of Costello's
physiognomy coincides with a disavowal of love in his response to her
questions "Is this love, Paul? Have we found love at last?": "No [...] this
is not love. This is something else. Something less" (263). Costello's
reply to this response, "And is that your last word, do you think?" (263),
suggests the necessarily inseparable nature of fidelity and betrayal.

Importantly, in this regard, Rayment's "last word" is a variant of the
standard accusation, in Coetzee's fiction, of abandonment, of parental impiety, of the parent's inability to love the child well enough. As much is
connoted by the intersection of the metaphor of following with the trope
of childbirth in the novel. Under inspiration, Costello bears Rayment in
order for him to bear the invisible. She is both mother and midwife. Accordingly, her following – indeed, persecution – of him sometimes takes
the form of an adjuration to deliver an infant. We twice read that she
"urges" him to "push," a word that he associates with "a woman in
labour" (83, 204). Alternatively, she urges him to speak, to "*Say* something" (100), an adjuration that recalls the medical officer's instruction to
Michael K in the principal of the failed childbirth scenes in *Life & Times
of Michael K*. In this context, Paul Rayment's "final word" may be read as
an accusation of abandonment. *J'accuse*: the text accuses the writer of
having abandoned it. For most of the novel, as we have seen, it is Ray-

ment, the text-figure, whom Costello accuses of inadequate love. The ending changes this: what is now at stake is the writer's betrayal of the text. What is at stake is Costello's betrayal of Rayment, her infidelity, her following through *not* following.

In order to divine the nature of Costello's not-following, one has to consider the relationship of which her relationship to Rayment is but a figure: namely, that between J.M. Coetzee and the novel entitled *Slow Man*. In this novel, this writer constantly parodies the ability of language and narrative to invest with substance his gift of self and thereby thematize unconditional hospitality. So, for instance, the word 'care', through deliberate overuse, becomes increasingly ambivalent and eventually signifies only the dissonance between itself and what it claims to signify. The most obvious example of such parody, however, may be found in the contrived nature of the novel's presentation of the narrative of Paul Rayment's *Bildung*. *Slow Man* does not present itself as Paul Rayment's growth to love, but as a *literary* representation of such a development. Through its sheer artificiality, contrivance, and stylized nature, this narrative representation parodies itself and therefore Rayment's progression from "slow man" to "rocket man" (258), from emotional torpor to the point at which the child, Ljuba, whose name coyly and tritely signifies "love" (30), smiles on him for the first time in the novel (258). The tropes of the child and the follower thus suggest that Rayment, now capable of love, is able to follow the invisible, the child. Yet, even as they suggest this, their extravagant, indeed farcical, nature draws attention to their tropological status and, in the process, they come to parody their representational claims. In fact, farce announces itself as farce when Ljuba, after smiling at Rayment, incredulously observes: "You aren't Rocket Man, you're Slow Man!" (258). The novel's parody of its metaphors and what they purport to metaphorize continues when Costello suggests to Rayment, whom she has earlier described as her "knight with the doleful countenance" (256), that they tour around Australia in motorized bath chairs. Through this allusion to Don Quixote and Sancho Panza, the metaphor of following turns in on itself and indicates that the text cannot follow what it purports to follow.

By means of his use of parody, Coetzee thus constantly foregrounds his novel's separation from what it professes to "represent," to follow. As a representation, it is different from, separate from, what it purports to present. It comes after, is the past of, what it seeks to render present. Indeed,

as we have seen, the *Augenblick* or instant of exposure to alterity is dia-
chronous, not "assemblable in a recollection of a representable representation."[28] Precisely this divorce is emphasized by the work's self-reflexive
depiction of Costello's inspiration, which, even as it claims to present the
moment of the text's coming into being, exposes its exile from that
moment by revealing itself to be merely a representation thereof. The
work lays bare the ineluctable pastness of the event of its inspiration by
presenting Elizabeth Costello as a surrogate author, and thereby, in fact,
distancing itself from its actual ontogenesis: i.e. the moment of J.M. Coetzee's inspiration with Costello, the character, the sentence *he* is sentenced
to speak. *Slow Man* is belated, too late, too slow.

Through his use of parody, then, Coetzee, in the very process of following the text, breaks company with it. In effect, he stages the aporia
evident in the question that Blanchot asks of the writing process, and to
which I referred in my discussion of *Disgrace*: "How can I recover it, how
can I turn around and look at what exists *before*, if all my power consists
of making it into what exists *after*?".[29] The novel always comes *after*. It
follows. Coetzee's parodic subversion of the novel's following of the invisible is, of course, a betrayal of sorts. It is for this reason that Rayment,
the text-figure in *Slow Man*, questions the nature of the love that Costello,
the writer-figure, feels has come into being in their relationship. It is also
for this reason that, after Rayment's "last word," the novel concludes with
his formal farewell to Costello, with their breaking of company.

The point I wish to emphasise, though, is that Coetzee's use of parody
makes of his following of the text a pursuit, a persecution, and that this
not-following is, in fact, necessary for him to follow the text *and* the invisible faithfully and authentically. His betrayal or abandonment of the
work is therefore a form of fidelity. Tellingly, in this regard, this writer, in
having his novel suggest that it may be the disabling condition for unconditional hospitality, opens it to this very experience. It should here again
be noted that, rather than presenting Paul Rayment's growth to love, Coetzee presents his novel's failure to present this development. He makes the
novel's narrative form signify not presence but a failure thereof and, in the
process, indicate the limitlessness that its limits inevitably imply. While it
may not have the ability to present love – may well be the very condition

---

[28] Levinas, *Otherwise Than Being*, 51.
[29] Blanchot, "Literature and the Right to Death," 327.

of impossibility for it – the novel thus does have the ability to gesture beyond itself, to gesture towards what is not just different from but more than (indeed, infinitely other than) its form and medium. By investing it with this capacity to point beyond its "givenness"[30] and thereby, crucially, to distance itself from itself, Coetzee opens out the form of his novel not to its opposite but, as Derrida puts it in a discussion of language and hospitality, to "an other than itself which is no longer *its* other."[31] In failing to name, invite, and thereby control, the invisible, the novel opens itself to the possibility of being visited, invaded, possessed, and controlled by it. After all, and I have emphasized this point throughout this study, its inability to master what it seeks, but fails, to present precludes this novel from not only including this otherness in, but also excluding it from, its textual economy. If it is hospitable, then, the text is so despite itself. Despite itself, *Slow Man* holds itself open to, lets itself be haunted by, what is other than itself.

Although this argument is staged in Coetzee's earlier novels, it is clarified and developed, rather than simply repeated, in *Slow Man* by the trope of following. In order to follow the invisible, Coetzee must both obey and break the rules of language and the novel. Simply to follow the text would be profoundly irresponsible. To enable *it* to break company with the invisible and thereby be possessed by it, the writer must abandon the text. The form of the abandonment in question: i.e. Coetzee's use of parody, is therefore, paradoxically, an act of remaining true not only to the invisible but also to the work. Parody, as Coetzee well knows, pays homage to what it attacks, betrays.[32] It is not one or the other but both at the same time. Coetzee betrays the work to be true to it; he interrupts his following of the work in order to follow both it and the invisible. The betrayal at issue is an unavoidable part of this fidelity.

---

[30] Adorno, *Aesthetic Theory*, 67, 386.

[31] Jacques Derrida, *Acts of Religion*, ed. & intro. Gil Anidjar (New York: Routledge, 2002): 362.

[32] While Coetzee does not use the term, parody is constantly implied in his essay entitled "What is a Classic? A Lecture," in *Stranger Shores: Essays 1986–1999* (2001; London: Vintage, 2002): 1–19. I am thinking, in particular, of his concluding comment that criticism and interrogation, "no matter how hostile," are "what the classic uses to define itself and to ensure its survival" (19). See also Geertsema's insightful commentary on Coetsee's essay in "'Traductions': J.M. Coetzee and the Violent 'Invention' of the Classic," *Current Writing: Text and Reception in Southern Africa* 8.1 (1996): 45–60.

I have thus far limited my discussion of the trope of following to the relationship between writer, text and the invisible. Quite obviously, though, this trope has a bearing on the reader's reading of the work. In responding to the command of the invisible, the writer writes and as soon as s/he does so a reader is implied by this relationship – from the first, then, the reader is implicated in the writer's relationship to the invisible. Not only the writer but also the reader follows the work that "plods" after the invisible. The logic of following that informs the writer's relationship to the text therefore also informs the reader's relationship to it. In effect, the novel leads the reader; it is the reader's guide, and a wholly unreliable one at that. Accordingly, the reader must distrust the work. In *Age of Iron*, where the analogy between Vercueil as messenger and text as messenger amplifies the metaphor of following to include the reader, the necessity for such distrust is directly articulated in Mrs Curren's injunction to her daughter:

> I tell you the story of this morning mindful that the storyteller, from her office, claims the place of right. It is through my eyes that you see; the voice that speaks in your head is mine. Through me alone do you find yourself here on these desolate flats, smell the smoke in the air, see the bodies of the dead, hear the weeping, shiver in the rain. It is my thoughts that you think, my despair that you feel [...]. To me your sympathies flow; your heart beats with mine.
>
> Now, my child, flesh of my flesh, my best self, I ask you to draw back. I tell you this story not so that you will feel for me but so that you will learn how things are. It would be easier for you, I know, if the story came from someone else, if it were a stranger's voice sounding in your ear. But the fact is, there is no one else. I am the only one. I am the one writing: I, I. So I ask you: attend to the writing, not to me. If lies and pleas and excuses weave among the words, listen for them. Do not pass them over, do not forgive them easily. Read all, even this adjuration, with a cold eye.[33]

If the reader is to follow the text faithfully, s/he must do so through not following, which is to say betraying, it.

---

[33] Coetzee, *Age of Iron*, 95–96. See Geertsema's discussion of this passage in "'We Embrace To Be Embraced': Irony in an Age of Iron," *English in Africa* 24.1 (1997): 96–97; see also "Irony and Otherness," 255.

In *Slow Man*, Coetzee's use of parody has much the same effect as Mrs Curren's injunction: it serves as a narrative strategy through which the work urges the reader to distrust and ultimately betray it. The irony is patent: in reading this novel, one follows the metaphor of following only to find that to follow the text responsibly one must not follow its metaphors. Or so it seems. On reflection, it becomes clear that the further irony is that, if one simply obeys the text's injunction not to follow it, one, of course, follows it and is therefore still too credulous and trusting in one's relationship to the untrustworthy. As Mrs Curren's words indicate, one must disobey even the injunction to disobey. What is here at stake once more is the absence of a clear-cut opposition between the *acoluthon* and the *anacoluthon*. To disobey it, one must first obey the text. The point, then, is not *not* to follow the text, but not to follow it *in* following it: one must interrupt the logic that informs the text's economy. Mrs Curren's argument is ultimately the same as Dostoevsky's when he tells Maximov that the reader must be the arm, be the axe, *and* be the skull. To read like this is precisely *not* to follow the text *in* following it. Like Elizabeth Costello's following of Paul Rayment, the reader must pursue the text: i.e. follow *and* guide it. To follow it faithfully, the reader must betray the text. To trust it, s/he must distrust it.

Should one manage to read in this way, one will have guided the work to a point at which it exposes one to what it, through its failure to present (the very slowness which renders it an unreliable guide), has been unable to exclude from its economy. One will have encountered an otherness which the text hosts despite itself. Indeed, one will have been exposed to an alterity that haunts the text. It is to the novel's deeply self-reflexive projection of the reader's exposure to this otherness and its possible effect on him or her that I now turn.

℘ ঽ

My use of the word 'haunted' is quite deliberate. If the text's hospitality consists in its inability either to include or to exclude the alterity with which it is concerned, it may be inferred that the otherness in question is spectral, neither present nor absent. Although it fails to present its writer's unconditional hospitality, his gift of self, *Slow Man* is nonetheless haunted by his ghost. Its hospitality is an effect of its inspiration and possession by what it is unable to possess, over which it cannot exert conceptual control.

What we have here, then, is very similar to what we found in *Age of Iron* in Mrs Curren's description of her letter to her daughter, its projected recipient: "These words, as you read them, if you read them, enter you and draw breath again. They are, if you like, my way of living on."[34] In my discussion of this description, I observed that this character's words, by echoing those of Christ to his disciples at the Last Supper, liken the text to the Eucharist, the archetypal self-sacrificing gift of love. That is, they figure the text as the Host that hosts the writer's ghost.

As Mrs Curren's description indicates, this transubstantiation, in the course of which the writer as host becomes guest and ghost, has a direct effect on the reader, the unwitting recipient of the spectral gift of self. In *Slow Man*, Coetzee thematizes just this process by depicting the novel as a site of the dead, an underworld of sorts which, in turn, figures reading as a descent into the realm of the dead. The association of the novel with the abode of the dead is already evident in the suggestion that the accident with which the novel opens kills Paul Rayment. Once he recovers his senses in the hospital, he reflects on "the lurking question of what exactly it was that happened on Magill Road to blast him into this dead place" (4). The use of the word "blast," here is not incidental, as is emphasized by the fact that the motorist responsible for the accident, described as "the angel of death" (122), bears the name "Blight," which in fact means "blast." By implication, Paul Rayment's "fall" is a katabasis, a blowing downwards, a descent into the underworld. Rayment himself reflects on having, Alice-like, "tumble[d] down a dark hole" (122), and Elizabeth Costello, in discussing the accident with him, refers to the "life you were about to depart" (83), and describes Magill Road as "the very portal to the abode of the dead" (83). Finally, it is not only the hospital that is described as a place of the dead, "a cocoon of dead air" (3): Rayment's apartment is a "funeral parlour" (227), and Adelaide a "graveyard" (231). Given this association of the novel's settings with death, it is not surprising that Rayment should refer to himself as being "caught in limbo" (112). Like Costello (120, 160), he, in a further extension of the air-motif, is depicted as a spirit, "*A figure without substance, ghostly, beyond anger and desire*" (224). Both he and Costello, then, are like air: "blank," "colourless," and "featureless," lacking in form and substance (120, 160).

---

[34] Coetzee, *Age of Iron*, 120.

In depicting itself as a place of the dead, *Slow Man* describes reading not only as a descent into the underworld but also as an attempt to raise the dead. By imaging its reading as a katabasis, this text, in fact, implies that *it* must inspire the reader to invest it – the host of the writer's spectral gift of self – with form and substance. The novel must inspire the reader to animate it. This much is intimated by two of the work's images of reading. In the first, Paul Rayment encounters one of Elizabeth Costello's novels, appropriately entitled *The Fiery Furnace* (119), and after reading a couple of passages, snaps the book shut, reflecting that "He is not going to expose himself to any more of the colourless, odourless, inert, and depressive gas given off by its pages" (120). Immediately thereafter, he reads a passage from Costello's notebook describing a woman davening over a dying body: i.e. "Rocking stiffly back and forth at the bedside, her hands over her ears, her eyes wide open, unblinking, as though afraid she might miss the moment when, like a spurt of gas, the soul will leave the body" (121). These instances of the air-motif serve to associate expiration with inspiration, spirit with ghost, and, through their common root, *gast*, ghost with guest. Indeed, in German, Dutch, and Afrikaans the word 'gas' is also homonymously linked to 'guest'.[35] Collectively, these associations allude not only to the possibility that the reader may be inspired by the text, but also to the nature of such inspiration. The suggestion is that what the reader is exposed to in reading is neither in nor outside the novel. What may inspire him or her, then, is the trace of the absence of what has inspired the text and which it, in failing to present, fails to keep out.

To read in the manner imaged in the novel is therefore to risk opening oneself to the guest, the ghost, that the text hosts despite itself, that it has been possessed by owing to its inability to possess it. Were this to happen,

---

[35] I must thank Johan Geertsema for reminding me of Coetzee's discussion of the word 'gas' in his essay on Gerrit Achterberg's "Ballade van de Gasfitter" ("Achterberg's 'Ballade van de Gasfitter': The Mystery of I and You," in *Doubling the Point*, 73–75). Apart from reflecting on its homonyms, Coetzee examines this word's symbolic import in the poem. Especially insightful, in this regard, is his argument that the gasfitter is a figure of the poet, and that the gas, which "enters every home" as guest, symbolizes "the spirit, ghostly, overwhelmingly, coming upon us with fatal power, smelling of the void, tamed only by the *dichter*-priest" (73). Gas, and Coetzee reminds his reader that the word derives from the Greek 'chaos' (73), is infinity, the void. The writer, who mediates between its powers and the structural "needs of man" (73), is thus a "secretary of the invisible." My argument is partly that, should the reader be exposed to the invisible in his or her reading of the text, s/he too becomes its secretary.

the reader would, in his or her turn, be possessed by what possesses the text. As we have seen, precisely this notion of reading as possession through inspiration is invoked in *Age of Iron* in the dying Mrs Curren's comparison of her letter to her daughter, who is to receive and read it only after her mother's death, to a moth, a comparison which alludes to the mythological representation of the soul as a butterfly emerging from a dying person's mouth. In drawing this comparison, it may be recalled, Mrs Curren equates her letter with her spirit, her breath, her ghost:

> It is not my soul that will remain with you but the spirit of my soul, the breath, the stirring of the air about these words, the faintest of turbulence traced in the air by the ghostly passage of my pen over the paper your fingers now hold. (118–19)

To be inspired by the text is to be exposed to (indeed, to be invaded by) "the colourless, odourless, inert, and depressive gas given off" by its "pages." While the reader under inspiration becomes the host of the text, it is only in having been taken hostage by it. S/he hosts the work through losing the ability to extend an invitation to it.

Differently put, the reader forfeits subjective volition through losing the ability to possess the novel conceptually, to integrate it into an already formed conceptual system. The text inspires the reader by exceeding the expectations and intentions that s/he brings to his or her encounter with it. That is, it inspires the reader by surprising him or her. Once again, the ghost-metaphor intimates as much. In figuring inspiration as the novel's possession of the reader, it also implies that the reader, in being haunted by the text, is shocked, horrified, rendered aghast by it. To be inspired is to be *caught* unawares. Indeed, the word "surprise" derives in part from *prehendere* 'to catch', as Coetzee intimates in the opening sentence of the novel: "THE BLOW CATCHES him from the right, sharp and surprising and painful [...]" (1). The reader's inability to comprehend the text, to grasp it with his or her mind, enables it to surprise him or her.[36]

---

[36] Ironically, in referring to the accident, Paul Rayment asks Elizabeth Costello the following questions: "Am I alive or dead? Did something happen to me on Magill Road that I have failed to grasp?" (233). This irony inevitably extends to the reader's response to the novel's play with the etymology of words such as "surprise," "grasp," "comprehend," and, indeed, "ghost," "guest," and "gas." While Coetzee invites the reader to follow such etymologies and thereby establish the novel's coherence, the

Unconditional hospitality is inspiration, surprise, which is to say an accident in which the reader, the host, "goes absent" (1). In being haunted by the text, s/he is possessed, unhomed, and, as the etymology of the word 'haunt' connotes, becomes a *haimaz*, a home,[37] for this visitor. The words "goes absent" come from the opening passage of the novel, which describes Paul Rayment's accident. As I have indicated, this opening scene may be read as an allegory of writerly inspiration. It can, of course, also be read less as an allegory of the reader's inspiration by the novel than as the event thereof, the pre-reflective moment in which s/he, in following them, is seized and possessed by the words on the page and thereby dispossessed of self. In other words, the scene seeks to be the moment or instant in which reading loses its status as a willed action and becomes an event.

As the reader reads the novel's opening pages, then, s/he, quite uncannily, reads of what may be happening in the very moment of reading the novel's opening pages. S/he reads of the possibility of "going absent" in reading, of being inspired by Paul Rayment's expiration, his "last word" (263), his giving up of the ghost, his last gasp, "the gasp when he hit the road, the breath going out of him in a whoosh," and which, he speculates, could be "interpreted as [...] a last word" (83). For, in such a reading, it is the novel which is a hospital, a "dead place," a "cocoon of dead air" (3). To apply Costello's description of Magill Road, the novel's opening setting, to the text as a whole, the novel, in the event of the accident of inspiration, becomes "the very portal to the abode of the dead" (83). Its words, like air, are "colourless, odourless, inert" (120). To read them is to read of being inspired by them to animate the writer's spirit by which they are haunted. The reader's task is to make flesh the word, to breathe life into it. In this regard, Mrs Curren's aforementioned words to her daughter, the internal reader in *Age of Iron*, also apply to the reader of

---

etymologies concerned all signify the text's desire to interrupt precisely this interpretative procedure, to slip the reader's conceptual grasp. In his aforementioned email correspondence with me, Johan Geertsema explains the "paradoxical effect" of Coetzee's use of etymology, particularly false etymology, in *Age of Iron* and *Slow Man*: "[such etymologies] serve to connect, thread together and render coherent the web of the text. But such rendering coherent is of course precisely what the text wishes to interrupt even as it encourages/demands it" (7 November 2007; see also "Irony and Otherness," 253–54).

[37] *The Concise Oxford Dictionary of Current English* (6th ed. 1976).

Slow Man: "These words, as you read them, if you read them, enter you and draw breath again. They are, if you like, my way of living on."

Under inspiration, then, the reader is faced with the very responsibility that confronts the writer: i.e. to animate the word, to make of language a home for the other. As in the case of writerly responsibility, the issue at stake here is not whether or not this task can be accomplished but the fact that, in the event of being inspired by the text, the reader is charged with the responsibility for doing so. S/he undertakes this task not because s/he thinks that it is possible to complete it, but because s/he has no say in the matter. In fact, rather than undertake it, s/he is assigned it. Reading is an event in which the reader, as Dostoevsky puts it, gives him-/herself up.[38] S/he cannot but care generously, which is to say selflessly.

It is tempting to conclude that the reader's inspiration is the *telos* towards which the novel progresses, and that, should it attain this goal, it will have secured, in the event of its own reading, a re-enactment of the unconditional hospitality that produced it, but which it is unable to thematize. While unable to represent such generous care, *Slow Man* will have secured a performance thereof in its reception. Such a conclusion would, however, overlook the ateleological dimension of the aesthetic and ethical task concerned. It would overlook the fact that the reader's task is not a finite *task* but an infinite *responsibility*. Like the previous novels, this work attempts to pass to the reader the burden of responsibility for completing a task that its characters and author have failed to fulfil. *Slow Man* charges the reader with the responsibility of presenting what Costello has failed to present, what Rayment has failed to present, and, indeed, what Coetzee has failed to present owing to the insufficiency of language. What the reader must present is not just what language cannot present, but that which it is unable to exclude from the text's economy. Precisely because it cannot be excluded, the unpresentable ceaselessly demands to be included, to come into being. The reader is accordingly charged with a responsibility that cannot be discharged, and which therefore continues once s/he lays down the book. In terms of Coetzee's intersecting metaphors, the reader's actions in the world will continue to be haunted by the demand of the unpresentable even after s/he has finished reading the novel. His or her actions in the present will be informed, mediated by the

---

[38] Coetzee, *The Master of Petersburg*, 47.

moment (indeed, instant or *Augenblick*) of his or her inspiration, the im-memorial event of his or her self-sacrificing generosity.

By implication, the novel follows the reader beyond the space of read-ing. Ironically, the reader, in following the work as an *anacoluthon*: i.e. by persecuting it, by guiding it in its pursuit of the invisible, is inspired by the invisible. S/he becomes a "secretary of the invisible," which is to say that s/he no longer simply pursues but is pursued by the invisible beyond the bounds of the text that s/he thinks s/he has 'finished'. Like Paul Ray-ment, who, "haunted by the idea of doing good" (155), eventually follows the Jokić family, the reader's relations in the present in the realm of con-ditional hospitality will be inspired by, and consequently inflected with, the ethic of absolute hospitality. In the terms of Levinas' argument about the social effect of the self's singular relation to the human other, they will be conducted "in the trace of transcendence, in illeity";[39] they will be interrupted by unconditional care's insistence on coming into being.

In my discussion of *Age of Iron*, I argued that this text projects its desire to pursue and preside over the reader's worldly actions by means of the image of the Furies. The portrayal of Mrs Curren's letter as a Fury sig-nifies the novel's desire relentlessly to pursue its reader, imaged here as a perverter of respectful relations. In *Slow Man*, Paul Rayment, and thus the work itself, is portrayed as wishing to be a guardian angel that "hovers" over and protects others (see, for example, 224). Even more striking, however, is the implicit analogy between the text's pursuit of the reader and that of Sinbad by the old man of the river. In burdening the reader with responsibility for what has not yet emerged, the novel "descends" on his or her shoulders. It pursues *and* guides the reader in his or her social interactions. Costello's aforementioned words to Rayment apply equally to the text's relationship to its reader: "Most of the time you won't notice I am here. Just a touch on the shoulder, now and then, left or right, to keep you on the path" (87). The novel as *acoluthon* and *anacoluthon* seeks to interrupt, mediate, even justify, the reader's relations in the realm of con-ditional hospitality. What is at stake in *Slow Man*'s bid to affect the reader is therefore an attempt to extend the scope of ethical concern to everyone irrespective of identity.

Should the reader be moved to responsibility in the course of his or her singular engagement with the novel, s/he will no longer be in a position to

---

[39] Levinas, *Otherwise Than Being*, 158.

choose freely and autonomously his or her other commitments, to decide independently and rationally to what or whom s/he will extend care and concern. His or her relationships will no longer be determined solely by the calculus of invitation and, accordingly, the kind of differential exclusion that engenders ethical indifference.

If the novel's ethic of hospitality is to work, the pre-reflective experience of reading must affect the reader's conscious and reflective life. The moment of reading must approximate the attentionality of the reader-figure in the ending of *Foe*: i.e. it must be an *Augenblick*, a blink of the eye, in which the reader's intentional consciousness is interrupted not only by what it fails to include but also by what it fails to exclude. In other words, Susan Barton's sexual experience with Cruso on the island in *Foe*, which I discussed in my third chapter, is exactly the effect that *Slow Man* wishes to have on its reader:

> "We yield to a stranger's embrace or give ourselves to the waves; for the blink of an eyelid our vigilance relaxes; we are asleep; and when we awake, we have lost the direction of our lives."[40]

Elsewhere, Barton reflects on the way in which such ecstatic experiences remain with one as an "after-memory" (104) or, in Blanchot's description of ecstasy, an "extratemporal memory or remembrance of a past which has never been lived in the present (and thus a stranger to all *Erlebnis*)."[41] It is because she can "summon back nothing distinct" that the "after-memory" remains with her and ceaselessly insists on being remembered (104). In aspiring to make of the reading experience an *Augenblick*, *Slow Man* seeks to remain with and in the reader as an insubstantial "after-memory" which cannot be, and so incessantly demands to be, "summoned" back.

Slow Man thus seeks to drive the reader mad. It should be recalled from my discussion of the Fury image in *Age of Iron* that the Furies, in their pursuit and persecution of those who had perverted respectful relations, drove them mad. Should *Slow Man* follow and so remain with the reader, and constantly demand that s/he render possible an impossibility, it will have precisely this effect on him or her. In requiring him or her to make of the same a home for the other, to be infinitely responsible despite being a

[40] Coetzee, *Foe*, 30.
[41] Blanchot, *The Unavowable Community*, 18–19.

finite being, it will drive him or her mad. It will do so by ensuring that
s/he is always unequal to his or her infinite responsibility, and so never
able to love well enough, always necessarily guilty of betrayal, of
irresponsibility. Burdened with a form of responsibility that exacts
irresponsibility, the reader will find him-/herself in a double bind and,
as Derrida argues, "When you want to make someone mad, you put him
or her under a double bind, insisting on it, not just for a minute but *constantly*. If the double bind is the condition for responsibility, or ethics,
then ethics are mad."[42]

Nevertheless, should the novel have this effect on the reader, it will
have changed him or her, freed him or her from his or her self-entrapment.
Ultimately, the *Bildung* that is really at issue in this novel is that of not
Paul Rayment but of an equally slow man or woman – the reader. *Slow
Man* seeks to save the reader. In terms of the Levinasian notion of an "inspiration that is already expiration" (182),[43] it endeavours to free the
reader "by breathing from closure in [him or her]self" (180).

℘ ঽ

Coetzee's bid to make of the reading of his novel an attentional event is,
of course, quite paradoxical. After all, this endeavour blurs the boundaries
between host and visitor: the novel, which hosts the writer's spectral gift
of self, wishes to possess the reader, to *make* of him or her a host and of
itself his or her visitor. The text, by implication, tries to control what cannot be controlled: it must induce an accidental reading which, were it to
happen, could not be an accident. In order to do this, it must enact an
opening for the reader, and so await his or her arrival. As aspirant visitor,
it must await the arrival of the reader as host. In doing so, it must actively
prevent this host from inviting it, surprise him or her, and thereby ensure
that it will be received with unconditional hospitality.

In the process of contriving such a reception, the novel cannot but
await, and therefore invite, a certain kind of reader. It expects a reading
that will surprise it and so enable it to enact what it cannot represent. That
is, it intends an attentional reading. In the process, it paradoxically awaits
that which, were it to come, would do so despite its intentions and against

[42] Derrida, "Following Theory: Jacques Derrida," interview, in *life. after. theory*, 36.
[43] Levinas, *Otherwise Than Being*, 182.

its expectations. Indeed, *Slow Man* announces its expectation of the unexpected in the passage in which the woman davens over the dying body.
While I previously discussed this passage as an image of reading, the
shifting roles of host and visitor in the novel require – indeed, exact –
additional readings, including one in which the scene allegorizes the paradox of expecting the unexpected. In the excerpt from Elizabeth Costello's
notebook, the woman who waits for a "spurt of gas" to leave the body on
the bed does so with "hands over her ears, her eyes wide open, unblinking" (121). The woman awaits what Levinas calls "invisible air" (180);
she awaits that which, were it to come, would come unseen, unexpectedly
and unbeknownst to her. She wishes to see what can only come in an
Augenblick.

The novel expects "invisible air" by aspiring to be "invisible air," to be
what affects a reader who, were s/he to be affected, would be so not only
despite him-/herself but also despite the novel's intentions. *Slow Man* is
thus self-consciously aware that it awaits a reader who is wholly other and
to whose arrival, should it transpire, it will be quite oblivious. That is, the
text is aware that the time of awaiting is without term, that to all intents
and purposes the attentional reader is always yet to come. By extension,
the novel knows that the visitation of the host/visitor it awaits exceeds the
time of arrival and departure, that the instant of arrival is always deferred
because the reader it awaits is always more than it expects.

I have discussed many of these paradoxes in my readings of Coetzee's
earlier work. In *Slow Man*, however, the debate on awaiting what would
not be recognized if it were to arrive is extended. This novel makes it
quite clear that the apparent futility of this endeavour is itself a sign of the
fact that awaiting is an intention that escapes the writer's intention. The
novel's awaiting of, and attempt to inspire and affect, the reader is itself
an effect of Coetzee's inspiration. Indeed, the text's self-conscious obsession with its own reading is a trace of the pastness of the attentional
moment of this inspiration. *Slow Man* is haunted by the unconditional
hospitality through which it has come into being but of which it is merely
a trace. In other words, its desire to possess the reader, to assert control
over the reader's reading of the novel, is beyond its control. Differently
put, its attempt to assert control is an effect of a *loss* of control. In fact, it
is the necessary and inevitable, because wholly involuntary, aesthetic response to the ethical imperative to make of language a home for the other.

Significantly, too, in this regard, the novel's endeavour to possess the reader must be seen in the context of its depiction of itself as the writer's spectral gift of self. In terms of the ethic and aesthetic of hospitality, it follows from this depiction that the text is a response to the writer's inspiration and possession by the otherness of the recipient of his gift. He gives himself to the reader in being taken hostage by him or her. However, if this gift is to be received by the reader, it must surprise him or her. In order to give himself to the reader, Coetzee must therefore possess and control the reader. The novel's attempt to do so is thus itself a function of the recipient's possession of the giver of the gift.

It follows that *Slow Man* is a trace of Coetzee's inspiration by the otherness of the reader whom it seeks to inspire. It is itself an effect of its writer's inspiration by what it awaits to inspire and to be animated by. To use the term that Mrs Curren applies to the effect that Vercueil's otherness has had on her and the effect that, she suspects, her otherness has had on him, the novel awaits a "mutual election,"[44] a notion that relies on, even as it dismantles, the opposition between host and visitor.

❦ ❧

---

[44] Coetzee, *Age of Iron*, 179.

Conclusion

⹁

I N AN ESPECIALLY PERCEPTIVE, even prescient, comment on
Coetzee's writing, Michael Valdez Moses points out that the Magistrate's "repudiation of the Empire," in *Waiting for the Barbarians*,
"implicitly rejects all political regimes, none of which may lay claim to a
philosophically defensible conception of right."[1] What is at stake in this
novel is not just Empire's negative construction of itself; it is also that this
is how all communities constitute themselves. Thus Moses suggests that
Waiting for the Barbarians poses the following question: "How will the
State that follows establish its claim to justice except by discriminating
itself, its form, from the Other which lies outside it?"[2] As I pointed out in
the opening chapter of this study, community (and a community always
underlies the state) necessarily defines itself in opposition to what it is not.
That is, it defines itself through conflict. Its very existence presupposes
conflict.[3]

One of my contentions in this study has been that Coetzee's writing,
owing to its awareness of the conflictual process by which community
erects itself, must continue to attempt to rival history, to contrive a degree
of autonomy, and therefore that his novels, despite being grounded in
specific times and places, cannot help concerning themselves with the
same issues. To a greater or lesser extent, they tell the "same story." Accordingly, the reluctance to follow history of which we read in "Into the
Dark Chamber," and which is staged in Mrs Curren's decision, in *Age of
Iron*, to decline Mr Thabane's invitation to name the state's atrocities in
Guguletu and, rather, to find her "own words" is again evident in *Disgrace*, notwithstanding the momentous changes in South African history

---

[1] Moses, "The Mark of Empire," 123.
[2] "The Mark of Empire," 123.
[3] See Strong, "Foreword," xv.

in the interval between the writing of the two novels. So, for instance, as Sikhumbuzo Mngadi has indicated,[4] Lurie's separation, in the latter novel, from his daughter while she is being violated in her bedroom quite clearly evokes Coetzee's description, in this essay, of the artist's inability to enter the dark chamber.[5] The difference, of course, is that while the essay refers to the problems attendant on representing, or following, the apartheid state's violence, the novel has at its centre an act of violence that is perpetrated after the demise of the apartheid state. While apartheid may have ended, Coetzee's point seems to be, the history of the ostensibly new South African community still erects itself in the old manner: i.e. through a logic of collective discrimination which is, by definition, hostile to otherness, to singularity. This is why Lurie's task is so strongly reminiscent of the kind of quest on which the protagonists of the apartheid novels embark. Like them, he must find the child of which history is the death and do so in his "own words." Already during his daughter's rape, I pointed out, he begins to imagine what is happening in the bedroom become dark chamber. The trick, and this I also pointed out, is to do so without following history.

As with the apartheid narratives, then, *Disgrace* must attempt to interrupt history by opening itself to what history damages. It must follow the other rather than history. The same is true of *Slow Man*. If anything, this novel, notwithstanding its Australian provenance, is, as we have seen, Coetzee's clearest fictional elaboration to date of the philosophical and aesthetic implications of the trope of following. In the introduction to this study, I indicated that the Australian Elizabeth Costello, like Magda, her South African thematic forebear, is a secretary of the invisible. She seeks to follow the invisible rather than history. Importantly, *Slow Man* selfreflexively announces these similarities: it is aware of its iterative nature. It is aware that it continues a story that the other novels in the oeuvre of which it is a part have all started but failed to complete. It is also aware that it, too, because of its inadequacy, its slowness, will fail to end this story. What Johan Geertsema once said of *Age of Iron* is equally true of *Slow Man*: "The novel is at once constituted by the attempt to render otherness and the attempt to render that rendering problematic."[6]

---

[4] Mngadi, "Reconsidering the Copula, 'and,' in 'Literature *and* Politics'," 30.
[5] Coetzee, "Into the Dark Chamber," 363.
[6] Geertsema, "Irony and Otherness," 259.

Nevertheless, in telling the "same story" that the South African fiction does, a novel like *Slow Man* changes this story. On the most obvious of levels, we find that the motif of following elucidates the conflicted nature of aesthetic and ethical responsibility. Less obviously, however, *Slow Man* simply alters the concerns, themes, and motifs of Coetzee's oeuvre by quite intentionally forming a new context that both enables their repetition and ensures that they change in being repeated. As Derrida is aware, there is alteration in every repetition.[7] In turn, the new context constituted by this novel alters the overriding context of the oeuvre it joins. While it is self-evidently the case that any writer who adds to his or her oeuvre alters all the texts that form that oeuvre, I must emphasize that, with *Slow Man*, such alteration becomes a conscious strategy in Coetzee's writing, a way of interrupting the story dictated by the invisible – a way of following the invisible by not following it. Thus, this novel's parody of its narrative not only means that *it* cannot be the "same story" that its author has previously told, but also that it changes the previous fiction. Since Paul Rayment's *Bildung* (and the tropes that figure it) is remarkably similar to what the protagonists of some of the earlier novels undergo, Coetzee's parody of it comments on his entire fictional project. After reading *Slow Man*, one responds differently to the oeuvre of which it is part. By repeating it, this writer interrupts the "same story," and thereby makes sure that it cannot remain quite the same.

In the previous chapter, I noted that Elizabeth Costello, in *Slow Man*, parodies the fluid author–text relationship by comparing it to a relationship in which leader and follower become increasingly indistinguishable: namely, that of Don Quixote and Sancho Panza. Read in this context, a passage such as the one in *Age of Iron* in which Mrs Curren likens her car to Rocinante,[8] and thus her relationship with Vercueil to Don Quixote's relationship to Sancho Panza, signifies differently from the way in which it previously signified. *Slow Man* alters this passage's position in the oeuvre and this brings about a shift in its field of signification. The Quixote references in *Slow Man* change *Age of Iron* by affecting the reader's response to it. The story can no longer be the same. In fact, the story now increasingly seems to parody itself.

---

[7] Jacques Derrida, "Signature, Event, Context," in *Margins of Philosophy*, tr. Alan Bass (*Marges de la philosophie*, 1972; Brighton: Harvester, 1982): 307–30.
[8] Coetzee, *Age of Iron*, 16.

A further instance of a passage that changes or to which the reader responds differently after having encountered *Slow Man*'s self-parody is the scene in *Disgrace* in which Lurie, plunking away on a toy banjo in a yard in Africa, hopes for a "note of immortal longing" which, were it to sound, would be recognized not by him but possibly by "the scholars of the future."[9] In the context of *Slow Man*'s self-parody, this scene invites being read as an allegory of the absurdity and futility of the artist's quixotic responsibility for what has not emerged and which cannot emerge. Similarly, one now cannot help but wonder about Cruso and Friday's apparently futile labour on the island in *Foe*. When Barton asks him who will seed the terraces they have prepared, Cruso, with "sorry dignity," replies with these words: "The planting is reserved for those who come after us and have the foresight to bring seed."[10] From the perspective of *Slow Man*, what we have in these novels begins to look suspiciously like a parody of the writer's secretarial responsibility for the invisible.

If *Slow Man* tells the "same story" that Coetzee has previously told – the "slow story" dictated by the invisible – it does so by interrupting it, and thereby making of it a different story. In the process, this novel changes the reader's response to this story; it changes the way in which s/he follows it. After *Slow Man*, it becomes clear that Coetzee has always been quite aware of the lugubrious nature and comic potential of his fictional project: in the examples cited, this endeavour is likened to composing an opera on a toy banjo, and to futile labour on a desert island which may or may not be visited by someone or other in times to come. Evidently, Coetzee pokes fun at his literary intentions. The irony, of course, is that his use of parody in *Slow Man* does not simply denigrate his project. It also becomes a way of furthering it: by parodying the narrative of his novel, I have argued, this writer seeks to open it to what it excludes. In parodying his ambitions in *Slow Man*, Coetzee paradoxically seeks to realize them, thereby paying homage to the slowness of the very story he attacks. What we have here is a clear case of betting on all the numbers; a strategy for which the protagonist of *The Master of Petersburg* shows some appreciation.

ᘔ ᘔ

---

[9] Coetzee, *Disgrace*, 214.
[10] Coetzee, *Foe*, 33.

Works Cited

───────── ঽ

Adams, Percy. *Travel Literature and the Evolution of the Novel* (Lexington: U of Kentucky P, 1983).

Adorno, Theodor W. *Aesthetic Theory*, tr. C. Lenhardt, ed. Gretel Adorno & Rolf Tiedemann (*Ästhetische Theorie*, 1970; London: Routledge & Kegan Paul, 1984).

——. *Minima Moralia: Reflections from Damaged Life*, tr. E.F.N. Jephcott (*Minima Moralia: Reflexionen aus dem beschädigten Leben*, 1951; London: Verso, 1978).

——. *Negative Dialectics*, tr. E.B. Ashton (*Negative Dialektik*, 1966; London: Routledge & Kegan Paul, 1973).

——, & Max Horkheimer. *Dialectic of Enlightenment*, tr. John Cumming (*Dialektik der Aufklärung*, 1944; London: Verso, 1997).

Anker, Willem. "Bewaarder van die Stilte: Gedagtes oor J.M. Coetzee se Etiek van Skryf," *Journal of Literary Studies* 22.1–2 (2006): 113–37.

Ashcroft, Bill. "Irony, Allegory and Empire: *Waiting for the Barbarians* and *In the Heart of the Country*," in *Critical Essays on J.M. Coetzee*, ed. Kossew, 100–16.

Attridge, Derek. *J.M. Coetzee and the Ethics of Reading: Literature in the Event* (Scottsville: U of KwaZulu–Natal P & Chicago: U of Chicago P, 2005).

——. *The Singularity of Literature* (London: Routledge, 2004).

Attwell, David. *J.M. Coetzee: South Africa and the Politics of Writing* (Berkeley: U of California P, 1993).

——. "Race in *Disgrace*," *Interventions* 4.3 (2002): 331–41.

Authorised King James Version of the Holy Bible (London: Collins, n.d.).

Baines, Anthony. "Lyre," in *The New Oxford Companion to Music*, ed. Denis Arnold (Oxford: Oxford UP, 1983), vol. 2.

Baker, Geoffrey. "The Limits of Sympathy: J.M. Coetzee's Evolving Ethics of Engagement," *ARIEL: A Review of International English Literature* 36.1–2 (2005): 27–49.

Batten, Charles L. *Pleasurable Instruction: Form and Convention in Eighteenth-Century Travel Literature* (Berkeley: U of California P, 1978).

Bauman, Zygmunt. *Postmodern Ethics* (Oxford: Blackwell, 1993).

Beard, Margot. "Lessons from the Dead Masters: Wordsworth and Byron in J.M. Coetzee's *Disgrace*," *English in Africa* 34.1 (2007): 59–77.

Benjamin, Walter. *Illuminations*, tr. Harry Zohn, ed. & intro. Hannah Arendt (*Schriften*, 1955; London: Fontana, 1973).

——. "On Some Motifs in Baudelaire," in *Illuminations*, 152–96.

——. "The Work of Art in the Age of Mechanical Reproduction," in *Illuminations*, 211–44.

Beressem, Hanjo. "*Foe*: The Corruption of Words," *Matatu: Journal for African Culture and Society* 2.3–4 (1988): 222–35.

Berlin, Isaiah. *The Roots of Romanticism*, ed. Henry Hardy (London: Chatto & Windus, 1999).

Bethlehem, Louise. "Aneconomy in an Economy of Melancholy: Embodiment and Gendered Identity in J.M. Coetzee's *Disgrace*," *African Identities* 1.2 (2003): 167–85.

——. "Pliant/Compliant; Grace/*Disgrace*; Plaint/Complaint," *Scrutiny2* 7.1 (2002): 20–24.

Blanchot, Maurice. *The Infinite Conversation*, tr. Susan Hanson (*L'Entretien infini*, 1969; Minneapolis: U of Minnesota P, 1995).

——. "Literature and the Right to Death," in *The Work of Fire*, tr. Charlotte Mandell (*La Part du feu*, 1949; Stanford CA: Stanford UP, 1995). 300–43.

——. "Orpheus' Gaze" (1955), in *The Siren's Song*, 177–81.

——. *The Siren's Song: Selected Essays by Maurice Blanchot*, ed. & intro. Gabriel Josipovici, tr. Sacha Rabinovitch (Brighton: Harvester, 1982).

——. *The Unavowable Community*, tr. Pierre Joris (*La Communauté inavouable*, 1983; Barrytown NY: Station Hill, 1988).

——. "Where Now? Who Now?", in *The Siren's Song*, 192–98.

——. *The Writing of the Disaster*, tr. Ann Smock (*Écriture du désastre*, 1980; Lincoln: U of Nebraska P, 1995).

Boehmer, Elleke. "Not Saying Sorry, Not Speaking Pain: Gender Implications in *Disgrace*," *Interventions* 4.3 (2002): 342–51.

Bongie, Chris. "'Lost in the Maze of Doubting': J.M. Coetzee's *Foe* and the Politics of (Un)likeness," *Modern Fiction Studies* 39.2 (1993): 261–81.

Borch, Merete Falck et al., ed. *Bodies and Voices: The Force-Field of Representation and Discourse in Colonial and Postcolonial Studies* (Cross/Cultures 94; Amsterdam & New York: Rodopi, 2008).

Briganti, Chiara. "'A Bored Spinster with a Locked Diary': The Politics of Hysteria in *In the Heart of the Country*, in *Critical Essays on J.M. Coetzee*, ed. Kossew, 84–99.

Canepari–Labib, Michela. *Old Myths – Modern Empires: Power, Language and Identity in J.M. Coetzee's Work* (Oxford: Peter Lang, 2005).

Carchidi, Victoria. "At Sea on a Desert Island: Defoe, Tournier and Coetzee," in *Literature and Quest*, ed. Christine Arkinstall (Amsterdam & Atlanta GA: Rodopi, 1993): 75–88.

Carr, David. *Time, Narrative and History* (Bloomington: Indiana UP, 1986).

Coetzee, J.M. "Achterberg's 'Ballade van de Gasfitter': The Mystery of I and You," in *Doubling the Point*, 69–90.

——. *Age of Iron* (London: Secker & Warburg, 1990).

——. "The Agentless Sentence as Rhetorical Device," in *Doubling the Point*, 170–80.

——. *Diary of a Bad Year* (London: Harvill Secker, 2007).

——. *Disgrace* (London: Secker & Warburg, 1999).

——. *Dusklands* (Johannesburg: Ravan, 1974).

——. *Doubling the Point: Essays and Interviews*, ed. David Attwell (Cambridge MA: Harvard UP, 1992).

——. *Elizabeth Costello: Eight Lessons* (London: Secker & Warburg, 2003).

——. "Erasmus' *Praise of Folly*: Rivalry and Madness," *Neophilologus* 76.1 (1992): 1–18.

——. *Foe* (Johannesburg: Ravan, 1986).

——. "Idleness in South Africa," in *White Writing*, 163–77.

——. *In the Heart of the Country* (1977; Johannesburg: Ravan, 1978).

——. "Into the Dark Chamber: The Writer and the South African State," in *Doubling the Point*, 361–68.

——. "Jerusalem Prize Acceptance Speech," in *Doubling the Point*, 96–99.

——. *Life & Times of Michael K* (Johannesburg: Ravan, 1983).

——. *The Master of Petersburg* (London: Secker & Warburg, 1994).

——. "The Novel Today," *Upstream* 6.1 (1988): 2–5.

——. "Reading the South African Landscape," in *White Writing*, 163–77.

——. *Slow Man* (London: Secker & Warburg, 2005).

——. *Waiting for the Barbarians* (Johannesburg: Ravan, 1981.)

——. "What is a Classic? A Lecture," in *Stranger Shores. Essays 1986–1999* (2001; London: Vintage, 2002): 1–19.

——. *White Writing: On the Culture of Letters in South Africa* (New Haven CT: Radix, 1988).

Coleridge, Samuel Taylor. *The Complete Poetical and Dramatic Works of Samuel Taylor Coleridge*, ed. James Dykes Campbell (London: Macmillan, 1893).

——. *Biographia Literaria* (London: Dent, 1956.)

The Concise Oxford Dictionary of Current English (6th ed. 1976).

Cornwell, Gareth. "'He and His Man': Allegory and Catachresis in J.M. Coetzee's Nobel Lecture," *English in Africa* 34.1 (2007): 97–114.

——. "Realism, Rape, and J.M. Coetzee's *Disgrace*," *Critique: Studies in Contemporary Fiction* 43.4 (2002): 307–22.

Critchley, Simon. *Very Little … Almost Nothing: Death, Philosophy, Literature* (London: Routledge, 1997).

Defoe, Daniel. *Robinson Crusoe* (1719; London: Dent, 1975).

De Graef, Ortwin. "Suffering, Sympathy, Circulation: Smith, Wordsworth, Coetzee (But there's a dog)," *European Journal of English Studies* 7.3 (2003): 311–31.

De Jong, Marianne. "An Incomplete Repression: *The Master of Petersburg* and *Stavrogin's Confession*," *Slavic Almanach* 3.3–4 (1995): 48–75.

——. "Is the Writer Ethical? The Early Novels of J.M. Coetzee up to *Age of Iron*," *Journal of Literary Studies* 20.1–2 (2004): 71–93.

Derrida, Jacques. *Acts of Religion*, ed. & intro. Gil Anidjar (New York: Routledge, 2002).

——. "Adieu," in *The Work of Mourning*, ed. & tr. Pascale–Anne Brault & Michael Naas (*Chaque fois unique, la fin du monde*, 1996; Chicago: U of Chicago P, 2001): 200–209.

——. "The Animal that therefore I Am (More to Follow)," tr. David Wills, *Critical Inquiry* 28 (2002): 369–418.

——. "Following Theory: Jacques Derrida," interview, in *life. after. theory*, ed. Michael Payne & John Schad (London: Continuum, 2003): 1–51.

——. *The Gift of Death*, tr. David Wills (*Donner la mort in L'ethique du don: Jacques Derrida et la pensee du don*, 1992; Chicago: U of Chicago P, 1995).

——. *Of Hospitality: Anne Dufourmantelle Invites Jacques Derrida to Respond*, tr. Rachel Bowlby (*De l'hospitalité: Anne Dufourmantelle invite Jacques Derrida à répondre*, 1997; Stanford C A: Stanford U P, 2000).

——. "Signature, Event, Context," in *Margins of Philosophy*, tr. Alan Bass (*Marges de la philosophie*, 1972; Brighton: Harvester, 1982): 307–30.

——. *Specters of Marx: The State of the Debt, the Work of Mourning and the New International*, tr. Peggy Kamuf, intro. Bernd Magnus & Stephen Cullenberg (*Spectres de Marx: L'État de la dette, le travail du deuil et la nouvelle Internationale*, 1993; New York: Routledge, 1994).

Donovan, Josephine. "'Miracles of Creation': Animals in J.M. Coetzee's Work," *Michigan Quarterly Review* 43.1 (2004): 78–93; online http://name.umdl.umich .edu/act2080.0043.112 (8 June 2008).

Dostoevsky, Fyodor. *The Devils*, tr. & intro. David Magarshack (*Besy*, 1871; Harmondsworth: Penguin, 2nd ed. 1971).

Douthwaite, John. "Melanie: Voice and its Suppression in J.M. Coetzee's *Disgrace*" *Current Writing: Text and Reception in Southern Africa* 13.1 (2001): 130–60.

Dovey, Teresa. *The Novels of J.M. Coetzee: Lacanian Allegories* (Craighall: Ad. Donker, 1988).

Duncan, Ian. "Narrative Authority in J.M. Coetzee's *Age of Iron*," *Tydskrif vir Letterkunde* 43.2 (2006): 174–85.

Durrant, Sam. *Postcolonial Narrative and the Work of Mourning: J.M. Coetzee, Wilson Harris, and Toni Morrison* (Albany: State U of New York P, 2004).

———. "J.M. Coetzee, Elizabeth Costello, and the Limits of the Sympathetic Imagination," in *J.M. Coetzee and the Idea of the Public Intellectual*, ed. Jane Poyner (Athens: Ohio UP, 2006): 118–34.

Eckstein, Barbara. "The Body, The Word, and the State: J.M. Coetzee's *Waiting for the Barbarians*," *Novel: A Forum on Fiction* 22.2 (1989): 175–98.

Farred, Grant. "Bulletproof Settlers: The Politics of Offense in the New South Africa," in *Whiteness: A Critical Reader*, ed. Mike Hill (New York: New York UP, 1997): 65–77.

Findlay, John N. "Foreword," in Hegel, *Phenomenology of Spirit*, v–xxx.

Fowles, John. *The French Lieutenant's Woman* (1969; London: Triad/Granada, 1977).

Gallagher, Susan VanZanten. *A Story of South Africa: J.M. Coetzee's Fiction in Context* (Cambridge MA: Harvard UP, 1991).

Gardiner, Allan. "J.M. Coetzee's *Dusklands*: Colonial Encounters of the Robinsonian Kind," *World Literature Written in English* 27.2 (1987): 174–84.

Gaylard, Gerald. "Mastering Arachnophobia: The Limits of Self-Reflexivity in African Fiction," *Journal of Commonwealth Literature* 37.1 (2002): 85–99.

Geertsema, Johan. "Irony and Otherness: A Study of Some Recent South African Narrative Fiction" (doctoral dissertation, University of Cape Town, 1999).

———. "'Traductions': J.M. Coetzee and the Violent 'Invention' of the Classic," *Current Writing: Text and Reception in Southern Africa* 8.1 (1996): 45–60.

———. "'We Embrace To Be Embraced': Irony in an Age of Iron," *English in Africa* 24.1 (1997): 89–102.

Graham, Lucy. "'Yes, I am giving him up': Sacrificial Responsibility and Likeness with Dogs in J.M. Coetzee's Recent Fiction," *Scrutiny2* 7.1 (2000): 4–15.

Graves, Robert. *The Greek Myths* (Harmondsworth: Penguin, 2nd ed. 1960), vol. 1.

Green, Martin. *Dreams of Adventure, Deeds of Empire* (London: Routledge & Kegan Paul, 1979).

Grimal, Pierre. *The Dictionary of Classical Mythology*, tr. A.P. Maxwell–Hyslop (*Dictionnaire de la mythologie grecque et romaine*, 1951; Oxford: Blackwell, 1986).

Hamilton, Grant. "J.M. Coetzee's *Dusklands*: The Meaning of Suffering," *Journal of Literary Studies* 21.3–4 (2005): 296–314.

Hansen, Miriam. "Mass Culture as Hieroglyphic Writing: Adorno, Derrida, Kracauer," *New German Critique* 56 (Spring–Summer 1992): 43–73.

Hayes, Patrick. "'An Author I Have Not Read': Coetzee's *Foe*, Dostoevsky's *Crime and Punishment*, and the Problem of the Novel," *Review of English Studies* 57.230 (2006): 273–90.

Head, Dominic. *J.M. Coetzee* (Cambridge: Cambridge UP, 1997).

Hegel, Georg Wilhelm Friedrich. *Aesthetics: Lectures on Fine Art*, tr. Thomas M. Knox (*Vorlesungen über die Ästhetik*, 1843; Oxford: Clarendon, 1975), vol. 1.

———. *Phenomenology of Spirit*, tr. Arnold V. Miller (*Phänomenologie des Geistes*, 1807; Oxford: Oxford UP, 1977).

Heidegger, Martin. *Being and Time*, tr. John Macquarrie & Edward Robinson (*Sein und Zeit*, 1927; London: SCM, 1962).

Helgesson, Stefan. *Writing in Crisis: Ethics and History in Gordimer, Ndebele and Coetzee* (Scottsville: U of KwaZulu–Natal P, 2004).

Herron, Tom. "The Dog Man: Becoming Animal in Coetzee's *Disgrace*," *Twentieth-Century Literature* 51.4 (2005): 467–90.

Hesiod. *The Poems of Hesiod*, tr. R.M. Frazer (Norman: U of Oklahoma P, 1983).

Holland, Michael. "*'Plink-Plunk'*: Unforgetting the Present in Coetzee's *Disgrace*," *Interventions* 4.3 (2002): 395–404.

Horrel, Georgina. "Postcolonial *Disgrace*: (White) Women and (White) Guilt in the 'New' South Africa," in *Bodies and Voices*, ed. Borch et al., 17–31.

Huggan, Graham. "Philomela's Retold Story: Silence, Music, and the Post-Colonial Text," *Journal of Commonwealth Literature* 25.1 (1990): 12–23.

——, & Stephen Watson, ed. *Critical Perspectives on J.M. Coetzee* (Houndmills: Macmillan, 1996).

Jacobs, J.U. "Writing a New Nation: South African Fiction After Apartheid," in *Latitude 63° North: Proceedings of the 8th International Region and Nation Conference*, ed. David Bell (Östersund, Sweden, 2002): 23–42.

JanMohamed, Abdul R. "The Economy of Manichean Allegory: The Function of Racial Difference in Colonialist Literature," in "*Race," Writing, and Difference*, ed. Henry Louis Gates, Jr. (Chicago: U of Chicago P, 1986): 78–106.

Jolly, Rosemary. *Colonization, Violence, and Narration in White South African Writing: André Brink, Breyten Breytenbach, and J.M. Coetzee* (Athens: Ohio UP, 1996).

Kossew, Sue, ed. *Critical Essays on J.M. Coetzee* (New York: G.K. Hall, 1998).

——. *Pen and Power: A Post-Colonial Reading of J.M. Coetzee and André Brink* (Cross/Cultures 27; Amsterdam & Atlanta GA: Rodopi, 1996).

——. "The Politics of Shame and Redemption in J.M. Coetzee's *Disgrace*," *Research in African Literatures* 34.2 (2003): 155–62.

Lawlan, Rachel. "*The Master of Petersburg*: Confession and Double Thoughts in Coetzee and Dostoevsky," *ARIEL: A Review of International English Literature* 29.2 (1998): 131–57.

Lebdai, Benaouda. "Identity: Bodies and Voices in Coetzee's *Disgrace* and Bouraoui's *Garçon manqué*," in *Bodies and Voices*, ed. Borch et al., 33–43.

Levinas, Emmanuel. *Collected Philosophical Papers*, tr. Alphonso Lingis (Dordrecht: Martinus Nijhoff, 1987).

——. *Existence and Existents*, tr. Alphonso Lingis (*De l'existence à l'existant*, 1947; The Hague: Martinus Nijhoff, 1978).

——. *Otherwise Than Being or Beyond Essence*, tr. Alphonso Lingis (*Autrement qu'être ou au-delà de l'essence*, 1974; The Hague: Martinus Nijhoff, 1981).

——. "Philosophy and the Idea of Infinity" (1957), in *Collected Philosophical Papers*, 47–59.

——. "Reality and its Shadow" (1948), in *Collected Philosophical Papers*, 1–13.

——. *Totality and Infinity: An Essay on Exteriority*, tr. Alphonso Lingis. (*Totalité et infini: Essai sur l'extériorité*, 1961; Dordrecht: Kluwer Academic, 1991).

Lingis, Alphonso. "Introduction" to Levinas, *Otherwise Than Being*, xi–xxxix.

Llewelyn, John. *Emmanuel Levinas: The Genealogy of Ethics* (London: Routledge, 1995).

Macaskill, Brian. "Charting J.M. Coetzee's Middle Voice: *In the Heart of the Country*," in *Critical Essays on J.M. Coetzee*, ed. Kossew, 66–83.

——, & Jeanne Colleran. "Interfering with 'The Mind of Apartheid'," *Pretexts* 4.1 (1992): 67–84.

——. "Reading History, Writing Heresy: The Resistance of Representation and the Representation of Resistance in J.M. Coetzee's *Foe*," *Contemporary Literature* 33.3 (1992): 432–57.

MacLeod, Lewis. "'Do We of Necessity Become Puppets in a Story?' Or Narrating the World: On Speech, Silence, and Discourse in J.M. Coetzee's *Foe*," *Modern Fiction Studies* 52.1 (2006): 1–18.

Maes–Jelinek, Hena. "The Muse's Progress: 'Infinite Rehearsal' in J.M. Coetzee's *Foe*," in *A Shaping of Connections*, ed. Maes–Jelinek et al., 232–42.

——, Kirsten Holst Petersen, & Anna Rutherford, ed. *A Shaping of Connections: Commonwealth Literature Studies – Then and Now* (Sydney: Dangaroo, 1989).

Maher, Susan Naramore. "Confronting Authority: J.M. Coetzee's *Foe* and the Remaking of *Robinson Crusoe*," *International Fiction Review* 18.1 (1991): 34–40.

May, Brian. "J.M. Coetzee and the Question of the Body," *Modern Fiction Studies* 47.2 (2001): 391–420.

Meffan, James, & Kim L. Worthington. "Ethics before Politics: J.M. Coetzee's *Disgrace*," in *Mapping the Ethical Turn: A Reader in Ethics, Culture, and Literary Theory*, ed. Todd F. Davis & Kenneth Womack (Charlottesville & London: UP of Virginia, 2001): 131–50.

Merivale, Patricia. "Audible Palimpsests: Coetzee's Kafka," in *Critical Perspectives on J.M. Coetzee*, ed. Huggan & Watson, 52–67.

Miller, J. Hillis. "Prosopopeia in Hardy and Stevens," in *Tropes, Parables, Performatives*, 245–59.

——. *Reading Narrative*, (Norman: U of Oklahoma P, 1998).

——. "Topography and Tropography in Thomas Hardy's *In Front of the Landscape*," in *Tropes, Parables, Performatives*, 195–212.

——. *Tropes, Parables, Performatives: Essays on Twentieth-Century Literature* (Durham NC: Duke UP, 1991).

——. *Versions of Pygmalion* (Cambridge MA: Harvard UP, 1990).

Mngadi, Sikhumbuzo. "Reconsidering the Copula, 'and,' in 'Literature *and* Politics,'
    and Some Thoughts on 'Progressive Formalism'." *Alternation* 11.1 (2004): 25–43.

Moran, Shane. "To Criticise the Critic: *Disgrace*," *Alternation* 8.2 (2001): 216–28.

Moses, Michael Valdez. "Solitary Walkers: Rousseau and Coetzee's *Life and Times of
    Michael K*," *South Atlantic Quarterly* 93.1 (1994): 131–56.

——. "The Mark of Empire: Writing, History, and Torture in Coetzee's *Waiting for
    the Barbarians*," *Kenyon Review* 15.1 (1993): 115–27.

Nancy, Jean–Luc. *The Inoperative Community*, tr. & ed. Peter Connor et al. (*La Com-
    munauté désœuvrée*, 1986; Minneapolis: U of Minnesota P, 1991).

Neumann, Anne Waldron. "Escaping the 'Time of History'? Present Tense and the
    Occasion of Narration in J.M. Coetzee's *Waiting for the Barbarians*," *Journal of
    Narrative Technique* 20.1 (1990): 65–86.

Newman, Judie. *The Ballistic Bard: Postcolonial Fictions* (London: Arnold, 1995).

Olsen, Lance. "The Presence of Absence: Coetzee's *Waiting for the Barbarians*,"
    ARIEL: A Review of International English Literature 16.2 (1985): 47–56.

Ovid. *Metamorphoses*, tr. Rolfe Humphries (Bloomington: Indiana UP, 1955).

Oxford English Dictionary Online (http://dictionary.oed.com/).

Parry, Benita. "Speech and Silence in the Fictions of J.M. Coetzee," in *Writing South
    Africa: Literature, Apartheid, and Democracy*, ed. Derek Attridge & Rosemary
    Jolly (Cambridge & New York: Cambridge UP, 1998): 149–65.

Pearlman, E. "Robinson Crusoe and the Cannibals," *Mosaic* 10 (1976): 39–55.

Pechey, Graham. "Coetzee's Purgatorial Africa: The Case of *Disgrace*," *Interventions*
    4.3 (2002): 374–83.

Penner, Dick. *Countries of the Mind: The Fiction of J.M. Coetzee* (Westport CT:
    Greenwood, 1989).

Petersen, Kirsten Holst. "An Elaborate Dead End? A Feminist Reading of Coetzee's
    Foe," in *A Shaping of Connections*, ed. Maes–Jelinek et al., 243–52.

Phelan, James. "Present Tense Narration, Mimesis, the Narrative Norm, and the Posi-
    tioning of the Reader in *Waiting for the Barbarians*," in *Understanding Narrative*,
    ed. James Phelan & Peter J. Rabinowitz (Columbus: Ohio UP, 1994): 222–45.

Popescu, Monica. "Waiting for the Russians: Coetzee's *The Master of Petersburg* and
    the Logic of Late Postcolonialism," *Current Writing: Text and Reception in South-
    ern Africa* 19.1 (2007): 1–20.

Post, Robert M. "The Noise of Freedom: J.M. Coetzee's *Foe*," *Critique: Studies in
    Contemporary Fiction* 30.3 (1989): 143–54.

Rajan, Tilottama. *Dark Interpreter: The Discourse of Romanticism* (Ithaca NY: Cor-
    nell UP, 1980).

Ravindranathan, Thangam. "*Amor Matris*: Language and Loss in J.M. Coetzee's *Age
    of Iron*," *Safundi: The Journal of South African and American Studies* 8.4 (2007):
    395–411.

Rimmon–Kenan, Shlomith. *Narrative Fiction: Contemporary Poetics* (1983; London: Routledge, 2nd ed. 2002).

Roberts, Sheila. "'Post-Colonialism, or the House of Friday': J.M. Coetzee's *Foe*," *World Literature Written in English* 31.1 (1991): 87–92.

Rogers, Pat. "Crusoe's Home," *Essays in Criticism* 24 (1974): 375–90.

Said, Edward. "Orientalism Reconsidered," *Cultural Critique* 1 (1985): 89–107.

Schlegel, Friedrich. "Athenäum Fragments," in *Philosophical Fragments*, tr. P. Firchow (Minneapolis: U of Minnesota P, 1991): 18–93.

Segall, Kimberly Wedeven. "Pursuing Ghosts: The Traumatic Sublime in J.M. Coetzee's *Disgrace*," *Research in African Literatures* 36.4 (2005): 40–54.

Smith, Neville. "Difference and J.M. Coetzee's *Disgrace*," *Journal of Literary Studies* 23.2 (2007): 200–16.

Soovik, Ene–Reet. "Prisoners of the Present: Tense and Agency in J.M. Coetzee's *Waiting for the Barbarians* and M. Atwood's *The Handmaid's Tale*," *Interlitteraria* 8 (2003): 259–75.

Spivak, Gayatri Chakravorty. "Theory in the Margin: Coetzee's *Foe* Reading Defoe's *Crusoe/Roxana*," *English in Africa* 17.2 (1990): 1–23.

Steiner, George. "Master and Man," review of *Waiting for the Barbarians*, *New Yorker* (12 July 1982): 102–103.

Stratton, Florence. "Imperial Fictions: J.M. Coetzee's *Disgrace*," *ARIEL: A Review of International English Literature* 33.3–4 (2002): 83–104.

Strong, Tracy B. "Foreword," in Carl Schmitt, *Political Theology* (Chicago: U of Chicago P, 2005): vii–xxxv.

Taylor, Jane. "The Impossibility of Ethical Action," review of J.M. Coetzee's *Disgrace*, *Mail & Guardian* (23–29 July 1999): 25.

Tiffin, Helen. "Post-Colonial Literatures and Counter-Discourse," *Kunapipi* 9.3 (1987): 17–34.

Tolstoy, Leo. "What Men Live By" (1885), in *Twenty-Three Tales*, tr. Louise & Aylmer Maude (London: Oxford UP, 1906): 55–82.

Van Lierop, Karin. "A Mythical Interpretation of J.M. Coetzee's *Life and Times of Michael K*," *Commonwealth: Essays & Studies* 9.1 (1986): 44–49.

Wade, Jean–Philipe. "Doubling Back on J.M. Coetzee," *English in Africa* 21.1–2 (1994): 191–219.

Watson, Stephen. "Colonialism and the Novels of J.M. Coetzee" (1986), in *Critical Perspectives on J.M. Coetzee*, ed. Huggan & Watson, 13–36.

——. "The Writer and the Devil: J.M. Coetzee's *The Master of Petersburg*," *New Contrast* 22.4 (1994): 47–61.

Wenzel, Jennifer. "Keys to the Labyrinth: Writing, Torture, and Coetzee's Barbarian Girl," *Tulsa Studies in Women's Literature* 15.1 (1996): 61–71.

Wicomb, Zoë. "Translations in the Yard of Africa," *Journal of Literary Studies* 18.3–4 (2002): 209–23.

Wittenberg, Hermann. "Imperial Space and the Discourse of the Novel," *Journal of Literary Studies* 13.1–2 (1997): 127–50.

Woodward, Wendy. "Dog Stars and Dog Souls: The Lives of Dogs in *Triomf* by Marlene van Niekerk and *Disgrace* by J.M. Coetzee," *Journal of Literary Studies* 17.3–4 (2001): 90–119.

Wordsworth, William. *The Prelude*, ed. J.C. Maxwell (Harmondsworth: Penguin, 1971).

——. *Poetical Works*, ed. Thomas Hutchinson (Oxford: Oxford U P, 1936).

Wright, Derek. "Black Earth, White Myth: Coetzee's *Michael K*," *Modern Fiction Studies* 38.2 (1992): 435–44.

Wright, Laura. *Writing "Out of All the Camps": J.M. Coetzee's Narratives of Displacement* (New York: Routledge, 2006).

Wright, Laurence. "David Lurie's Learning and the Meaning of J.M. Coetzee's *Disgrace*," in *Austerities: Essays on J.M. Coetzee*, ed. Michael Neill & Graham Bradshaw (London: Ashgate [forthcoming]).

Yeoh, Gilbert. "Love and Indifference in J.M. Coetzee's *Age of Iron*," *Journal of Commonwealth Literature* 38.3 (2003): 107–34.

——. "Negotiating Foundations: Nation, Homeland and Land in J.M. Coetzee's *Disgrace*," *A R I E L : A Review of International English Literature* 35.3–4 (2004): 1–38.

Zamora, Lois Parkinson. "Allegories of Power in the Fiction of J.M. Coetzee," *Journal of Literary Studies* 2.1 (1986): 1–15.

ᘏ ৡ

Index

—— ୨

LIBRARY, UNIVERSITY OF CHESTER

Lightning Source UK Ltd.
Milton Keynes UK
UKOW041632280213

206965UK00001B/32/P